PEARSON
COMMON CORE
Literature

Common Core
Companion Workbook

THE BRITISH TRADITION

D1361730

PEARSON

UPPER SADDLE RIVER, NEW JERSEY • BOSTON, MASSACHUSETTS
CHANDLER, ARIZONA • GLENVIEW, ILLINOIS

ISBN-13: 978-0-13-327113-3
ISBN-10:   0-13-327113-7
1 2 3 4 5 6 7 8 9 10 V016 17 16 15 14 13

Table of Contents

The instruction and activities in this book are organized around the Common Core State Standards for English and Language Arts.

Reading Standards for Literature   1

Reading Standards for Informational Texts   89

Informational Text 4: Determine the meaning of words and phrases as they are used in a text, including figurative, connotative, and technical meanings; analyze how an author uses and refines the meaning of a key term or terms over the course of a text (e.g., how Madison defines *faction* in *Federalist No. 10*).

Informational Text 5: Analyze and evaluate the effectiveness of the structure an author uses in his or her exposition or argument, including whether the structure makes points clear, convincing, and engaging.

Informational Text 6: Determine an author's point of view or purpose in a text in which the rhetoric is particularly effective, analyzing how style and content contribute to the power, persuasiveness, or beauty of the text.

Informational Text 7: Integrate and evaluate multiple sources of information presented in different media or formats (e.g., visually, quantitatively) as well as in words in order to address a question or solve a problem.

Informational Text 8: Delineate and evaluate the reasoning in seminal U.S. texts, including the application of constitutional principles and use of legal reasoning (e.g., in U.S. Supreme Court majority opinions and dissents) and the premises, purposes, and arguments in works of public advocacy (e.g., *The Federalist,* presidential addresses).

Informational Text 9: Analyze seventeenth-, eighteenth-, and nineteenth-century foundational U.S. documents of historical and literary significance (including The Declaration of Independence, the Preamble to the Constitution, the Bill of Rights, and Lincoln's Second Inaugural Address) for their themes, purposes, and rhetorical features.

Informational Text 10: By the end of grade 12, read and comprehend literary nonfiction at the high end of the grades 11–CCR text complexity band independently and proficiently.

Writing Standards   185

Writing 1: Write arguments to support claims in an analysis of substantive topics
or texts, using valid reasoning and relevant and sufficient evidence.

a. Introduce precise, knowledgeable claim(s), establish the significance of the
claim(s), distinguish the claim(s) from alternate or opposing claims, and create
an organization that logically sequences claim(s), counterclaims, reasons, and
evidence.

b. Develop claim(s) and counterclaims fairly and thoroughly, supplying the most
relevant evidence for each while pointing out the strengths and limitations of
both in a manner that anticipates the audience's knowledge level, concerns,
values, and possible biases.

c. Use words, phrases, and clauses as well as varied syntax to link the major
sections of the text, create cohesion, and clarify the relationships between
claim(s) and reasons, between reasons and evidence, and between claim(s)
and counterclaims.

d. Establish and maintain a formal style and objective tone while attending to
the norms and conventions of the discipline in which they are writing.

e. Provide a concluding statement or section that follows from and supports the
argument presented.

Writing 2: Write informative/explanatory texts to examine and convey complex
ideas, concepts, and information clearly and accurately through the effective
selection, organization, and analysis of content.

a. Introduce a topic; organize complex ideas, concepts, and information so
that each new element builds on that which precedes it to create a unified
whole; include formatting (e.g., headings), graphics (e.g., figures, tables), and
multimedia when useful to aiding comprehension.

b. Develop the topic thoroughly by selecting the most significant and relevant
facts, extended definitions, concrete details, quotations, or other information
and examples appropriate to the audience's knowledge of the topic.

c. Use appropriate and varied transitions and syntax to link the major sections of
the text, create cohesion, and clarify the relationships among complex ideas
and concepts.

d. Use precise language, domain-specific vocabulary, and techniques such as
metaphor, simile, and analogy to manage the complexity of the topic.

e. Establish and maintain a formal style and objective tone while attending to the norms and conventions of the discipline in which students are writing.

f. Provide a concluding statement or section that follows from and supports the information or explanation presented (e.g., articulating implications or the significance of the topic).

Writing 3: Write narratives to develop real or imagined experiences or events using effective technique, well-chosen details, and well-structured event sequences.

a. Engage and orient the reader by setting out a problem, situation, or observation and its significance, establishing one or multiple point(s) of view, and introducing a narrator and/or characters; create a smooth progression of experiences or events.

b. Use narrative techniques, such as dialogue, pacing, description, reflection, and multiple plot lines, to develop experiences, events, and/or characters.

c. Use a variety of techniques to sequence events so that they build on one another to create a coherent whole and build toward a particular tone and outcome (e.g., a sense of mystery, suspense, growth, or resolution).

d. Use precise words and phrases, telling details, and sensory language to convey a vivid picture of the experiences, events, setting, and/or characters.

e. Provide a conclusion that follows from and reflects on what is experienced, observed, or resolved over the course of the narrative.

Writing 4: Produce clear and coherent writing in which the development, organization, and style are appropriate to task, purpose, and audience.

Writing 5: Develop and strengthen writing as needed by planning, revising, editing, rewriting, or trying a new approach, focusing on addressing what is most significant for a specific purpose and audience.

Writing 6: Use technology, including the Internet, to produce, publish, and update individual or shared writing products in response to ongoing feedback, including new arguments or information.

Writing 7: Conduct short as well as more sustained research projects to answer a question (including a self-generated question) or solve a problem; narrow or broaden the inquiry when appropriate; synthesize multiple sources on the subject, demonstrating understanding of the subject under investigation.

Writing 8: Gather relevant information from multiple authoritative print and digital sources, using advanced searches effectively; assess the strengths and limitations of each source in terms of the task, purpose, and audience; integrate information into the text selectively to maintain the flow of ideas, avoiding plagiarism and overreliance on any one source and following a standard format for citation.

Writing 9: Draw evidence from literary or informational texts to support analysis, reflection, and research.

a. Apply *grades 11–12 Reading standards* to literature (e.g., "Demonstrate knowledge of eighteenth-, nineteenth- and early-twentieth-century foundational works of American literature, including how two or more texts from the same period treat similar themes or topics").

b. Apply *grades 11–12 Reading standards* to literary nonfiction (e.g., "Delineate and evaluate the reasoning in seminal U.S. texts, including the application of constitutional principles and use of legal reasoning [e.g., in U.S. Supreme Court Case majority opinions and dissents] and the premises, purposes, and arguments in works of public advocacy [e.g., *The Federalist,* presidential addresses]").

Writing 10: Write routinely over extended time frames (time for research, reflection, and revision) and shorter time frames (a single sitting or a day or two) for a range of tasks, purposes, and audiences.

Speaking and Listening Standards   278

Speaking and Listening 1: Initiate and participate effectively in a range of collaborative discussions (one- on-one, in groups, and teacher-led) with diverse partners on grades 11–12 topics, texts, and issues, building on others' ideas and expressing their own clearly and persuasively.

a. Come to discussions prepared, having read and researched material under study; explicitly draw on that preparation by referring to evidence from texts and other research on the topic or issue to stimulate a thoughtful, well-reasoned exchange of ideas.

b. Work with peers to promote civil, democratic discussions and decision-making, set clear goals and deadlines, and establish individual roles as needed.

c. Propel conversations by posing and responding to questions that probe reasoning and evidence; ensure a hearing for a full range of positions on a topic or issue; clarify, verify, or challenge ideas and conclusions; and promote divergent and creative perspectives.

d. Respond thoughtfully to diverse perspectives; synthesize comments, claims, and evidence made on all sides of an issue; resolve contradictions when possible; and determine what additional information or research is required to deepen the investigation or complete the task.

Language Standards   313

Language 1: Demonstrate command of the conventions of standard English grammar and usage when writing or speaking.

  a. Apply the understanding that usage is a matter of convention, can change over time, and is sometimes contested.

  b. Resolve issues of complex or contested usage, consulting references (e.g., *Merriam-Webster's Dictionary of English Usage, Garner's Modern American Usage*) as needed.

Language 2: Demonstrate command of the conventions of standard English capitalization, punctuation, and spelling when writing.

a. Observe hyphenation conventions.

b. Spell correctly.

Language 3: Apply knowledge of language to understand how language functions in different contexts, to make effective choices for meaning or style, and to comprehend more fully when reading or listening.

a. Vary syntax for effect, consulting references (e.g., Tufte's *Artful Sentences*) for guidance as needed; apply an understanding of syntax to the study of complex texts when reading.

Language 4: Determine or clarify the meaning of unknown and multiple-meaning words and phrases based on grades 11–12 reading and content, choosing flexibly from a range of strategies.

a. Use context (e.g., the overall meaning of a sentence, paragraph, or text; a word's position or function in a sentence) as a clue to the meaning of a word or phrase.

b. Identify and correctly use patterns of word changes that indicate different meanings or parts of speech (e.g., conceive, conception, conceivable).

c. Consult general and specialized reference materials (e.g., dictionaries, glossaries, thesauruses), both print and digital, to find the pronunciation of a word or determine or clarify its precise meaning, its part of speech, its etymology, or its standard usage.

d. Verify the preliminary determination of the meaning of a word or phrase (e.g., by checking the inferred meaning in context or in a dictionary).

Language 5: Demonstrate understanding of figurative language, word relationships, and nuances in word meanings.

    a. Interpret figures of speech (e.g., hyperbole, paradox) in context and analyze their role in the text.

    b. Analyze nuances in the meaning of words with similar denotations.

Language 6: Acquire and use accurately general academic and domain-specific words and phrases, sufficient for reading, writing, speaking, and listening at the college and career readiness level; demonstrate independence in gathering vocabulary knowledge when considering a word or phrase important to comprehension or expression.

Performance Tasks   338

About the *Common Core Companion*

The Common Core Companion student workbook provides instruction and practice in the Common Core State Standards. The standards are designed to help all students become college and career ready by the end of grade 12. Here is a closer look at this workbook:

Reading Standards

Reading Standards for Literature and Informational Texts are supported with instruction, examples, and multiple copies of worksheets that you can use over the course of the year. These key standards are revisited in the Performance Tasks section of your workbook.

Writing Standards

Full writing workshops are provided for Writing standards 1, 2, 3, and 8. Writing standards 4, 5, 6, 7, 9, and 10 are supported with direct instruction and worksheets that provide targeted practice. In addition, writing standards are revisited in Speaking and Listening activities and in Performance Tasks.

Speaking and Listening Standards

Detailed instruction and practice are provided for each Speaking and Listening standard. Additional opportunities to master these standards are provided in the Performance Tasks.

Language Standards

Explicit instruction and detailed examples support each Language standard. In addition, practice worksheets and graphic organizers provide additional opportunities for students to master these standards.

Performance Tasks

Using the examples in the Common Core framework as a guide, we provide opportunities for you to test your ability to master each reading standard, along with tips for success and rubrics to help you evaluate your work.

Reading Standards
for Literature

Literature 1

> 1. **Cite strong and thorough textual evidence to support analysis of what the text says explicitly as well as inferences drawn from the text, including determining where the text leaves matters uncertain.**

Explanation

To support your ideas about a piece of literature, you need to provide strong evidence, passages from the text that are related to the point you are making and that prove that point. Use such evidence, for instance, when analyzing **explicit details**, information that the writer provides directly, such as "he walked with a stoop" or "she regularly showed up late." Analyze these details to see which are the most important in conveying a character's personality and back up your analysis with evidence from the text.

You would also use textual evidence to support **inferences** about a work. For example, you might make inferences about a character's secret motives based on her actions, thoughts, feelings, or effect on others. Another type of inference relates to **ambiguity**, the effect created when an aspect of a work can be interpreted in two or more different ways. Writers sometimes create ambiguity to express complex ideas, perhaps even to demonstrate for readers that many aspects of life are uncertain. In pointing out an ambiguity, cite strong evidence that it could be interpreted in more than one way.

Examples

The following passages from a discussion of a short story illustrate the use of textual evidence.
- (a) an analysis of what the text says explicitly

  … Of all the explicit details about Zella presented in the first paragraph, the following is the most important in establishing her brashness: "Zella wore wide leather belts studded with metal gizmos she picked up at the hardware store." Other details, relating to her love of spaniels and her dislike of science fiction, do not suggest she is necessarily either bold or shy.
- (b) inferences about what the text suggests

  … Yet, in the end, Zella seems insecure and fragile. After the scene where she dances wildly on the pavement for her friends, she goes home to sit in the dark yard behind her apartment building, twisting her hair around her finger as she stares into space. That is not what a confident person would do.
- (c) the determination of an ambiguity in the text

  … The reader is never certain whether the things that Zella brags about to her friends are really true. Since there are no witnesses, we have to take Zella's word for all the outrageous things she claims to have done before moving to Mayfield. Perhaps this ambiguity is the writer's way of preserving a sense of mystery about her.

Academic Vocabulary

inference conclusion based on the reader's experience, reasoning, and details from the text
ambiguity aspect of a text that can be interpreted in two or more possible ways

Apply the Standard

Use the worksheets that follow to help you apply the standard as you read. Several copies of each worksheet have been provided for you to use with a number of different selections.

Name _____ Date _____ Selection _____

Citing Textual Evidence: Supporting an Analysis of What a Text Says Explicitly

In the left column, write a brief summary of a play or story you have read. Then, in the right column, cite textual evidence to support your choices of the most important details to include in the summary

Summary of Story or Play Title:	Textual Evidence to Support Your Choice of the Most Important Details

A

Name _____ Date _____ Selection _____

Citing Textual Evidence: Supporting an Analysis of What a Text Says Explicitly

In the left column, write a brief summary of a play or story you have read. Then, in the right column, cite textual evidence to support your choices of the most important details to include in the summary

Summary of Story or Play Title:	Textual Evidence to Support Your Choice of the Most Important Details

B

Name _____ Date _____ Selection _____

Citing Textual Evidence: Supporting an Analysis of What a Text Says Explicitly

In the left column, write a brief summary of a play or story you have read. Then, in the right column, cite textual evidence to support your choices of the most important details to include in the summary

Summary of Story or Play Title:	Textual Evidence to Support Your Choice of the Most Important Details

For use with Literature 1

Name _____ Date _____ Selection _____

Citing Textual Evidence: Supporting an Analysis of What a Text Says Explicitly

In the left column, write a brief summary of a play or story you have read. Then, in the right column, cite textual evidence to support your choices of the most important details to include in the summary

Summary of Story or Play Title:	Textual Evidence to Support Your Choice of the Most Important Details

Name _____ Date _____ Selection _____

Citing Textual Evidence: Supporting an Analysis of What a Text Says Explicitly

In the left column, write a brief summary of a play or story you have read. Then, in the right column, cite textual evidence to support your choices of the most important details to include in the summary

Summary of Story or Play Title:	Textual Evidence to Support Your Choice of the Most Important Details
1.	

Name _____ Date _____ Selection _____

Citing Textual Evidence: Supporting an Analysis of What a Text Says Explicitly

In the left column, write a brief summary of a play or story you have read. Then, in the right column, cite textual evidence to support your choices of the most important details to include in the summary

Summary of Story or Play Title:	Textual Evidence to Support Your Choice of the Most Important Details

For use with Literature 1

Name _____ Date _____ Selection _____

Citing Textual Evidence: Supporting Inferences

In the left column of the organizer, state inferences that you have made about a story or a play. In the right column, support each inference by citing strong evidence from the text. Place quotation marks around any direct quotations you use.

My Inference	Details That Support My Inference
1.	
2.	
3.	
4.	

A

Name _____ Date _____ Selection _____

Citing Textual Evidence: Supporting Inferences

In the left column of the organizer, state inferences that you have made about a story or a play. In the right column, support each inference by citing strong evidence from the text. Place quotation marks around any direct quotations you use.

My Inference	Details That Support My Inference
1.	
2.	
3.	
4.	

For use with Literature 1

Name _____ Date _____ Selection _____

Citing Textual Evidence: Supporting Inferences

In the left column of the organizer, state inferences that you have made about a story or a play. In the right column, support each inference by citing strong evidence from the text. Place quotation marks around any direct quotations you use.

My Inference	Details That Support My Inference
1.	
2.	
3.	
4.	

C

For use with Literature 1

Name _____ Date _____ Selection _____

Citing Textual Evidence: Supporting Inferences

In the left column of the organizer, state inferences that you have made about a story or a play. In the right column, support each inference by citing strong evidence from the text. Place quotation marks around any direct quotations you use.

My Inference	Details That Support My Inference
1.	
2.	
3.	
4.	

D

For use with Literature 1

Name _____ Date _____ Selection _____

Citing Textual Evidence: Supporting Inferences

In the left column of the organizer, state inferences that you have made about a story or a play. In the right column, support each inference by citing strong evidence from the text. Place quotation marks around any direct quotations you use.

My Inference	Details That Support My Inference
1.	
2.	
3.	
4.	

Name _____ Date _____ Selection _____

Citing Textual Evidence: Supporting Inferences

In the left column of the organizer, state inferences that you have made about a story or a play. In the right column, support each inference by citing strong evidence from the text. Place quotation marks around any direct quotations you use.

My Inference	Details That Support My Inference
1.	
2.	
3.	
4.	

F

Literature 2

> 2. **Determine two or more themes or central ideas of a text and analyze their development over the course of the text, including how they interact and build on one another to produce a complex account; provide an objective summary of the text.**

Explanation

The **theme** of a literary work is the central idea or insight into life it explores. The theme is not the subject of a text, as for example "war" or "sports" might be, but the insight that the work conveys about its subject. Following are examples of common themes that writers explore: the danger of reckless ambition, the destructive force of jealousy, and the importance of loyalty. Some literary works may have **multiple themes** that interact to give the work a sense of complexity and depth.

Instead of directly stating a theme, writers often imply or suggest it. In those cases, you can determine the theme by considering elements such as the following: hints contained in a work's title and people, places, and things, described so vividly that they become symbols suggesting deeper meanings. You can also analyze the development of a theme by seeing how an important character changes over the course of a work.

To start determining themes and analyzing their development, write an **objective summary**.

Examples

- **Summary** The following summary identifies a story's main character, conflicts, and key events.

  An engineer is assigned the complicated job of building a massive bridge. Several problems hold up the project, but the engineer comes up with creative solutions for each. However, she also pushes her workers and takes unnecessary risks. She manages to finish the project on time, but one worker is seriously injured on the job.

- **Multiple Themes** One theme is the importance of willpower. Several elements in the story help develop this theme: the story's title ("Accomplishing the Impossible"); the determination that the main character shows; and a flashback revealing she was a determined student. A second, but related, theme that the story explores is the harmful effects that a willful person can have on others.

- **Analysis of How Themes Interact** A successful analysis of the story would cite textual evidence to indicate the presence of these two themes. It would also cite details showing how the themes interact to provide the positive and negative aspects of perseverance.

Academic Vocabulary

theme the central idea that a literary work explores
objective summary brief restatement of the central idea and key details of a work that does not express a judgment of the work

Apply the Standard

Use the worksheets that follow to help you apply the standard as you read. Several copies of each worksheet have been provided for you to use with a number of different selections.

Name _____ Date _____ Selection _____

Summarizing a Text

In the left-hand column of the organizer, list the most important elements of the text. Then, use the information from your list to write an objective summary in the column on the right. Remember not to include your own judgments and interpretations of the work.

Main Characters and Traits	Summary
	....
	....
	....
	....
Central Conflict and Events	....
	....
	....
	....
	....
	....
	....
	....
Climax and Resolution	....
	....
	....
	....
	....
	....
	....

A

Name _____ Date _____ Selection _____

Summarizing a Text

In the left-hand column of the organizer, list the most important elements of the text. Then, use the information from your list to write an objective summary in the column on the right. Remember not to include your own judgments and interpretations of the work.

Main Characters and Traits	Summary
Central Conflict and Events	....
Climax and Resolution	....

For use with Literature 2

Name _____ Date _____ Selection _____

Summarizing a Text

In the left-hand column of the organizer, list the most important elements of the text. Then, use the information from your list to write an objective summary in the column on the right. Remember not to include your own judgments and interpretations of the work.

Main Characters and Traits	Summary
Central Conflict and Events	....
Climax and Resolution	....

C

Name _____ Date _____ Selection _____

Summarizing a Text

In the left-hand column of the organizer, list the most important elements of the text. Then, use the information from your list to write an objective summary in the column on the right. Remember not to include your own judgments and interpretations of the work.

Main Characters and Traits	Summary
	....
	....
	....
	....
Central Conflict and Events	....
	....
	....
	....
	....
	....
	....
Climax and Resolution	....
	....
	....
	....
	....
	....

For use with Literature 2

Name _____ Date _____ Selection _____

Summarizing a Text

In the left-hand column of the organizer, list the most important elements of the text. Then, use the information from your list to write an objective summary in the column on the right. Remember not to include your own judgments and interpretations of the work.

Main Characters and Traits	Summary
	....
	....
	....
	....
Central Conflict and Events	....
	....
	....
	....
	....
	....
	....
Climax and Resolution	....
	....
	....
	....
	....
	....

E

Name _____ Date _____ Selection _____

Summarizing a Text

In the left-hand column of the organizer, list the most important elements of the text. Then, use the information from your list to write an objective summary in the column on the right. Remember not to include your own judgments and interpretations of the work.

Main Characters and Traits	Summary
Central Conflict and Events	....
Climax and Resolution	....

F

Name _____ Date _____ Selection _____

Determining Themes and Analyzing Their Development and Interaction

Keeping your summary in mind, determine two different themes in the text. First, state the themes and provide textual details that reveal each one. Then, tell how the themes interact in the text to produce a complex account.

Theme 1:	Theme 2:
Supporting Textual Details: 1. 2. 3.	**Supporting Textual Details:** 1. 2. 3.

How the Themes Interact to Produce a Complex Account

For use with Literature 2

Name _____ Date _____ Selection _____

Determining Themes and Analyzing Their Development and Interaction

Keeping your summary in mind, determine two different themes in the text. First, state the themes and provide textual details that reveal each one. Then, tell how the themes interact in the text to produce a complex account.

Theme 1:	Theme 2:
Supporting Textual Details: 1. 2. 3.	**Supporting Textual Details:** 1. 2. 3.

How the Themes Interact to Produce a Complex Account

Name _____ Date _____ Selection _____

Determining Themes and Analyzing Their Development and Interaction

Keeping your summary in mind, determine two different themes in the text. First, state the themes and provide textual details that reveal each one. Then, tell how the themes interact in the text to produce a complex account.

Theme 1:	Theme 2:
Supporting Textual Details: 1. 2. 3.	**Supporting Textual Details:** 1. 2. 3.

How the Themes Interact to Produce a Complex Account

For use with Literature 2

Name _____ Date _____ Selection _____

Determining Themes and Analyzing Their Development and Interaction

Keeping your summary in mind, determine two different themes in the text. First, state the themes and provide textual details that reveal each one. Then, tell how the themes interact in the text to produce a complex account.

Theme 1:	Theme 2:
Supporting Textual Details: 1. 2. 3.	**Supporting Textual Details:** 1. 2. 3.

How the Themes Interact to Produce a Complex Account

D

Name _____ Date _____ Selection _____

Determining Themes and Analyzing Their Development and Interaction

Keeping your summary in mind, determine two different themes in the text. First, state the themes and provide textual details that reveal each one. Then, tell how the themes interact in the text to produce a complex account.

Theme 1:	Theme 2:
Supporting Textual Details: 1. 2. 3.	**Supporting Textual Details:** 1. 2. 3.

How the Themes Interact to Produce a Complex Account

E

Name _____ Date _____ Selection _____

Determining Themes and Analyzing Their Development and Interaction

Keeping your summary in mind, determine two different themes in the text. First, state the themes and provide textual details that reveal each one. Then, tell how the themes interact in the text to produce a complex account.

Theme 1:	Theme 2:
Supporting Textual Details: 1. 2. 3.	**Supporting Textual Details:** 1. 2. 3.

How the Themes Interact to Produce a Complex Account

Literature 3

> 3. **Analyze the impact of the author's choices regarding how to develop and relate elements of a story or drama (e.g., where a story is set, how the action is ordered, how the characters are introduced and developed).**

Explanation

As an author develops a story or drama, he or she makes deliberate choices regarding the major literary elements described below. These choices determine the impact of the work.

- **Setting** is the time and place of the action. It may also include the social and cultural dimensions, including the customs, rituals, and beliefs. For example, a harsh natural setting may serve both as a dramatic backdrop to the action of the plot and also as a kind of antagonist in a human versus nature conflict. The cultural dimensions of the setting may play an important role in determining the outlook and decisions of characters.
- **Plot** is the linked sequence of events in a literary work. Authors can present the plot in chronological order. However, authors can also change this pattern, beginning in the middle of the action and later introducing flashbacks that reveal past events. An author's decisions with regard to the structure or pacing of the plot will influence the mood of the story and how the readers or audience will react to characters.
- **Characterization** is the way authors create and develop characters. In **direct characterization**, a writer simply states a character's traits. When using **indirect characterization,** a writer reveals a character through: (1) words, thoughts, or actions of the character; (2) descriptions of the character; or (3) what others say about the character or how they react.

Examples

Charles Dickens sets his story *The Christmas Carol* in mid-nineteenth century London, a time and place where the poor suffered great hardships. Dickens opens his story on Christmas Eve, when special attention is given to the plight of the poor. He then uses both direct and indirect characterization to contrast the stingy, rich, Scrooge and the kindly, poor Bob Cratchit. After setting the scene and establishing the basic social issues, he centers the plot on an internal conflict—a moral struggle within Scrooge. Dickens resolves the conflict with the transformation of Scrooge. Dickens's choices regarding the setting, plot, and characterization effectively dramatize the story's message, that people should be loving and kind to one another at all times of the year.

Academic Vocabulary

direct characterization the process of developing a character by directly expressing his or her traits;

indirect characterization the process of developing by using telling details to hint at his or her traits

Apply the Standard

Use the worksheets that follow to help you apply the standard as you read. (Filling out both worksheets for the same story or drama will help you answer the final question on the "Analyzing Setting and Plot" worksheet.) Several copies of each worksheet have been provided for you to use with a number of different selections.

Name _____ Date _____ Selection _____

Analyzing Characterization

Use the character wheel to analyze the author's characterization of the main character in a story or drama.

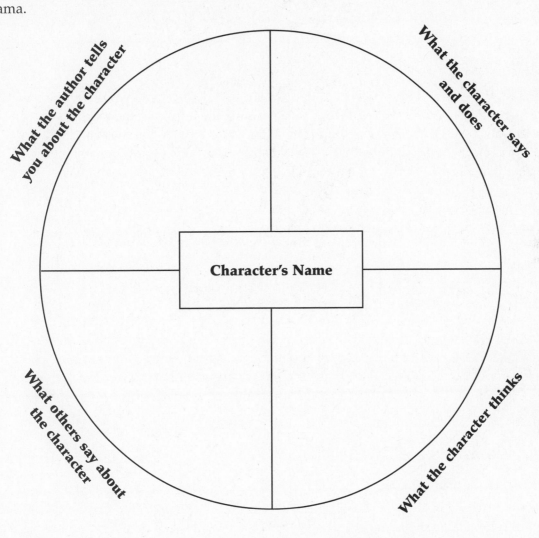

In your own words, describe the character's personality, how he or she develops over the course of the selection, and the impact of that development on the reader or audience.

....

....

....

....

....

For use with Literature 3

Name _____ Date _____ Selection _____

Analyzing Characterization

Use the character wheel to analyze the author's characterization of the main character in a story or drama.

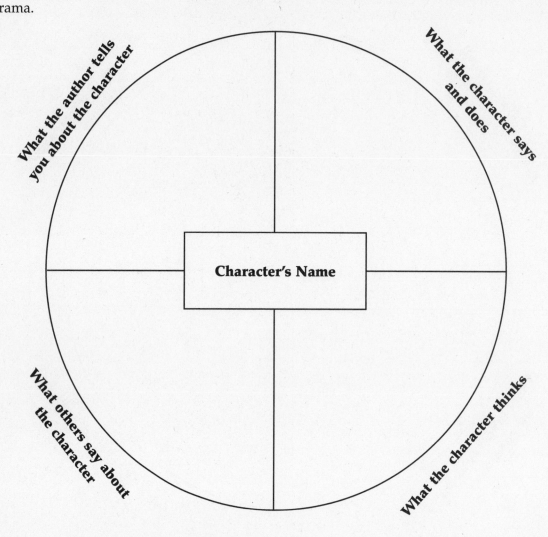

In your own words, describe the character's personality, how he or she develops over the course of the selection, and the impact of that development on the reader or audience.

....

....

....

....

....

For use with Literature 3

Name _____ Date _____ Selection _____

Analyzing Characterization

Use the character wheel to analyze the author's characterization of the main character in a story or drama.

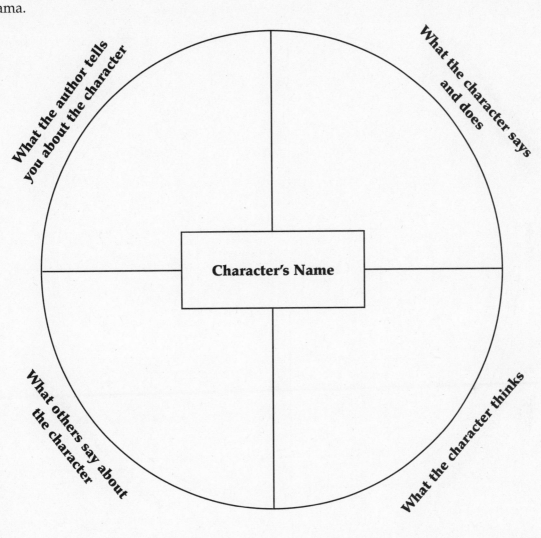

What the author tells you about the character

What the character says and does

Character's Name

What others say about the character

What the character thinks

In your own words, describe the character's personality, how he or she develops over the course of the selection, and the impact of that development on the reader or audience.

....

....

....

....

....

C

Name _____ Date _____ Selection _____

Analyzing Characterization

Use the character wheel to analyze the author's characterization of the main character in a story or drama.

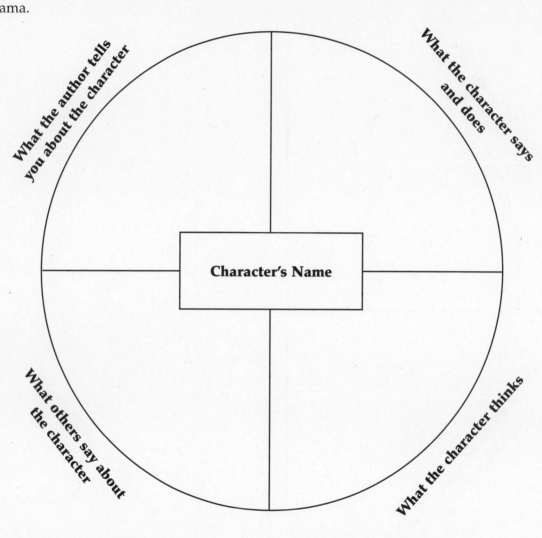

What the author tells you about the character

What the character says and does

Character's Name

What others say about the character

What the character thinks

In your own words, describe the character's personality, how he or she develops over the course of the selection, and the impact of that development on the reader or audience.

....

....

....

....

....

D

Name _____ Date _____ Selection _____

Analyzing Characterization

Use the character wheel to analyze the author's characterization of the main character in a story or drama.

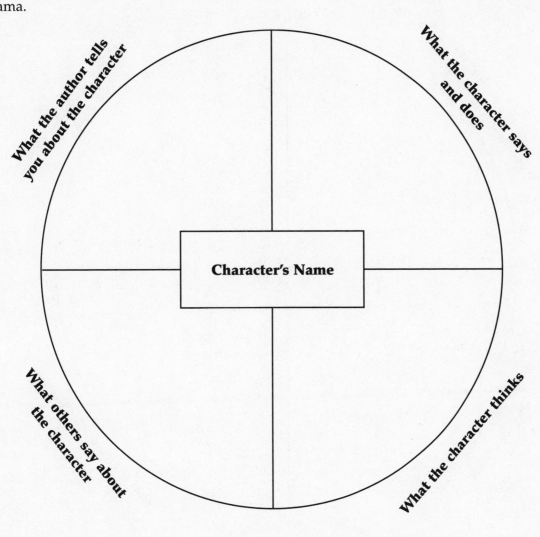

What the author tells you about the character

What the character says and does

Character's Name

What others say about the character

What the character thinks

In your own words, describe the character's personality, how he or she develops over the course of the selection, and the impact of that development on the reader or audience.

....

....

....

....

....

E

Name _____ Date _____ Selection _____

Analyzing Characterization

Use the character wheel to analyze the author's characterization of the main character in a story or drama.

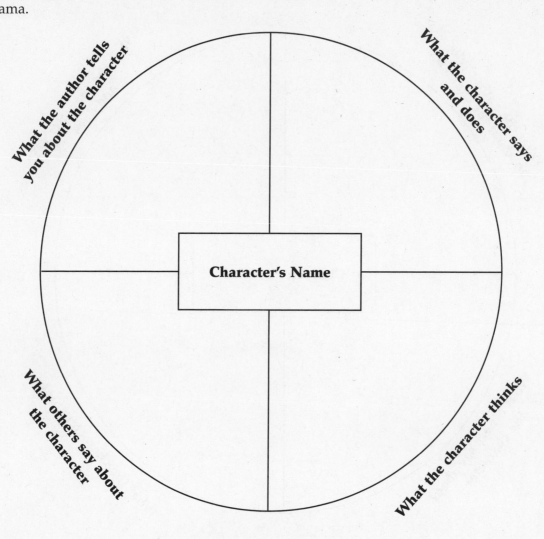

What the author tells you about the character

What the character says and does

Character's Name

What others say about the character

What the character thinks

In your own words, describe the character's personality, how he or she develops over the course of the selection, and the impact of that development on the reader or audience.

....

....

....

....

....

Name _____ Date _____ Selection _____

Analyzing Setting and Plot

Use the graphic organizer to identify the key elements of setting and plot in a story or drama. Then, keeping in mind your work on the "Analyzing Characterization" organizer, answer the question below the chart.

SETTING
Time:
Place:
PLOT
3 Key Events:
1...
2...
3...
Conflict:
Climax:
Resolution:

Describe the way in which these elements relate to the development of the main character and the impact that the interaction of all the work's elements has on readers.

....

....

....

....

....

A

Name _____ Date _____ Selection _____

Analyzing Setting and Plot

Use the graphic organizer to identify the key elements of setting and plot in a story or drama. Then, keeping in mind your work on the "Analyzing Characterization" organizer, answer the question below the chart.

SETTING   **Time:**   **Place:**
PLOT   **3 Key Events:**   1. ....   2. ....   3. ....   **Conflict:**   **Climax:**   **Resolution:**

Describe the way in which these elements relate to the development of the main character and the impact that the interaction of all the work's elements has on readers.

....

....

....

....

....

Name _____ Date _____ Selection _____

Analyzing Setting and Plot

Use the graphic organizer to identify the key elements of setting and plot in a story or drama. Then, keeping in mind your work on the "Analyzing Characterization" organizer, answer the question below the chart.

SETTING   **Time:**   **Place:**
PLOT   **3 Key Events:**   1. ....   2. ....   3. ....   **Conflict:**   **Climax:**   **Resolution:**

Describe the way in which these elements relate to the development of the main character and the impact that the interaction of all the work's elements has on readers.

....

....

....

....

....

C

Name _____ Date _____ Selection _____

Analyzing Setting and Plot

Use the graphic organizer to identify the key elements of setting and plot in a story or drama. Then, keeping in mind your work on the "Analyzing Characterization" organizer, answer the question below the chart.

SETTING
 	
  Time:
 	
  Place:

PLOT
 	
  3 Key Events:
 	
  1. ....
 	
  2. ....
 	
  3. ....
 	
  Conflict:
 	
  Climax:
 	
  Resolution:

Describe the way in which these elements relate to the development of the main character and the impact that the interaction of all the work's elements has on readers.

....

....

....

....

....

For use with Literature 3

Name _____ Date _____ Selection _____

Analyzing Setting and Plot

Use the graphic organizer to identify the key elements of setting and plot in a story or drama. Then, keeping in mind your work on the "Analyzing Characterization" organizer, answer the question below the chart.

SETTING

   Time:

   Place:

PLOT

   3 Key Events:

   1. ....

   2. ....

   3. ....

   Conflict:

   Climax:

   Resolution:

Describe the way in which these elements relate to the development of the main character and the impact that the interaction of all the work's elements has on readers.

....

....

....

....

....

For use with Literature 3

Name _____ Date _____ Selection _____

Analyzing Setting and Plot

Use the graphic organizer to identify the key elements of setting and plot in a story or drama. Then, keeping in mind your work on the "Analyzing Characterization" organizer, answer the question below the chart.

SETTING

   Time:

   Place:

PLOT

   3 Key Events:

   1. ....

   2. ....

   3. ....

   Conflict:

   Climax:

   Resolution:

Describe the way in which these elements relate to the development of the main character and the impact that the interaction of all the work's elements has on readers.

....

....

....

....

....

For use with Literature 3

Literature 4

> **4. Determine the meaning of words and phrases as they are used in the text, including figurative and connotative meanings; analyze the impact of specific word choices on meaning and tone, including words with multiple meanings or language that is particularly fresh, engaging, or beautiful. (Include Shakespeare as well as other authors.)**

Explanation

Good writers choose words that will enrich the meaning of their work and create a distinctive tone, or attitude toward the subject. To achieve such effects, they pay attention to these qualities of language:

- **Connotative meanings,** or the ideas, emotions, images and associations of a word.
- **Multiple meanings** of words that can signify two or more things.
- **Figurative language,** or words that go beyond their dictionary meanings

  simile: a comparison of two unlike things using the word *like* or *as*

  metaphor: a comparison in which something is described as though it were something else

Examples

In the opening speech from *Richard III*, William Shakespeare uses connotative meanings, figurative language, and multiple-meaning words to engage the audience and suggest Richard's unhappiness with the present state of affairs. His brother, Edward IV, has just become king, but Richard wants the throne for himself. Shakespeare's word choices convey Richard's sarcastic tone and hint at his ambitions.

> **Richard:** Now is the winter of our discontent
> Made glorious summer by this son of York;
> And all the clouds that low'r'd upon our house
> In the deep bosom of the ocean buried.

Connotative meanings — *Glorious* usually has positive connotations, but Richard suggests that "glorious summer" is the official view of things and not one he shares.

Figurative language — The new reign is metaphorically described as a passage from winter to summer.

Multiple meanings — The phrase "son of York" refers to Edward IV's status as the "son" of Richard, Duke of York, to the "sun" on the badge Edward IV adopted, and to the metaphorical summer of his reign.

Academic Vocabulary

connotation the images, feelings, ideas, and associations a word calls to mind

figurative language writing or speech that is not meant to be taken literally

Apply the Standard

Use the worksheets that follow to help you apply the standard as you read. Several copies of each worksheet have been provided for you to use with different literature selections.

- Understanding Connotations, Figurative Language, and Multiple-Meaning Words
- Understanding the Impact of Word Choice on Meaning and Tone

Name _____ Date _____ Selection _____

Understanding Connotations, Figurative Language, and Multiple-Meaning Words

Use the charts shown below to determine figurative and connotative meanings and the definitions of multiple-meaning words in a text you have read.

Use of Figurative Language	Meaning
1.	
2.	
3.	

Word or Phrase from the Text	Connotation
1.	
2.	
3.	

Passage with Multiple-Meaning Word	Meaning 1	Meaning 2
1.		
2.		
3.		

For use with Literature 4

Name _____ Date _____ Selection _____

Understanding Connotations, Figurative Language, and Multiple-Meaning Words

Use the charts shown below to determine figurative and connotative meanings and the definitions of multiple-meaning words in a text you have read.

Use of Figurative Language	Meaning
1.	
2.	
3.	

Word or Phrase from the Text	Connotation
1.	
2.	
3.	

Passage with Multiple-Meaning Word	Meaning 1	Meaning 2
1.		
2.		
3.		

Name _____ Date _____ Selection _____

Understanding Connotations, Figurative Language, and Multiple-Meaning Words

Use the charts shown below to determine figurative and connotative meanings and the definitions of multiple-meaning words in a text you have read.

Use of Figurative Language	Meaning
1.	
2.	
3.	

Word or Phrase from the Text	Connotation
1.	
2.	
3.	

Passage with Multiple-Meaning Word	Meaning 1	Meaning 3
1.		
2.		
3.		

C

Name _____ Date _____ Selection _____

Understanding Connotations, Figurative Language, and Multiple-Meaning Words

Use the charts shown below to determine figurative and connotative meanings and the definitions of multiple-meaning words in a text you have read.

Use of Figurative Language	Meaning
1.	
2.	
3.	

Word or Phrase from the Text	Connotation
1.	
2.	
3.	

Passage with Multiple-Meaning Word	Meaning 1	Meaning 2
1.		
2.		
3.		

For use with Literature 4

Name _____ Date _____ Selection _____

Understanding Connotations, Figurative Language, and Multiple-Meaning Words

Use the charts shown below to determine figurative and connotative meanings and the definitions of multiple-meaning words in a text you have read.

Use of Figurative Language	Meaning
1.	
2.	
3.	

Word or Phrase from the Text	Connotation
1.	
2.	
3.	

Passage with Multiple-Meaning Word	Meaning 1	Meaning 2
1.		
2.		
3.		

E

Name _____ Date _____ Selection _____

Understanding Connotations, Figurative Language, and Multiple-Meaning Words

Use the charts shown below to determine figurative and connotative meanings and the definitions of multiple-meaning words in a text you have read.

Use of Figurative Language	Meaning
1.	
2.	
3.	

Word or Phrase from the Text	Connotation
1.	
2.	
3.	

Passage with Multiple-Meaning Word	Meaning 1	Meaning 2
1.		
2.		
3.		

For use with Literature 4

Name _____ Date _____ Selection _____

Understanding the Impact of Word Choice on Meaning and Tone

In the left column, list examples of figurative and connotative meanings and multiple-meaning words from the text. In the right column, explain how each word choice influences the meaning and tone of the text

Examples of Figurative and Connotative Meanings and Multiple-Meaning Words	How the Word Choice Impacts Meaning and Tone
1.	
2.	
3.	
4.	
5.	

A

Name _____ Date _____ Selection _____

Understanding the Impact of Word Choice on Meaning and Tone

In the left column, list examples of figurative and connotative meanings and multiple-meaning words from the text. In the right column, explain how each word choice influences the meaning and tone of the text

Examples of Figurative and Connotative Meanings and Multiple-Meaning Words	How the Word Choice Impacts Meaning and Tone
1.	
2.	
3.	
4.	
5.	

For use with Literature 4

Name _____ Date _____ Selection _____

Understanding the Impact of Word Choice on Meaning and Tone

In the left column, list examples of figurative and connotative meanings and multiple-meaning words from the text. In the right column, explain how each word choice influences the meaning and tone of the text

Examples of Figurative and Connotative Meanings and Multiple-Meaning Words	How the Word Choice Impacts Meaning and Tone
1.	
2.	
3.	
4.	
5.	

C

Name _____ Date _____ Selection _____

Understanding the Impact of Word Choice on Meaning and Tone

In the left column, list examples of figurative and connotative meanings and multiple-meaning words from the text. In the right column, explain how each word choice influences the meaning and tone of the text

Examples of Figurative and Connotative Meanings and Multiple-Meaning Words	How the Word Choice Impacts Meaning and Tone
1.	
2.	
3.	
4.	
5.	

D

Name _____ Date _____ Selection _____

Understanding the Impact of Word Choice on Meaning and Tone

In the left column, list examples of figurative and connotative meanings and multiple-meaning words from the text. In the right column, explain how each word choice influences the meaning and tone of the text

Examples of Figurative and Connotative Meanings and Multiple-Meaning Words	How the Word Choice Impacts Meaning and Tone
1.	
2.	
3.	
4.	
5.	

E

Name _____ Date _____ Selection _____

Understanding the Impact of Word Choice on Meaning and Tone

In the left column, list examples of figurative and connotative meanings and multiple-meaning words from the text. In the right column, explain how each word choice influences the meaning and tone of the text

Examples of Figurative and Connotative Meanings and Multiple-Meaning Words	How the Word Choice Impacts Meaning and Tone
1.	
2.	
3.	
4.	
5.	

F

Literature 5

> **5.** **Analyze how an author's choices concerning how to structure specific parts of a text (e.g., the choice of where to begin or end a story, the choice to provide a comedic or tragic resolution) contribute to its overall structure and meaning as well as its aesthetic impact.**

Explanation

Specific choices that authors make regarding a work's structure influence its total design, meaning, and **aesthetic,** or artistic impact on a reader. Following are some examples:

- Authors must choose how to structure the **plot,** the linked sequence of events in a literary work. For example, a story can begin with the earliest event in a sequence and continue, in chronological order, to the last event. Authors can begin in the middle of things so that readers are immediately plunged into uncertainty. A device called a frame story can introduce one or more characters who then tell a story-within-a-story. This allows authors to develop the same theme in parallel tales. The choice of a work's form will guide the writer in developing and resolving a story's conflict. In a comic work, various mishaps and misunderstandings will come out right in the end. However, the resolution of a tragedy will involve the downfall and destruction of the main character.

- From the outset, authors must also make a structural choice regarding a story's **point of view,** the perspective from which it is told. A narrator who is outside the action but knows what every character thinks will provide readers with a complete picture of events (omniscient point of view). Readers may not get such a complete picture from a character who participates in the action and tells the story (first person point of view).

Example

Joseph Conrad's choices in structuring his story "The Lagoon" affect its design, tone, and meaning. Conrad's overall design involves a frame story and a story-within-a-story. At the beginning of the frame story, told from the limited third person point of view, a character called "the white man" is being ferried to the lonely hut of his "Malay friend" Arsat. In the story-within-a-story, Arsat's brother dies; in the frame story, Arsat's wife dies. These resolutions and the final image of Arsat alone on the shore suggest that, in a dangerous world, love can lead to betrayal and suffering.

Academic Vocabulary

aesthetic taking into account artistic issues, rather than social, political, or philosophical ones

plot linked sequence of events in a literary work

point of view vantage point from which a work is told

Apply the Standard

Use the worksheet that follows to help you apply the standard as you read. Several copies of the worksheet have been provided for you to use with different literature selections.

- Analyzing the Impact of an Author's Structural Choices

Name _____ Date _____ Selection _____

Analyzing the Impact of an Author's Structural Choices

Use the graphic organizer to describe an author's specific structural choices and explain how they influence a work's design, meaning, and aesthetic effect on readers.

Structural Choices	Effect on Design, Meaning, Aesthetic Impact
Point of View	
Where to Begin Story	
How to Narrate Events (devices such as frame story, flashback)	
How to Resolve Story	

A

For use with Literature 5

Name _____ Date _____ Selection _____

Analyzing the Impact of an Author's Structural Choices

Use the graphic organizer to describe an author's specific structural choices and explain how they influence a work's design, meaning, and aesthetic effect on readers.

Structural Choices	Effect on Design, Meaning, Aesthetic Impact
Point of View	
Where to Begin Story	
How to Narrate Events (devices such as frame story, flashback)	
How to Resolve Story	

B

For use with Literature 5

Name _____ Date _____ Selection _____

Analyzing the Impact of an Author's Structural Choices

Use the graphic organizer to describe an author's specific structural choices and explain how they influence a work's design, meaning, and aesthetic effect on readers.

Structural Choices	Effect on Design, Meaning, Aesthetic Impact
Point of View	
Where to Begin Story	
How to Narrate Events (devices such as frame story, flashback)	
How to Resolve Story	

For use with Literature 5

Name _____ Date _____ Selection _____

Analyzing the Impact of an Author's Structural Choices

Use the graphic organizer to describe an author's specific structural choices and explain how they influence a work's design, meaning, and aesthetic effect on readers.

Structural Choices	Effect on Design, Meaning, Aesthetic Impact
Point of View	
Where to Begin Story	
How to Narrate Events (devices such as frame story, flashback)	
How to Resolve Story	

D

Name _____ Date _____ Selection _____

Analyzing the Impact of an Author's Structural Choices

Use the graphic organizer to describe an author's specific structural choices and explain how they influence a work's design, meaning, and aesthetic effect on readers.

Structural Choices	Effect on Design, Meaning, Aesthetic Impact
Point of View	
Where to Begin Story	
How to Narrate Events (devices such as frame story, flashback)	
How to Resolve Story	

E

For use with Literature 5

Name _____ Date _____ Selection _____

Analyzing the Impact of an Author's Structural Choices

Use the graphic organizer to describe an author's specific structural choices and explain how they influence a work's design, meaning, and aesthetic effect on readers.

Structural Choices	Effect on Design, Meaning, Aesthetic Impact
Point of View	
Where to Begin Story	
How to Narrate Events (devices such as frame story, flashback)	
How to Resolve Story	

F

Literature 6

> 6. **Analyze a case in which grasping point of view requires distinguishing what is directly stated in a text from what is really meant (e.g., satire, sarcasm, irony, or understatement).**

Explanation

To clearly understand an author's point of view, readers must distinguish between what is stated in a text and what the author really means. Literary writers sometimes use the following techniques:

- **Satire** is writing that ridicules or exposes the faults of specific individuals, groups, institutions, or humanity in general. Satire uses indirection by saying the opposite of what it means or by treating seriously something that is actually ridiculous.

- **Irony** involves a discrepancy between what is stated and what is meant or between what is expected and what actually happens. **Verbal irony** occurs when someone says something that deliberately contradicts what he or she actually means. **Dramatic irony** occurs when there is a contradiction between what a character thinks and what the reader or audience knows to be true.

- **Sarcasm** is a type of verbal irony in which the tone or attitude is particularly harsh or mocking. Sarcasm expresses scorn, contempt, or disapproval of a person or situation.

- **Understatement** is a figure of speech that deliberately says less than is intended. In describing a downpour using understatement, you might say, "It was a bit damp."

Examples

- **Satire** "The Rape of the Lock" by Alexander Pope satirizes the pettiness of high society in eighteenth-century England. Based on an actual event, the poem tells the tale of a young aristocrat who cuts a lock of hair from the head of a beautiful woman as a kind of prize. Because the trivial event created a scandal, Pope mockingly treats the incident as if it had enormous significance by telling it in the style of a classical epic poem.

- **Irony** In "Shooting an Elephant," George Orwell makes this ironic observation: "I perceived in this moment that when the white man turns tyrant it is his own freedom that he destroys." Irony is at work here because one would expect a tyrant to deprive others of freedom, not himself.

Academic Vocabulary

satire writing that uses humor to ridicule corruption or folly

irony contradiction between expectation and reality or between what is said and what is meant

Apply the Standard

Use the worksheet that follows to help you apply the standard as you read. Several copies of the worksheet have been provided for you to use with different literature selections.

- Distinguishing Between What Is Stated and What Is Meant

Name _____ Date _____ Selection _____

Distinguishing Between What Is Said and What Is Meant

Use the left column of the chart to list instances in which an author states something indirectly by using satire, irony, sarcasm, or understatement. In the column on the right, explain what the author really means.

Examples from the Text	Actual Meaning

Name _____ Date _____ Selection _____

Distinguishing Between What Is Said and What Is Meant

Use the left column of the chart to list instances in which an author states something indirectly by using satire, irony, sarcasm, or understatement. In the column on the right, explain what the author really means.

Examples from the Text	Actual Meaning

Name _____ Date _____ Selection _____

Distinguishing Between What Is Said and What Is Meant

Use the left column of the chart to list instances in which an author states something indirectly by using satire, irony, sarcasm, or understatement. In the column on the right, explain what the author really means.

Examples from the Text	Actual Meaning

Name _____ Date _____ Selection _____

Distinguishing Between What Is Said and What Is Meant

Use the left column of the chart to list instances in which an author states something indirectly by using satire, irony, sarcasm, or understatement. In the column on the right, explain what the author really means.

Examples from the Text	Actual Meaning

Name _____ Date _____ Selection _____

Distinguishing Between What Is Said and What Is Meant

Use the left column of the chart to list instances in which an author states something indirectly by using satire, irony, sarcasm, or understatement. In the column on the right, explain what the author really means.

Examples from the Text	Actual Meaning

E

For use with Literature 6

Name _____ Date _____ Selection _____

Distinguishing Between What Is Said and What Is Meant

Use the left column of the chart to list instances in which an author states something indirectly by using satire, irony, sarcasm, or understatement. In the column on the right, explain what the author really means.

Examples from the Text	Actual Meaning

Literature 7

> **7. Analyze multiple interpretations of a story, drama, or poem (e.g., recorded or live production of a play or recorded novel or poetry), evaluating how each version interprets the source text. (Include at least one play by Shakespeare and one play by an American dramatist.)**

Explanation

Dramas are written to be performed on stage or on film. Stories and poems can be read aloud and recorded. Each production of a play or recording of a story or poem is an **interpretation** that conveys an understanding of the work. Each interpretation may take a different approach to the **source text**, the original story, drama, or poem. Interpretations can remain faithful to the source texts, make subtle changes to emphasize particular themes, aim for historical accuracy, or make significant changes to reflect popular tastes. To analyze multiple interpretations of a story, drama, or poem, focus on elements like the following:

- **Characterization:** In an interpretation of a story, drama, or poem, actors or readers bring the characters to life. What aspects of the characters are emphasized? In what ways are the characters different from how you pictured them while reading the source text?

- **Setting:** In many interpretations of a play, the original setting is kept. Sometimes the setting is updated. How does a new setting alter your understanding of the play?

- **Mood or atmosphere:** Examine how each interpretation creates a mood or atmosphere. Is the mood or atmosphere appropriate to the source text?

- **Narrative elements:** Are any narrative elements from the source text—such as a subplot, character, or scene—left out? What, if any, new narrative elements are added?

- **Elements of the medium:** How are resources unique to the medium used in each interpretation? For example, a film adaptation of a play can use realistic, on-site settings, while a theater production must rely on lighting and constructed sets.

Examples

- One interpretation of William Shakespeare's play *The Tragedy of Macbeth* may strive for historical accuracy.

- Another production may set *The Tragedy of Macbeth* in the modern world. This modern interpretation may stress how the play's theme of ruthless ambition applies to our own times.

Academic Vocabulary

interpretation performance of a story, drama, or poem that conveys one understanding of the work
source text an original story, drama, or poem on which an interpretation is based

Apply the Standard

Use the worksheet that follows to help you apply the standard as you read. Several copies of the worksheet have been provided for you to use with different literature selections.

- Analyzing Multiple Interpretations

Name _____ Date _____ Selection _____

Analyzing Multiple Interpretations

Use the graphic organizer, below, to analyze and compare two interpretations of a story, drama, or poem. Explain how the elements in the left-hand column are developed in each interpretation.

Source Text:		
	Interpretation 1:	**Interpretation 2:**
1. Characterization		
2. Setting		
3. Mood or Atmosphere		
4. Narrative Elements		
5. Elements of the Medium		

A

Name _____ Date _____ Selection _____

Analyzing Multiple Interpretations

Use the graphic organizer, below, to analyze and compare two interpretations of a story, drama, or poem. Explain how the elements in the left-hand column are developed in each interpretation.

Source Text:		
	Interpretation 1:	**Interpretation 2:**
1. Characterization		
2. Setting		
3. Mood or Atmosphere		
4. Narrative Elements		
5. Elements of the Medium		

Name _____ Date _____ Selection _____

Analyzing Multiple Interpretations

Use the graphic organizer, below, to analyze and compare two interpretations of a story, drama, or poem. Explain how the elements in the left-hand column are developed in each interpretation.

Source Text:		
	Interpretation 1:	**Interpretation 2:**
1. Characterization		
2. Setting		
3. Mood or Atmosphere		
4. Narrative Elements		
5. Elements of the Medium		

C

For use with Literature 7

Name _____ Date _____ Selection _____

Analyzing Multiple Interpretations

Use the graphic organizer, below, to analyze and compare two interpretations of a story, drama, or poem. Explain how the elements in the left-hand column are developed in each interpretation.

Source Text:		
	Interpretation 1:	**Interpretation 2:**
1. Characterization		
2. Setting		
3. Mood or Atmosphere		
4. Narrative Elements		
5. Elements of the Medium		

D

Name _____ Date _____ Selection _____

Analyzing Multiple Interpretations

Use the graphic organizer, below, to analyze and compare two interpretations of a story, drama, or poem. Explain how the elements in the left-hand column are developed in each interpretation.

Source Text:		
	Interpretation 1:	**Interpretation 2:**
1. Characterization		
2. Setting		
3. Mood or Atmosphere		
4. Narrative Elements		
5. Elements of the Medium		

E

Name _____ Date _____ Selection _____

Analyzing Multiple Interpretations

Use the graphic organizer, below, to analyze and compare two interpretations of a story, drama, or poem. Explain how the elements in the left-hand column are developed in each interpretation.

Source Text:		
	Interpretation 1:	**Interpretation 2:**
1. Characterization		
2. Setting		
3. Mood or Atmosphere		
4. Narrative Elements		
5. Elements of the Medium		

Literature 9

> 9. **Demonstrate knowledge of eighteenth-, nineteenth-, and early twentieth-century foundational works of American literature, including how two or more texts from the same period treat similar themes or topics.**

Explanation

Foundational texts are influential, trend-setting works that initiate and develop the literary forms, topics, and themes characteristic of a time period. Just as a course in American literature requires knowledge of foundational American works, so a course in British literature requires knowledge of key British texts. In British as in American literature, characteristic topics or themes of a **literary period** arise from the historical events and cultural influences of that era. For example, the British Romantic poet William Wordsworth employed a simpler, more direct language than was common in previous poetry, and he conveyed a deep appreciation for the beauty of the natural world. In his use of a more down-to-earth diction, he was responding to events such as the French Revolution, and his view of nature reflects a new cultural appreciation of wilderness.

Examples

The chart below lists several foundational works of British literature:

Eighteenth Century	Nineteenth Century	Early Twentieth Century
• Jonathan Swift, *Gulliver's Travels* • Alexander Pope, "The Rape of the Lock" • Samuel Johnson, *A Dictionary of the English Language*	• William Wordsworth, *The Prelude* • Samuel Taylor Coleridge, *The Rime of the Ancient Mariner* • Charles Dickens, *Great Expectations* • Charlotte Brontë, *Jane Eyre*	• Virginia Woolf, *Mrs. Dalloway* • T.S. Eliot, "Preludes" • W.H. Auden, "In Memory of W. B. Yeats"

Writers from the same historical period often address similar key topics and themes. For instance, the positive influence of nature on human development is a theme in William Wordsworth's *The Prelude*. He also expresses reservations about the effects of urbanization, lamenting that the minds of many people have "been turned aside / From Nature's way." In his poem of the same era, *The Rime of the Ancient Mariner*, Samuel Taylor Coleridge explores a similar theme. A seaman expresses deep remorse and guilt for his thoughtless killing of an albatross, an innocent creature of Nature, and reminds others of the need to love "man and bird and beast."

Academic Vocabulary

foundational text work that initiates and develops the key forms, themes, and topics of a period

literary period era in which literary works reflect new perspectives characteristic of the time

Apply the Standard

Use the worksheet that follows to help you apply the standard as you read. Several copies of the worksheet have been provided for you to use with different literature selections.

• Comparing Works of a Period

Name _____ Date _____ Selection _____

Comparing Works of a Period

Use the chart, below, to compare two literary works of the same era that explore a common theme or topic.

Title of text 1: .... **Author:** ....

Title of text 2: .... **Author:** ....

Theme or topic common to both texts: ....

....

	Text 1	Text 2
What main points does the writer make about the theme or topic?		
What details does the writer use in exploring the theme or topic?		
In what ways is the literary form suited to the theme or topic?		
What is unique about the author's approach?		

A

Name _____ Date _____ Selection _____

Comparing Works of a Period

Use the chart, below, to compare two literary works of the same era that explore a common theme or topic.

Title of text 1: .... **Author:** ....

Title of text 2: .... **Author:** ....

Theme or topic common to both texts: ....

....

	Text 1	Text 2
What main points does the writer make about the theme or topic?		
What details does the writer use in exploring the theme or topic?		
In what ways is the literary form suited to the theme or topic?		
What is unique about the author's approach?		

Name _____ Date _____ Selection _____

Comparing Works of a Period

Use the chart, below, to compare two literary works of the same era that explore a common theme or topic.

Title of text 1: .... **Author:**..

Title of text 2: .... **Author:**..

Theme or topic common to both texts:..

....

	Text 1	**Text 2**
What main points does the writer make about the theme or topic?		
What details does the writer use in exploring the theme or topic?		
In what ways is the literary form suited to the theme or topic?		
What is unique about the author's approach?		

Name _____ Date _____ Selection _____

Comparing Works of a Period

Use the chart, below, to compare two literary works of the same era that explore a common theme or topic.

Title of text 1: .... **Author:**...

Title of text 2: .... **Author:**...

Theme or topic common to both texts: ....

....

	Text 1	Text 2
What main points does the writer make about the theme or topic?		
What details does the writer use in exploring the theme or topic?		
In what ways is the literary form suited to the theme or topic?		
What is unique about the author's approach?		

D

Name _____ Date _____ Selection _____

Comparing Works of a Period

Use the chart, below, to compare two literary works of the same era that explore a common theme or topic.

Title of text 1: .... **Author:** ....

Title of text 2: .... **Author:** ....

Theme or topic common to both texts: ....

....

	Text 1	Text 2
What main points does the writer make about the theme or topic?		
What details does the writer use in exploring the theme or topic?		
In what ways is the literary form suited to the theme or topic?		
What is unique about the author's approach?		

E

Name _____ Date _____ Selection _____

Comparing Works of a Period

Use the chart, below, to compare two literary works of the same era that explore a common theme or topic.

Title of text 1: .... **Author:** ....

Title of text 2: .... **Author:** ....

Theme or topic common to both texts: ....

....

	Text 1	Text 2
What main points does the writer make about the theme or topic?		
What details does the writer use in exploring the theme or topic?		
In what ways is the literary form suited to the theme or topic?		
What is unique about the author's approach?		

Literature 10

---

10. By the end of grade 12, read and comprehend literature, including stories, dramas, and poems, at the high end of the grades 11-CCR text complexity band independently and proficiently.

Explanation

Successful readers are able to independently read and comprehend **complex texts,** works that present difficulties as a result of challenging concepts, organization, language, or sentence structure.

Examples

Be aware of specific factors that can make texts difficult to read, including the following items:

Language

- The level of vocabulary is high, with many unfamiliar words.

- Sentences are long and involved, with one or more dependent clauses.

- The text contains long blocks of description unbroken by dialogue.

Writer's Style

- The writer uses figurative language, such as metaphors, similes, or personification.

- The writer's use of ambiguity, irony, symbolism, or satire makes the text less accessible.

Subject Matter

- The writer makes allusions to unfamiliar events, places, or people.

- Understanding the text requires special background or technical knowledge.

Successful readers employ strategies like these to master complex texts:

- Stay focused by setting a specific purpose for reading.

- Stop reading after a specified period of time and summarize what you have read. Then reread parts of the text as needed.

Academic Vocabulary

complex texts works with challenging concepts, organization, language, or sentence structure

paraphrase simplify and rephrase a passage in one's own words

visualize create a mental picture of characters or events in a text

Apply the Standard

Use the worksheet that follows to help you apply the standard as you read. Several copies of the worksheet have been provided for you to use with different literature selections.

- Comprehending Complex Texts

Name _____ Date _____ Selection _____

Comprehending Complex Texts

- Use the left-hand column of the graphic organizer to evaluate the complexity of the text that you are reading independently. For each category, list factors that make the selection difficult.

- Use the right-hand column to describe the strategy or strategies that helped you master each difficulty mentioned in the left-hand column.

Title: .... Writer: ....

Factors That Make the Text Complex	Helpful Reading Strategies
1. Language	
2. Writer's Style	
3. Subject Matter	
4. Other	

Rating the Text

In your opinion, how complex was the text you read? Rate the complexity of the text on a scale of one to ten, with one being "easy" and ten being "very difficult."

My Rating: ....

A

Name _____ Date _____ Selection _____

Comprehending Complex Texts

- Use the left-hand column of the graphic organizer to evaluate the complexity of the text that you are reading independently. For each category, list factors that make the selection difficult.

- Use the right-hand column to describe the strategy or strategies that helped you master each difficulty mentioned in the left-hand column.

Title: .... Writer: ....

Factors That Make the Text Complex	Helpful Reading Strategies
1. Language	
2. Writer's Style	
3. Subject Matter	
4. Other	

Rating the Text

In your opinion, how complex was the text you read? Rate the complexity of the text on a scale of one to ten, with one being "easy" and ten being "very difficult."

My Rating: ....

B

Name _____ Date _____ Selection _____

Comprehending Complex Texts

- Use the left-hand column of the graphic organizer to evaluate the complexity of the text that you are reading independently. For each category, list factors that make the selection difficult.

- Use the right-hand column to describe the strategy or strategies that helped you master each difficulty mentioned in the left-hand column.

Title: .... Writer: ....

Factors That Make the Text Complex	Helpful Reading Strategies
1. Language	
2. Writer's Style	
3. Subject Matter	
4. Other	

Rating the Text

In your opinion, how complex was the text you read? Rate the complexity of the text on a scale of one to ten, with one being "easy" and ten being "very difficult."

My Rating: ....

C

Name _____ Date _____ Selection _____

Comprehending Complex Texts

- • Use the left-hand column of the graphic organizer to evaluate the complexity of the text that you are reading independently. For each category, list factors that make the selection difficult.

- • Use the right-hand column to describe the strategy or strategies that helped you master each difficulty mentioned in the left-hand column.

Title: .... Writer: ....

Factors That Make the Text Complex	Helpful Reading Strategies
1. Language	
2. Writer's Style	
3. Subject Matter	
4. Other	

Rating the Text

In your opinion, how complex was the text you read? Rate the complexity of the text on a scale of one to ten, with one being "easy" and ten being "very difficult."

My Rating: ....

D

Name _____ Date _____ Selection _____

Comprehending Complex Texts

- Use the left-hand column of the graphic organizer to evaluate the complexity of the text that you are reading independently. For each category, list factors that make the selection difficult.

- Use the right-hand column to describe the strategy or strategies that helped you master each difficulty mentioned in the left-hand column.

Title: .... **Writer:** ....

Factors That Make the Text Complex	Helpful Reading Strategies
1. Language	
2. Writer's Style	
3. Subject Matter	
4. Other	

Rating the Text

In your opinion, how complex was the text you read? Rate the complexity of the text on a scale of one to ten, with one being "easy" and ten being "very difficult."

My Rating: ....

E

Name _____ Date _____ Selection _____

Comprehending Complex Texts

- Use the left-hand column of the graphic organizer to evaluate the complexity of the text that you are reading independently. For each category, list factors that make the selection difficult.

- Use the right-hand column to describe the strategy or strategies that helped you master each difficulty mentioned in the left-hand column.

Title: .... **Writer:** ....

Factors That Make the Text Complex	Helpful Reading Strategies
1. Language	
2. Writer's Style	
3. Subject Matter	
4. Other	

Rating the Text

In your opinion, how complex was the text you read? Rate the complexity of the text on a scale of one to ten, with one being "easy" and ten being "very difficult."

My Rating: ....

Reading Standards for Informational Text

Informational Text 1

> 1. **Cite strong and thorough textual evidence to support analysis of what the text says explicitly as well as inferences drawn from the text, including determining where the text leaves matters uncertain.**

Explanation

In an informational text, authors provide many **explicit details,** direct statements about the subject under discussion. In addition, authors suggest certain details or ideas, rather than expressing them directly. In order to understand this hinted-at information, readers must **draw inferences** from the text, making educated guesses based on what the text says explicitly and their own experience.

To support inferences, you will have to cite **textual evidence,** relevant and sufficient supporting information from the text, to support the inferences that you make.

Sometimes writers not only hint at ideas, but intentionally create **ambiguity.** They may do so in order to suggest the complexity of a subject and to prompt readers to think about it more deeply.

Examples

An informational text about Maya Lin provided explicit details like these to support the central idea of the text, namely, that she is a gifted artist:

- At the age of 21, in 1981, she won a competition for the design of the Vietnam Veterans Memorial. The competition was open to the public. Over 1,400 competitors submitted designs.

You might analyze details in an informational text by determining which ones provide support for the central idea and are therefore important enough to be included in a summary.

Authors may also imply or suggest information. The reader must draw inferences from the text—make educated guesses based on textual evidence, reasoning, and experience—to determine what the author is suggesting. For example, note the textual evidence, below, and the inference drawn from them:

- Several thousand personal items are left at the memorial each year.
- Visitors lining the stark black granite wall are openly weeping.
- Inference: People's experience of the memorial is both moving and intimate.

In one ambiguous passage from the informational text on Maya Lin, a veteran reaches out to touch the name of a fallen comrade and mourns his death. Readers are left to wonder whether the Memorial evokes loving memories of a lost buddy or emphasizes the fact that he is gone.

Academic Vocabulary

inference educated guess based on textual details, reasoning, and life experience
textual evidence items from a text that support an analysis of explicit details or an inference
ambiguity text that can be interpreted in two or more possible ways

Apply the Standard

Use the worksheets that follow to help you apply the standard as you read. Several copies of each worksheet have been provided for you to use with different informational texts.

- Using Textual Evidence to Support an Analysis of Explicit Details
- Using Textual Evidence to Support an Inference and Identify Ambiguity

Name _____ Date _____ Selection _____

Using Textual Evidence to Support an Analysis of Explicit Details

Use the graphic organizer, below, to analyze which explicit details in an informational text are the most important. In the left column, state one of the author's central ideas. In the middle column, note the most important explicit details from the text that back up the idea. In the right column, explain how evidence from the text supports your choice of important explicit details.

Informational Text: _____ Author: _____

Central Idea	Most Important Explicit Details Backing up Idea	Textual Evidence Supporting Choice of Explicit Details
1.		
2.		
3.		

A

Using Textual Evidence to Support an Analysis of Explicit Details

Use the graphic organizer, below, to analyze which explicit details in an informational text are the most important. In the left column, state one of the author's central ideas. In the middle column, note the most important explicit details from the text that back up the idea. In the right column, explain how evidence from the text supports your choice of important explicit details.

Informational Text: .... Author: ....

Central Idea	Most Important Explicit Details Backing up Idea	Textual Evidence Supporting Choice of Explicit Details
1.		
2.		
3.		

Name _____ Date _____ Selection _____

Using Textual Evidence to Support an Analysis of Explicit Details

Use the graphic organizer, below, to analyze which explicit details in an informational text are the most important. In the left column, state one of the author's central ideas. In the middle column, note the most important explicit details from the text that back up the idea. In the right column, explain how evidence from the text supports your choice of important explicit details.

Informational Text: .... Author: ....

Central Idea	Most Important Explicit Details Backing up Idea	Textual Evidence Supporting Choice of Explicit Details
1.		
2.		
3.		

Name _____ Date _____/_____ Selection _____

Using Textual Evidence to Support an Analysis of Explicit Details

Use the graphic organizer, below, to analyze which explicit details in an informational text are the most important. In the left column, state one of the author's central ideas. In the middle column, note the most important explicit details from the text that back up the idea. In the right column, explain how evidence from the text supports your choice of important explicit details.

Informational Text: .... Author: ....

Central Idea	Most Important Explicit Details Backing up Idea	Textual Evidence Supporting Choice of Explicit Details
1.		
2.		
3.		

Using Textual Evidence to Support an Analysis of Explicit Details

Use the graphic organizer, below, to analyze which explicit details in an informational text are the most important. In the left column, state one of the author's central ideas. In the middle column, note the most important explicit details from the text that back up the idea. In the right column, explain how evidence from the text supports your choice of important explicit details.

Informational Text: .... Author: ....

Central Idea	Most Important Explicit Details Backing up Idea	Textual Evidence Supporting Choice of Explicit Details
1.		
2.		
3.		

E

Name _____ Date _____ Selection _____

Using Textual Evidence to Support an Analysis of Explicit Details

Use the graphic organizer, below, to analyze which explicit details in an informational text are the most important. In the left column, state one of the author's central ideas. In the middle column, note the most important explicit details from the text that back up the idea. In the right column, explain how evidence from the text supports your choice of important explicit details.

Informational Text: .... Author: ....

Central Idea	Most Important Explicit Details Backing up Idea	Textual Evidence Supporting Choice of Explicit Details
1.		
2.		
3.		

Name _____ Date _____ Selection _____

Using Textual Details to Support an Inference and Identify Ambiguity

In the left column, enter inferences you draw from the text and ambiguities you identify. In the right column, explain how textual details support your inference or confirm a passage's ambiguity.

Informational Text: .... Author: ....

Inference	Textual Details Supporting Inference
1.	
2.	

Ambiguity	Textual Details Confirming Ambiguity
3.	
4.	

A

For use with Informational Text 1

Name _____ Date _____ Selection _____

Using Textual Details to Support an Inference and Identify Ambiguity

In the left column, enter inferences you draw from the text and ambiguities you identify. In the right column, explain how textual details support your inference or confirm a passage's ambiguity.

Informational Text: .... Author: ....

Inference	Textual Details Supporting Inference
1.	
2.	

Ambiguity	Textual Details Confirming Ambiguity
3.	
4.	

Name _____ Date _____ Selection _____

Using Textual Details to Support an Inference and Identify Ambiguity

In the left column, enter inferences you draw from the text and ambiguities you identify. In the right column, explain how textual details support your inference or confirm a passage's ambiguity.

Informational Text: .... Author: ....

Inference	Textual Details Supporting Inference
1.	
2.	

Ambiguity	Textual Details Confirming Ambiguity
3.	
4.	

C

Name _____ Date _____ Selection _____

Using Textual Details to Support an Inference and Identify Ambiguity

In the left column, enter inferences you draw from the text and ambiguities you identify. In the right column, explain how textual details support your inference or confirm a passage's ambiguity.

Informational Text: .... Author: ....

Inference	Textual Details Supporting Inference
1.	
2.	

Ambiguity	Textual Details Confirming Ambiguity
3.	
4.	

D

Name _____ Date _____ Selection _____

Using Textual Details to Support an Inference and Identify Ambiguity

In the left column, enter inferences you draw from the text and ambiguities you identify. In the right column, explain how textual details support your inference or confirm a passage's ambiguity.

Informational Text: .... Author: ....

Inference	Textual Details Supporting Inference
1.	
2.	

Ambiguity	Textual Details Confirming Ambiguity
3.	
4.	

For use with Informational Text 1

Name _____ Date _____ Selection _____

Using Textual Details to Support an Inference and Identify Ambiguity

In the left column, enter inferences you draw from the text and ambiguities you identify. In the right column, explain how textual details support your inference or confirm a passage's ambiguity.

Informational Text: .... Author: ....

Inference	Textual Details Supporting Inference
1.	
2.	

Ambiguity	Textual Details Confirming Ambiguity
3.	
4.	

For use with Informational Text 1

Informational Text 2

> 2. **Determine two or more central ideas of a text and analyze their development over the course of the text, including how they interact and build on one another to provide a complex analysis; provide an objective summary of the text.**

Explanation

The **central ideas** in an informational text are the key messages or insights the writer wishes to convey. Many nonfiction pieces—including essays and expository articles—develop two or more central ideas. As you read, note the central ideas the author presents. Then, analyze how they interact with one another, giving greater depth and complexity to the treatment of a **topic,** or subject. Creating an **objective summary** of a text can help you identify and focus on the central ideas.

Examples

- An article may focus on a single topic while providing two or more central ideas, A text about the Great Fire of London in 1666 may develop these two ideas:
  - The fire blazed for three days, taking the lives of only sixteen people but destroying more than eighty percent of the city and causing many to become homeless.
  - Despite the terrible damage, a new and better London—with wider streets and buildings made of brick, not wood—arose from the ruins.

The author develops these central ideas over the course of the text in order to analyze all the consequences of the Great Fire of London. The ideas interact with one another as the author compares the immediate devastating effects of the fire with its subsequent positive effects.

- Making an objective summary of such an article will help you to identify two central ideas and analyze how they interact:

  The Great Fire of London in 1666 caused enormous property losses, including the destruction of eighty percent of the city proper. Nonetheless, the rebuilding of the city after the fire brought many benefits, including wider streets, brick buildings, and the construction of St. Paul's Cathedral.

Academic Vocabulary

central ideas key messages or insights conveyed by a text

topic chief subject of a text

objective summary brief restatement of most important points in a text, without expressing an opinion

Apply the Standard

Use the worksheets that follow to help you apply the standard as you read. Several copies of each worksheet have been provided for you to use with different informational texts.

- Analyzing Central Ideas
- Summarizing Text

Name _____ Date _____ Selection _____

Analyzing Central Ideas

Use the top graphic organizer to state key details and central ideas of the text. Use the bottom graphic organizer to explain how the ideas build or interact over the course of the text.

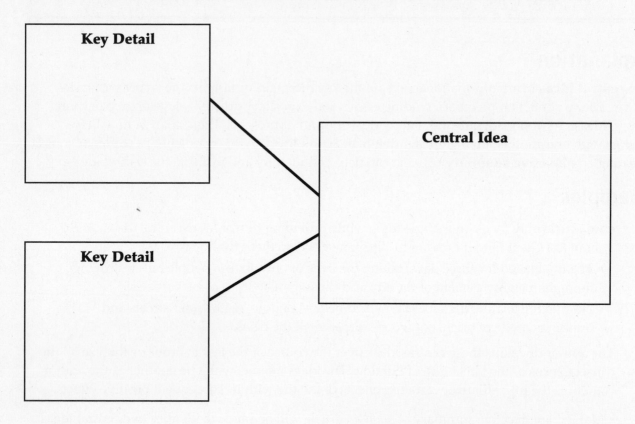

Key Detail

Key Detail

Central Idea

How the Ideas Interact

For use with Informational Text 2

Name _____ Date _____ Selection _____

Analyzing Central Ideas

Use the top graphic organizer to state key details and central ideas of the text. Use the bottom graphic organizer to explain how the ideas build or interact over the course of the text.

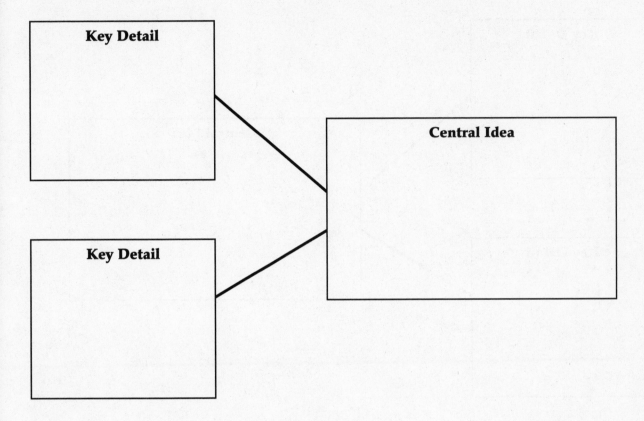

Key Detail

Key Detail

Central Idea

How the Ideas Interact

For use with Informational Text 2

Name _____ Date _____ Selection _____

Analyzing Central Ideas

Use the top graphic organizer to state key details and central ideas of the text. Use the bottom graphic organizer to explain how the ideas build or interact over the course of the text.

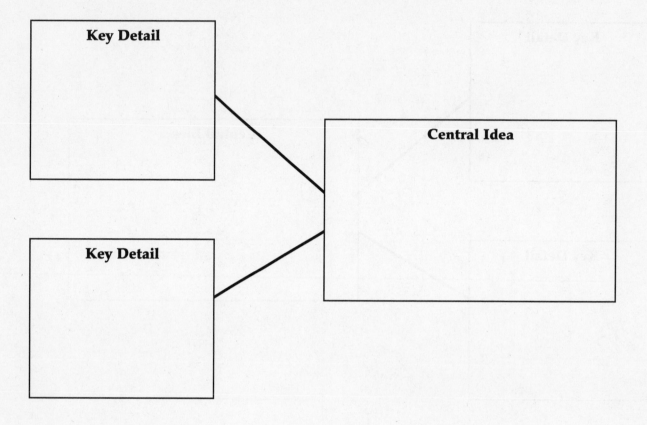

How the Ideas Interact

Name _____ Date _____ Selection _____

Analyzing Central Ideas

Use the top graphic organizer to state key details and central ideas of the text. Use the bottom graphic organizer to explain how the ideas build or interact over the course of the text.

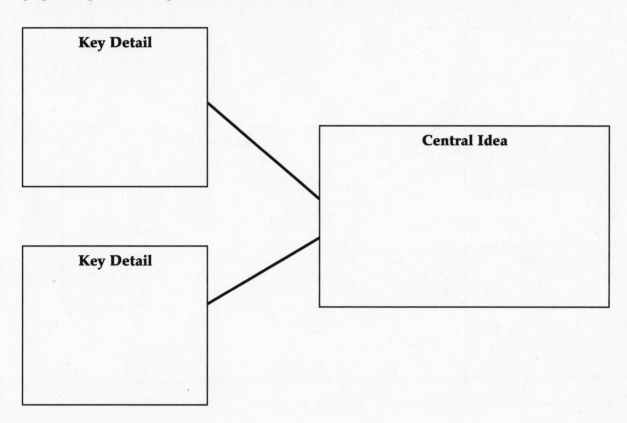

Key Detail

Key Detail

Central Idea

How the Ideas Interact

D

Name _____ Date _____ Selection _____

Analyzing Central Ideas

Use the top graphic organizer to state key details and central ideas of the text. Use the bottom graphic organizer to explain how the ideas build or interact over the course of the text.

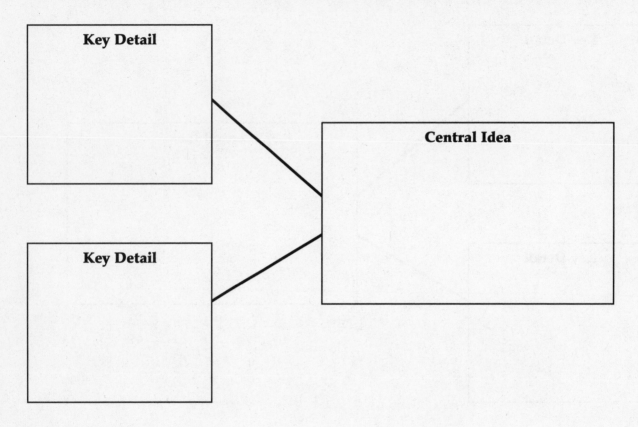

Key Detail

Key Detail

Central Idea

How the Ideas Interact

E

Name _____ Date _____ Selection _____

Analyzing Central Ideas

Use the top graphic organizer to state key details and central ideas of the text. Use the bottom graphic organizer to explain how the ideas build or interact over the course of the text.

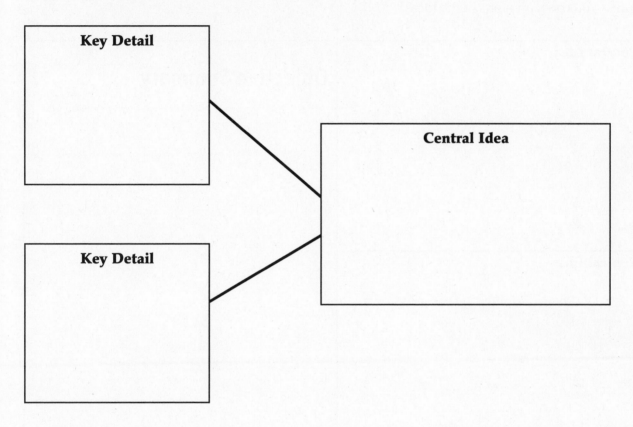

Key Detail

Key Detail

Central Idea

How the Ideas Interact

For use with Informational Text 2

Name _____ Date _____ Selection _____

Summarizing Text

In the left column of the graphic organizer, briefly state the central or essential ideas of the text. Then, use these ideas to write an objective summary in the right column, being careful not to express your own opinions of the ideas.

Central Idea	**Objective Summary** ....
Central Idea	
Central Idea	

A

Name _____ Date _____ Selection _____

Summarizing Text

In the left column of the graphic organizer, briefly state the central or essential ideas of the text. Then, use these ideas to write an objective summary in the right column, being careful not to express your own opinions of the ideas.

Central Idea	Objective Summary
Central Idea	
Central Idea	

For use with Informational Text 2

Name _____ Date _____ Selection _____

Summarizing Text

In the left column of the graphic organizer, briefly state the central or essential ideas of the text. Then, use these ideas to write an objective summary in the right column, being careful not to express your own opinions of the ideas.

Central Idea	Objective Summary ....
Central Idea	
Central Idea	

C

Name _____ Date _____ Selection _____

Summarizing Text

In the left column of the graphic organizer, briefly state the central or essential ideas of the text. Then, use these ideas to write an objective summary in the right column, being careful not to express your own opinions of the ideas.

Central Idea	Objective Summary ....
	....
	....
	....
	....
Central Idea	....
	....
	....
	....
	....
	....
	....
Central Idea	....
	....
	....
	....
	....
	....

For use with Informational Text 2

Name _____ Date _____ Selection _____

Summarizing Text

In the left column of the graphic organizer, briefly state the central or essential ideas of the text. Then, use these ideas to write an objective summary in the right column, being careful not to express your own opinions of the ideas.

Central Idea	**Objective Summary** ....
	....
	....
	....
	....
Central Idea	....
	....
	....
	....
	....
	....
	....
	....
Central Idea	....
	....
	....
	....
	....
	....

For use with Informational Text 2

Name _____ Date _____ Selection _____

Summarizing Text

In the left column of the graphic organizer, briefly state the central or essential ideas of the text. Then, use these ideas to write an objective summary in the right column, being careful not to express your own opinions of the ideas.

Central Idea	Objective Summary
Central Idea	
Central Idea	
Central Idea	

F

Informational Text 3

> 3. **Analyze a complex set of ideas or sequence of events and explain how specific individuals, ideas, or events interact and develop over the course of the text.**

Explanation

Science articles, history books, and reports are three examples of the wide variety of informational texts you will encounter in your reading. These texts can be challenging to read because they present a complex set of ideas or **sequence of events.** You can analyze and master such texts by using a multidraft reading strategy, as follows:

First Reading
- **Skim** and **scan** the text to gain a sense of the whole.
- Note high-level and subject-specific vocabulary.
- Note section headings, bulleted lists, and graphics like charts and tables.

Second Reading
- Read slowly and in depth, identifying the main idea and supporting details.
- Monitor your understanding and reread confusing or difficult passages.
- Use context clues to help define unfamiliar terms.
- Use reference materials to clarify terms or ideas that remain unclear.
- Clarify the relationships between the text and graphics.

Third Reading
- Analyze how individuals, ideas, or events interact and develop.
- Express your understanding of the work as a whole.

Example

The following notes come from a third reading of Arthur C. Clarke's 1945 science article "Extra-Terrestrial Relays: Can Rocket Stations Give World-Wide Radio Coverage?"

> Clarke first introduces several key ideas, some of which may have been familiar to readers: rockets can escape Earth's gravity and orbit the planet; soon, radio-steered and manned rockets will be possible; and many Earth-orbits are available. This initial development brings Clarke to a crucial concept, namely that in one particular orbit, an object will circle with the earth and therefore remain stationary above a spot. With this concept established, Clarke can present his revolutionary idea: Stationary satellites with the proper equipment can relay transmissions from one spot on earth to another. Beginning with concepts more familiar to readers, Clarke works his way toward a dramatically new idea, but one that he makes sound plausible. . . .

Academic Vocabulary

sequence of events events that occur in order, one after another
skim read quickly to discover the main ideas
scan look over to identify format and main features

Apply the Standard

Use the worksheet that follows to help you apply the standard as you read. Several copies have been provided for you to use with different informational texts.

- Analyzing the Development of Ideas and Events

Name _____ Date _____ Assignment _____

Analyzing the Development of Ideas and Events

Use the graphic organizer, below, to analyze a complex set of ideas or sequence of events in an informational text you have read recently. Then, answer the question at the bottom of the page.

Title: ....   Author: ....   Subject: ....

Analysis	
What does the text describe? ❏ a complex set of ideas ❏ a sequence of events	
Set of Ideas	**Sequence of Events**
Outline the main ideas and supporting details: I. 　A. 　.B. II. 　A. 　.B. III. 　A. 　B.	List the events in order: 1st Event: 2nd Event: 3rd Event: 4th Event:
How do ideas interact and develop over the course of the text?	**How do events interact and develop over the course of the text?** ....

For use with Literature 3

Name _____ Date _____ Assignment _____

Analyzing the Development of Ideas and Events

Use the graphic organizer, below, to analyze a complex set of ideas or sequence of events in an informational text you have read recently. Then, answer the question at the bottom of the page.

Title: ....   Author: ....   Subject: ....

Analysis
What does the text describe? ❏ a complex set of ideas ❏ a sequence of events

Set of Ideas	Sequence of Events
Outline the main ideas and supporting details: I. A. .B. II. A. .B. III. A. B.	List the events in order: 1st Event: 2nd Event: 3rd Event: 4th Event:
How do ideas interact and develop over the course of the text?	**How do events interact and develop over the course of the text?** ....

For use with Literature 3

Name _____ Date _____ Assignment _____

Analyzing the Development of Ideas and Events

Use the graphic organizer, below, to analyze a complex set of ideas or sequence of events in an informational text you have read recently. Then, answer the question at the bottom of the page.

Title:...........................   Author:...........................   Subject:...........................

Analysis
What does the text describe? ❏ a complex set of ideas ❏ a sequence of events

Set of Ideas	Sequence of Events

Outline the main ideas and supporting details:
 	
I.
 	
  A.
 	
  .B.
 	
II.
 	
  A.
 	
  .B.
 	
III.
 	
  A.
 	
  B.
	List the events in order:
	
	1st Event:
	
	2nd Event:
	
	3rd Event:
	
	4th Event:

How do ideas interact and develop over the course of the text?	**How do events interact and develop over the course of the text?** ....

C

Name _____ Date _____ Assignment _____

Analyzing the Development of Ideas and Events

Use the graphic organizer, below, to analyze a complex set of ideas or sequence of events in an informational text you have read recently. Then, answer the question at the bottom of the page.

Title: .... Author: .... Subject: ....

Analysis	
What does the text describe? ❏ a complex set of ideas ❏ a sequence of events	
Set of Ideas	**Sequence of Events**
Outline the main ideas and supporting details: I. 　A. 　.B. II. 　A. 　.B. III. 　A. 　B.	List the events in order: 1st Event: 2nd Event: 3rd Event: 4th Event:
How do ideas interact and develop over the course of the text?	**How do events interact and develop over the course of the text?** ....

D

Name _____ Date _____ Assignment _____

Analyzing the Development of Ideas and Events

Use the graphic organizer, below, to analyze a complex set of ideas or sequence of events in an informational text you have read recently. Then, answer the question at the bottom of the page.

Title: .... Author: .... Subject: ....

Analysis

What does the text describe?
- ❏ a complex set of ideas
- ❏ a sequence of events

Set of Ideas	Sequence of Events

Outline the main ideas and supporting details:
 	
I.
 	
  A.
 	
  .B.
 	
II.
 	
  A.
 	
  .B.
 	
III.
 	
  A.
 	
  B.
	List the events in order:
	
	1st Event:
	
	2nd Event:
	
	3rd Event:
	
	4th Event:

How do ideas interact and develop over the course of the text?	**How do events interact and develop over the course of the text?** ....

E

Name _____ Date _____ Assignment _____

Analyzing the Development of Ideas and Events

Use the graphic organizer, below, to analyze a complex set of ideas or sequence of events in an informational text you have read recently. Then, answer the question at the bottom of the page.

Title: .... Author: .... Subject: ....

Analysis	
What does the text describe? ❏ a complex set of ideas ❏ a sequence of events	
Set of Ideas	**Sequence of Events**

Outline the main ideas and supporting details:
 	
I.
 	
  A.
 	
  .B.
 	
II.
 	
  A.
 	
  .B.
 	
III.
 	
  A.
 	
  B.
	List the events in order:
	
	1st Event:
	
	2nd Event:
	
	3rd Event:
	
	4th Event:

How do ideas interact and develop over the course of the text?	**How do events interact and develop over the course of the text?** ....

Informational Text 4

> 4. Determine the meaning of words and phrases as they are used in a text, including figurative, connotative, and technical meanings; analyze how an author uses and refines the meaning of a key term or terms over the course of a text.

Explanation

When reading informational texts, you will come across words and phrases that are new to you or used in unfamiliar ways. **Figurative language** is writing not meant to be interpreted literally. Authors use figurative language to express ideas in a fresh way. Words also have **connotative meanings,** or emotions and feelings that are associated with them. Connotations can be positive, neutral or negative. Informational texts often include technical terms specifically related to a subject. Figuring out **technical meanings** is an important part of reading informational text.

Sometimes an author refines the meaning of a key term over the course of the text, introducing it in the opening paragraphs and later providing more and different examples or explanations. Authors add new layers of meaning to words on purpose. Pay special attention to words that authors repeat. They can often provide clues about the themes an author is trying to develop.

Examples

- **Figurative language** "The sound of the cicadas is like a buzz saw that cuts the night." The author uses a simile to help readers grasp that cicadas make a loud, harsh noise.

- **Connotations** Describing a scent as *pungent* creates a stronger impression than *overpowering.* Authors choose words carefully, because connotations affect readers' impressions.

- **Technical language.** Use context clues to figure out technical terms: "The Amazon rainforest is a lush <u>ecosystem</u> that contains an enormous variety of <u>species,</u> including some that are not found anyplace else on Earth." If the text does not provide context clues or definitions, check the terms' meanings in a dictionary.

Academic Vocabulary

connotative meaning the associations related to a word

figurative language writing that is not meant to be interpreted literally

technical meanings word meanings specifically related to a subject

Apply the Standard

Use the worksheets that follow to help you apply the standard as you read. Several copies of each worksheet have been provided for you to use with different informational texts.

- Understanding Connotations, Figurative Language, and Technical Terms

- Analyzing Key Terms

Name _____ Date _____ Assignment _____

Understanding Connotations, Figurative Language, and Technical Terms

Use the graphic organizers to analyze the connotations, figurative language, and technical terms found in informational text.

- In the top organizer, list words from the text that have **connotations** beyond their dictionary meanings. Circle the kind of connotation (*negative, positive,* or *neutral*) and supply the word's meaning.

- In the bottom organizer, list examples of **figurative language** or **technical terms,** and explain what the figures of speech mean or imply.

Connotations

Words with Connotations	Kind of Connotation (Circle one.)	Connotative Meaning
1.	negative positive neutral	
2.	negative positive neutral	
3.	negative positive neutral	
4.	negative positive neutral	

Figurative Language and Technical Terms

Figurative Language or Technical Term	What It Means or Implies
1.	
2.	
3.	
4.	

A

Name _____ Date _____ Assignment _____

Understanding Connotations, Figurative Language, and Technical Terms

Use the graphic organizers to analyze the connotations, figurative language, and technical terms found in informational text.

- In the top organizer, list words from the text that have **connotations** beyond their dictionary meanings. Circle the kind of connotation (*negative, positive,* or *neutral*) and supply the word's meaning.

- In the bottom organizer, list examples of **figurative language** or **technical terms,** and explain what the figures of speech mean or imply.

Connotations

Words with Connotations	Kind of Connotation (Circle one.)	Connotative Meaning
1.	negative positive neutral	
2.	negative positive neutral	
3.	negative positive neutral	
4.	negative positive neutral	

Figurative Language and Technical Terms

Figurative Language or Technical Term	What It Means or Implies
1.	
2.	
3.	
4.	

B   For use with Informational Text 4

Name _____ Date _____ Assignment _____

Understanding Connotations, Figurative Language, and Technical Terms

Use the graphic organizers to analyze the connotations, figurative language, and technical terms found in informational text.

- In the top organizer, list words from the text that have **connotations** beyond their dictionary meanings. Circle the kind of connotation (*negative, positive,* or *neutral*) and supply the word's meaning.

- In the bottom organizer, list examples of **figurative language** or **technical terms,** and explain what the figures of speech mean or imply.

Connotations

Words with Connotations	Kind of Connotation (Circle one.)	Connotative Meaning
1.	negative positive neutral	
2.	negative positive neutral	
3.	negative positive neutral	
4.	negative positive neutral	

Figurative Language and Technical Terms

Figurative Language or Technical Term	What It Means or Implies
1.	
2.	
3.	
4.	

C

Name _____ Date _____ Assignment _____

Understanding Connotations, Figurative Language, and Technical Terms

Use the graphic organizers to analyze the connotations, figurative language, and technical terms found in informational text.

- In the top organizer, list words from the text that have **connotations** beyond their dictionary meanings. Circle the kind of connotation (*negative, positive,* or *neutral*) and supply the word's meaning.

- In the bottom organizer, list examples of **figurative language** or **technical terms,** and explain what the figures of speech mean or imply.

Connotations

Words with Connotations	Kind of Connotation (Circle one.)	Connotative Meaning
1.	negative positive neutral	
2.	negative positive neutral	
3.	negative positive neutral	
4.	negative positive neutral	

Figurative Language and Technical Terms

Figurative Language or Technical Term	What It Means or Implies
1.	
2.	
3.	
4.	

D

Name _____ Date _____ Assignment _____

Understanding Connotations, Figurative Language, and Technical Terms

Use the graphic organizers to analyze the connotations, figurative language, and technical terms found in informational text.

- In the top organizer, list words from the text that have **connotations** beyond their dictionary meanings. Circle the kind of connotation (*negative, positive,* or *neutral*) and supply the word's meaning.

- In the bottom organizer, list examples of **figurative language** or **technical terms,** and explain what the figures of speech mean or imply.

Connotations

Words with Connotations	Kind of Connotation (Circle one.)	Connotative Meaning
1.	negative positive neutral	
2.	negative positive neutral	
3.	negative positive neutral	
4.	negative positive neutral	

Figurative Language and Technical Terms

Figurative Language or Technical Term	What It Means or Implies
1.	
2.	
3.	
4.	

E

Name _____ Date _____ Assignment _____

Understanding Connotations, Figurative Language, and Technical Terms

Use the graphic organizers to analyze the connotations, figurative language, and technical terms found in informational text.

- In the top organizer, list words from the text that have **connotations** beyond their dictionary meanings. Circle the kind of connotation (*negative, positive,* or *neutral*) and supply the word's meaning.

- In the bottom organizer, list examples of **figurative language** or **technical terms,** and explain what the figures of speech mean or imply.

Connotations

Words with Connotations	Kind of Connotation (Circle one.)	Connotative Meaning
1.	negative positive neutral	
2.	negative positive neutral	
3.	negative positive neutral	
4.	negative positive neutral	

Figurative Language and Technical Terms

Figurative Language or Technical Term	What It Means or Implies
1.	
2.	
3.	
4.	

F

For use with Informational Text 4

Name _____   Date _____   Assignment _____

Analyzing Key Terms

Use the graphic organizer to analyze several uses of a key term over the course of the text, and describe which context clues help you better understand the term.

Key Term	
What are textual examples of the key term?	How does context help further your understanding of the key term?
1.	
2.	
3.	
4.	
Summarize the understanding that you have of the key term after reading the entire text:	

A

Name _____ Date _____ Assignment _____

Analyzing Key Terms

Use the graphic organizer to analyze several uses of a key term over the course of the text, and describe which context clues help you better understand the term.

Key Term	
What are textual examples of the key term?	How does context help further your understanding of the key term?
1.	
2.	
3.	
4.	
Summarize the understanding that you have of the key term after reading the entire text:	

For use with Informational Text 4

Name _____ Date _____ Assignment _____

Analyzing Key Terms

Use the graphic organizer to analyze several uses of a key term over the course of the text, and describe which context clues help you better understand the term.

Key Term	
What are textual examples of the key term?	How does context help further your understanding of the key term?
1.	
2.	
3.	
4.	
Summarize the understanding that you have of the key term after reading the entire text:	

For use with Informational Text 4

Name _____ Date _____ Assignment _____

Analyzing Key Terms

Use the graphic organizer to analyze several uses of a key term over the course of the text, and describe which context clues help you better understand the term.

Key Term	
What are textual examples of the key term?	How does context help further your understanding of the key term?
1.	
2.	
3.	
4.	
Summarize the understanding that you have of the key term after reading the entire text:	

For use with Informational Text 4

Name _____ Date _____ Assignment _____

Analyzing Key Terms

Use the graphic organizer to analyze several uses of a key term over the course of the text, and describe which context clues help you better understand the term.

Key Term	
What are textual examples of the key term?	How does context help further your understanding of the key term?
1.	
2.	
3.	
4.	

Summarize the understanding that you have of the key term after reading the entire text:

E

Name _____ Date _____ Assignment _____

Analyzing Key Terms

Use the graphic organizer to analyze several uses of a key term over the course of the text, and describe which context clues help you better understand the term.

Key Term	
What are textual examples of the key term?	How does context help further your understanding of the key term?
1.	
2.	
3.	
4.	
Summarize the understanding that you have of the key term after reading the entire text:	

F

Informational Text 5

> **5. Analyze and evaluate the effectiveness of the structure an author uses in his or her exposition or argument, including whether the structure makes points clear, convincing, and engaging.**

Explanation

Writers deliberately structure, or organize, their ideas in order to make their points clear, convincing, and engaging. The structure of an **exposition** or **argument** can follow several different patterns of organization. Here are four common patterns of organization:

- **Chronological order** Listing steps in a process in the order in which they happen or should be done. Telling events in time order.

- **Cause-and-effect** Showing how one situation or condition causes or influences another

- **Comparison-and-contrast** Pointing out similarities and differences between items

- **Order of Importance** Proceeding from least important point to most important, or from most to least important point

Knowing the ways authors structure their writing can help you understand it more thoroughly and quickly. Look for these text structures when reading informational text.

Examples

- *Chronological order:* A writer who proposes a plan to improve the national economy may use this structure to list steps in the order in which they should be carried out.

- *Cause-and-effect:* This structure might be effective when explaining multiple causes leading to a war or multiple effects produced by it.

- *Comparison-and-contrast:* A writer attempting to persuade an audience of the advantages of one product over another might use this structure effectively.

- *Order of importance:* This structure would work well for a text that presents several reasons for building a new dam. Reasons could be presented from most important to least important, or vice versa.

Academic Vocabulary

argument the position that a writer presents, supported by evidence

exposition writing that explains a process or presents information

Apply the Standard

Use the worksheet that follows to help you apply the standard as you read. Several copies have been provided for you to use with different informational texts.

- Analyzing and Evaluating Structure

Name _____ Date _____ Assignment _____

Analyzing and Evaluating Structure

Writers can choose among several types of organization to structure their texts, such as:

chronological order   **comparison and contrast**

cause-and-effect order   **order of importance.**

Use this graphic organizer to analyze and evaluate the structure of the text you are reading.

1. What is the writer's central idea or argument?
2. What type of organization does the writer use?
3. What details from the text show this type of organization?
4. Is this the best type of organization for the text? Explain your answer.

For use with Informational Text 5

Name _____ Date _____ Assignment _____

Analyzing and Evaluating Structure

Writers can choose among several types of organization to structure their texts, such as:

chronological order   *comparison and contrast*

cause-and-effect order   *order of importance.*

Use this graphic organizer to analyze and evaluate the structure of the text you are reading.

1. What is the writer's central idea or argument?
2. What type of organization does the writer use?
3. What details from the text show this type of organization?
4. Is this the best type of organization for the text? Explain your answer.

Name _____ Date _____ Assignment _____

Analyzing and Evaluating Structure

Writers can choose among several types of organization to structure their texts, such as:

chronological order   *comparison and contrast*

cause-and-effect order   *order of importance.*

Use this graphic organizer to analyze and evaluate the structure of the text you are reading.

1. What is the writer's central idea or argument?
2. What type of organization does the writer use?
3. What details from the text show this type of organization?
4. Is this the best type of organization for the text? Explain your answer.

Name _____ Date _____ Assignment _____

Analyzing and Evaluating Structure

Writers can choose among several types of organization to structure their texts, such as:

chronological order   *comparison and contrast*

cause-and-effect order   *order of importance.*

Use this graphic organizer to analyze and evaluate the structure of the text you are reading.

1. What is the writer's central idea or argument?
2. What type of organization does the writer use?
3. What details from the text show this type of organization?
4. Is this the best type of organization for the text? Explain your answer.

For use with Informational Text 5

Name _____ Date _____ Assignment _____

Analyzing and Evaluating Structure

Writers can choose among several types of organization to structure their texts, such as:

chronological order   *comparison and contrast*

cause-and-effect order   *order of importance.*

Use this graphic organizer to analyze and evaluate the structure of the text you are reading.

1. What is the writer's central idea or argument?
2. What type of organization does the writer use?
3. What details from the text show this type of organization?
4. Is this the best type of organization for the text? Explain your answer.

E

Name _____ Date _____ Assignment _____

Analyzing and Evaluating Structure

Writers can choose among several types of organization to structure their texts, such as:

chronological order   *comparison and contrast*

cause-and-effect order   *order of importance.*

Use this graphic organizer to analyze and evaluate the structure of the text you are reading.

1. What is the writer's central idea or argument?
2. What type of organization does the writer use?
3. What details from the text show this type of organization?
4. Is this the best type of organization for the text? Explain your answer.

Informational Text 6

> 6. **Determine an author's point of view or purpose in a text in which the rhetoric is particularly effective, analyzing how style and content contribute to the power, persuasiveness or beauty of the text.**

Explanation

In an informational text, a writer's point of view is his or her position or perspective on an issue. A writer may explicitly state his or her point of view, telling readers exactly what he or she thinks. Other times writers may implicitly suggest a position in their arguments. You can determine a writer's point of view by paying close attention to the details and **rhetoric** he or she includes.

Rhetorical devices are the methods that writers use to emphasize their points and achieve their purpose. Below are several rhetorical devices:

- *Repetition* is the repeating of a word, phrase, or idea to add emphasis.

- *Rhetorical questions* are questions with obvious answers, such as, "Are we incapable of change?"

- *Parallelism* involves repeating similar grammatical structures to create rhythm or add emphasis.

- *Allusion* is a reference to a well-known person, event, place, literary work, or work of art.

Examples

- In his "Speech to Parliament: In Defense of the Lower Classes," George Gordon, Lord Byron poses the **rhetorical question:** "Can you commit a whole country to their own prisons?" The unstated answer (*no*) emphasizes Byron's defense of factory workers.

- In the "We Shall Fight on the Beaches" speech, Winston Churchill employs **repetition** to stress the urgency of defending Britain from German aggression: "<u>We shall</u> go on to the end, <u>we shall fight</u> in France, <u>we shall fight</u> on the seas and oceans, we shall fight with growing confidence and growing strength in the air, <u>we shall</u> defend our Island."

- "Work had become his own personal Gulag of sorts" has an allusion (gulags). It is an allusion to the network of horrible forced labor prisons in the former Soviet Union. In this sentence, the allusion helps convey the absolute unpleasantness of work.

Academic Vocabulary

rhetoric the art of writing or speaking effectively

Apply the Standard

Use the worksheets that follow to help you apply the standard as you read informational texts. Several copies of each worksheet have been provided for you.

- Determining Point of View

- Analyzing Effective Rhetoric

Name _____ Date _____ Selection _____

Determining Point of View

Use the graphic organizer below to determine the writer's point of view.

- Give details from the text that explicitly or implicitly reveal the writer's point of view.

- Paraphrase the author's viewpoint in your own words.

Title of Selection: ....

Details from the text:
1.
2.
3.
4.
5.

Author's point of view:

A

Name _____ Date _____ Selection _____

Determining Point of View

Use the graphic organizer below to determine the writer's point of view.

- Give details from the text that explicitly or implicitly reveal the writer's point of view.

- Paraphrase the author's viewpoint in your own words.

Title of Selection: ....

Details from the text:
1.
2.
3.
4.
5.

Author's point of view:

For use with Informational Text 6

Name _____ Date _____ Selection _____

Determining Point of View

Use the graphic organizer below to determine the writer's point of view.

- Give details from the text that explicitly or implicitly reveal the writer's point of view.

- Paraphrase the author's viewpoint in your own words.

Title of Selection: ....

Details from the text:
1.
2.
3.
4.
5.

Author's point of view:

C

Name _____ Date _____ Selection _____

Determining Point of View

Use the graphic organizer below to determine the writer's point of view.

- • Give details from the text that explicitly or implicitly reveal the writer's point of view.

- • Paraphrase the author's viewpoint in your own words.

Title of Selection: ....

Details from the text:
1.
2.
3.
4.
5.

Author's point of view:

Name _____ Date _____ Selection _____

Determining Point of View

Use the graphic organizer below to determine the writer's point of view.

- Give details from the text that explicitly or implicitly reveal the writer's point of view.

- Paraphrase the author's viewpoint in your own words.

Title of Selection: ....

Details from the text:
1.
2.
3.
4.
5.

Author's point of view:

E

Name _____ Date _____ Selection _____

Determining Point of View

Use the graphic organizer below to determine the writer's point of view.

- Give details from the text that explicitly or implicitly reveal the writer's point of view.

- Paraphrase the author's viewpoint in your own words.

Title of Selection: ....

Details from the text:
1.
2.
3.
4.
5.

Author's point of view:

F

Name _____ Date _____ Selection _____

Analyzing Effective Rhetoric

Use the graphic organizer below to analyze the rhetorical devices that are used in a text you are reading. (Note that the text you are analyzing may not include examples of each type.) Then answer the question at the bottom of the page.

Title of Selection: ....

Type of Rhetorical Device	Examples from the Text
Repetition:	
Rhetorical questions:	
Parallelism:	
Allusions:	

How does the author's use of these devices contribute to the power, persuasiveness, or beauty of

the text? ....

....

....

A

Name _____ Date _____ Selection _____

Analyzing Effective Rhetoric

Use the graphic organizer below to analyze the rhetorical devices that are used in a text you are reading. (Note that the text you are analyzing may not include examples of each type.) Then answer the question at the bottom of the page.

Title of Selection: ....

Type of Rhetorical Device	Examples from the Text
Repetition:	
Rhetorical questions:	
Parallelism:	
Allusions:	

How does the author's use of these devices contribute to the power, persuasiveness, or beauty of

the text? ....

....

....

Name _____ Date _____ Selection _____

Analyzing Effective Rhetoric

Use the graphic organizer below to analyze the rhetorical devices that are used in a text you are reading. (Note that the text you are analyzing may not include examples of each type.) Then answer the question at the bottom of the page.

Title of Selection: ....

Type of Rhetorical Device	Examples from the Text
Repetition:	
Rhetorical questions:	
Parallelism:	
Allusions:	

How does the author's use of these devices contribute to the power, persuasiveness, or beauty of

the text? ....

....

....

C

Name _____ Date _____ Selection _____

Analyzing Effective Rhetoric

Use the graphic organizer below to analyze the rhetorical devices that are used in a text you are reading. (Note that the text you are analyzing may not include examples of each type.) Then answer the question at the bottom of the page.

Title of Selection: ....

Type of Rhetorical Device	Examples from the Text
Repetition:	
Rhetorical questions:	
Parallelism:	
Allusions:	

How does the author's use of these devices contribute to the power, persuasiveness, or beauty of

the text? ....

....

....

D

Name _____ Date _____ Selection _____

Analyzing Effective Rhetoric

Use the graphic organizer below to analyze the rhetorical devices that are used in a text you are reading. (Note that the text you are analyzing may not include examples of each type.) Then answer the question at the bottom of the page.

Title of Selection: ....

Type of Rhetorical Device	Examples from the Text
Repetition:	
Rhetorical questions:	
Parallelism:	
Allusions:	

How does the author's use of these devices contribute to the power, persuasiveness, or beauty of

the text? ....

....

....

E

Name _____ Date _____ Selection _____

Analyzing Effective Rhetoric

Use the graphic organizer below to analyze the rhetorical devices that are used in a text you are reading. (Note that the text you are analyzing may not include examples of each type.) Then answer the question at the bottom of the page.

Title of Selection: ....

Type of Rhetorical Device	Examples from the Text
Repetition:	
Rhetorical questions:	
Parallelism:	
Allusions:	

How does the author's use of these devices contribute to the power, persuasiveness, or beauty of

the text? ....

....

....

F

Informational Text 7

> 7. **Integrate and evaluate multiple sources of information presented in different media or formats (e.g., visually, quantitatively) as well as in words in order to address a question or solve a problem.**

Explanation

When you investigate a topic, you may find several sources that present information in different formats. Visual formats include photographs, maps, and illustrations. **Quantitative** formats include charts, graphs, and tables. Oral formats include speeches and other types of audio material. Print information includes **primary source** documents—nonfiction works that are firsthand accounts of a specific historical period or event. Below are several examples of primary source documents:

- Diaries and journals are private, personal records of events. Diaries and journals often provide unique glimpses of real life during notable times. They contain valuable personal details that only a participant or an eyewitness can supply.

- A letter is a written message addressed to a specific reader or readers.

- A field report is a first-hand record of observations and data written by researchers in the field. Depending on their subjects, writers of field reports may include specialized scientific or technical language and illustrations.

- A government memorandum is a brief official message that summarizes reasons for a particular action and gives instructions on how it is to be performed.

In order to fully address a question or to solve a problem, it helps to integrate and evaluate several sources. Each source or format adds unique content to an in-depth understanding of a subject.

Examples

Several sources can help you address the question, "What was life like for the Allied soldiers fighting in Europe during World War II?" Newsreels and photographs show actual scenes of the war. Graphs and charts can provide statistics on battle casualties, war evacuations, and numbers of battleships. Maps of European battlefields illustrate troop movements or the sites of important battles.

Academic Vocabulary

primary source a first-hand document or recording of an event

quantitative containing data that deals with measurements or amounts

Apply the Standard

Use the worksheet that follows to help you apply the standard as you read informational texts. Several copies of the worksheet have been provided for you.

- Integrating and Evaluating Information

Name _____ Date _____ Selection _____

Integrating and Evaluating Information

Use this organizer to integrate and evaluate information from several sources. First, determine a question or problem that you will address by gathering information. Then select three different sources that present information about the subject in different formats (e.g., map, diary, letter, graph), and answer the questions.

What question or problem will you investigate? ....

....

....

Evaluating Information	Source 1	Source 2	Source 3
1. In what format is the information presented?			
2. Who is the author and what is the date of the source?			
3. What is the most helpful information the source provides?			

↓

Integrating Information: Think about what you've learned from all three sources. What conclusions can you draw about your topic?

A

Name _____ Date _____ Selection _____

Integrating and Evaluating Information

Use this organizer to integrate and evaluate information from several sources. First, determine a question or problem that you will address by gathering information. Then select three different sources that present information about the subject in different formats (e.g., map, diary, letter, graph), and answer the questions.

What question or problem will you investigate? ....

....

....

Evaluating Information	Source 1	Source 2	Source 3
1. In what format is the information presented?			
2. Who is the author and what is the date of the source?			
3. What is the most helpful information the source provides?			

↓

Integrating Information: Think about what you've learned from all three sources. What conclusions can you draw about your topic?

B

Name _____ Date _____ Selection _____

Integrating and Evaluating Information

Use this organizer to integrate and evaluate information from several sources. First, determine a question or problem that you will address by gathering information. Then select three different sources that present information about the subject in different formats (e.g., map, diary, letter, graph), and answer the questions.

What question or problem will you investigate? ....

....

....

Evaluating Information	Source 1	Source 2	Source 3
1. In what format is the information presented?			
2. Who is the author and what is the date of the source?			
3. What is the most helpful information the source provides?			

↓

Integrating Information: Think about what you've learned from all three sources. What conclusions can you draw about your topic?

Name _____ Date _____ Selection _____

Integrating and Evaluating Information

Use this organizer to integrate and evaluate information from several sources. First, determine a question or problem that you will address by gathering information. Then select three different sources that present information about the subject in different formats (e.g., map, diary, letter, graph), and answer the questions.

What question or problem will you investigate? ....

....

....

Evaluating Information	Source 1	Source 2	Source 3
1. In what format is the information presented?			
2. Who is the author and what is the date of the source?			
3. What is the most helpful information the source provides?			

↓

Integrating Information: Think about what you've learned from all three sources. What conclusions can you draw about your topic?

D

For use with Informational Text 7

Name _____ Date _____ Selection _____

Integrating and Evaluating Information

Use this organizer to integrate and evaluate information from several sources. First, determine a question or problem that you will address by gathering information. Then select three different sources that present information about the subject in different formats (e.g., map, diary, letter, graph), and answer the questions.

What question or problem will you investigate? ....

....

....

Evaluating Information	Source 1	Source 2	Source 3
1. In what format is the information presented?			
2. Who is the author and what is the date of the source?			
3. What is the most helpful information the source provides?			

↓

Integrating Information: Think about what you've learned from all three sources. What conclusions can you draw about your topic?

E

Name _____ Date _____ Selection _____

Integrating and Evaluating Information

Use this organizer to integrate and evaluate information from several sources. First, determine a question or problem that you will address by gathering information. Then select three different sources that present information about the subject in different formats (e.g., map, diary, letter, graph), and answer the questions.

What question or problem will you investigate? ....

....

....

Evaluating Information	Source 1	Source 2	Source 3
1. In what format is the information presented?			
2. Who is the author and what is the date of the source?			
3. What is the most helpful information the source provides?			

↓

Integrating Information: Think about what you've learned from all three sources. What conclusions can you draw about your topic?

For use with Informational Text 7

Informational Text 8

> 8. **Delineate and evaluate the reasoning in seminal U.S. texts, including the application of constitutional principles and use of legal reasoning (e.g., in U.S. Supreme Court majority opinions and dissents) and the premises, purposes, and arguments in works of public advocacy (e.g., *The Federalist*, presidential addresses).**

Explanation

Persuasion is writing that presents an argument, or message that is meant to move readers to think a certain way or take a specific action. Strong writers often rely on the following persuasive appeals to convince readers of their **premises: appeals to emotion** to influence readers' feelings; **appeals to logic** to show that an argument is correct; and **appeals to ethics** to show that a higher principle supports the idea.

Persuasive writers also use a variety of rhetorical devices to stress their key points and to move readers' emotions: restatement, repetition, parallelism, rhetorical questions, and allusions.

When you evaluate an argument—such as those in influential U.S. texts, Supreme Court opinions and dissents, and presidential addresses—look for uses of persuasive appeals and rhetorical devices. Ask if the writer has used sound evidence and reasoning to support his or her message.

Examples

Notice the appeals, reasoning, and rhetorical devices that Franklin D. Roosevelt used in his third inaugural address on January 20, 1941, to rouse the country's faith in democracy:

- **Appeal to logic; repetition; parallelism; restatement:** "We know [democracy] cannot die—because it is built on the unhampered initiative of individual men and women joined together in a common enterprise—an enterprise undertaken and carried through by the free expression of a free majority."

- **Appeal to emotion:** "We know it because democracy alone, of all forms of government, enlists the full force of men's enlightened will."

- **Allusion:** "[Democracy's] vitality was written into our own Mayflower Compact, into the Declaration of Independence, into the Constitution of the United States, into the Gettysburg Address."

Academic Vocabulary

reasoning: the use of logical thinking in order to draw conclusions

premise: basis of an argument

Apply the Standard

Use the worksheets that follow to help you apply the standard as you read informational texts. Several copies of each worksheet have been provided for you.

- Evaluating Reasoning

Name _____ Date _____ Selection _____

Evaluating Reasoning

Answer the questions in the graphic organizer to help you evaluate the reasoning in a text that pertains to governmental or legal matters.

Text: ....   **Writer:** ....

1. What main arguments or explanations are presented?	
2. What reasoning or evidence supports the writer's argument?	
3. What appeals does the writer make to emotions, logic, or ethics?	
4. What rhetorical devices does the writer use?	
5. What is the writer's main purpose in writing the text?	
6. Overall, would you say the argument is convincing or effective? Why or why not?	

A

Name _____ Date _____ Selection _____

Evaluating Reasoning

Answer the questions in the graphic organizer to help you evaluate the reasoning in a text that pertains to governmental or legal matters.

Text: .... **Writer:** ....

1. What main arguments or explanations are presented?	
2. What reasoning or evidence supports the writer's argument?	
3. What appeals does the writer make to emotions, logic, or ethics?	
4. What rhetorical devices does the writer use?	
5. What is the writer's main purpose in writing the text?	
6. Overall, would you say the argument is convincing or effective? Why or why not?	

For use with Informational Text 8

Name _____ Date _____ Selection _____

Evaluating Reasoning

Answer the questions in the graphic organizer to help you evaluate the reasoning in a text that pertains to governmental or legal matters.

Text: .... **Writer:** ....

1. What main arguments or explanations are presented?	
2. What reasoning or evidence supports the writer's argument?	
3. What appeals does the writer make to emotions, logic, or ethics?	
4. What rhetorical devices does the writer use?	
5. What is the writer's main purpose in writing the text?	
6. Overall, would you say the argument is convincing or effective? Why or why not?	

Name _____ Date _____ Selection _____

Evaluating Reasoning

Answer the questions in the graphic organizer to help you evaluate the reasoning in a text that pertains to governmental or legal matters.

Text: .... **Writer:** ....

1. What main arguments or explanations are presented?	
2. What reasoning or evidence supports the writer's argument?	
3. What appeals does the writer make to emotions, logic, or ethics?	
4. What rhetorical devices does the writer use?	
5. What is the writer's main purpose in writing the text?	
6. Overall, would you say the argument is convincing or effective? Why or why not?	

D

Name _____ Date _____ Selection _____

Evaluating Reasoning

Answer the questions in the graphic organizer to help you evaluate the reasoning in a text that pertains to governmental or legal matters.

Text: .... **Writer:** ....

1. What main arguments or explanations are presented?	
2. What reasoning or evidence supports the writer's argument?	
3. What appeals does the writer make to emotions, logic, or ethics?	
4. What rhetorical devices does the writer use?	
5. What is the writer's main purpose in writing the text?	
6. Overall, would you say the argument is convincing or effective? Why or why not?	

E

For use with Informational Text 8

Name _____ Date _____ Selection _____

Evaluating Reasoning

Answer the questions in the graphic organizer to help you evaluate the reasoning in a text that pertains to governmental or legal matters.

Text: ....   **Writer:** ....

1. What main arguments or explanations are presented?	
2. What reasoning or evidence supports the writer's argument?	
3. What appeals does the writer make to emotions, logic, or ethics?	
4. What rhetorical devices does the writer use?	
5. What is the writer's main purpose in writing the text?	
6. Overall, would you say the argument is convincing or effective? Why or why not?	

Informational Text 9

> **9. Analyze seventeenth-, eighteenth-, and nineteenth-century foundational U.S. documents of historical and literary significance (including The Declaration of Independence, the Preamble to the Constitution, the Bill of Rights, and Lincoln's Second Inaugural Address) for their themes, purposes, and rhetorical features.**

Explanation

Documents that helped to establish guiding principles for U.S. government, law, and society are known as foundational documents. In addition to having historical significance, many of these documents also have literary merit. Foundational documents from U.S. history include:

- **The Declaration of Independence:** a declaration of the colonies' independence from Britain, written in 1776 by Thomas Jefferson

- **Lincoln's Second Inaugural Address:** the address delivered on March 4, 1865, when the Civil War was nearly at an end. Lincoln urges the country to reunite in peace and charity.

To analyze a foundational document, first determine the purpose or aim of the author. The purpose of most historical documents is persuasion—an attempt to convince the audience to take an action or adopt an idea. Next, determine the theme of the work, or its central message or insight. Lastly, analyze the rhetorical devices the writer used to highlight his or her key points, such as:

- **Connotations:** the associations that a word calls to mind

- **Allusions:** references to well-known people, events, or texts

- **Repetition:** repeating a word or phrase

- **Parallelism:** repeating a grammatical structure

- **Appeals to emotion:** appeals to readers' feelings

- **Appeals to logic:** the use of reasoning

- **Appeals to ethics:** appeals to readers' principles

- **Figurative language:** language that is not intended to be interpreted literally

Examples

The purpose of President Lincoln's *Second Inaugural Address* was not to glory in victory but to advise against harsh treatment of the South. The theme running through the address is a plea for the country to heal by moving forward in a sense of brotherhood. In support of this idea, Lincoln makes an allusion to the Bible ("but let us judge not, that we be not judged").

Apply the Standard

Use the worksheet that follows to help you apply the standard as you read informational texts. Several copies of each worksheet have been provided for you.

- Analyzing Historical Documents

Name _____ Date _____ Selection _____

Analyzing Historical Documents

Answer the questions in the graphic organizer to analyze a historical document.

Selection: ....

1. When was the document written? What main historical events were happening at that time?	
2. What is the writer's main purpose?	
3. What key points does the writer make?	
4. What is the theme of the work? (Synthesize the key points you listed in #3.)	
5. What rhetorical devices are employed? Give four examples from the text.	**a.**
	b.
	c.
	d.
6. What makes this document significant? Does it have both historical and literary significance? Explain.	

Name _____ Date _____ Selection _____

Analyzing Historical Documents

Answer the questions in the graphic organizer to analyze a historical document.

Selection: ....

1. When was the document written? What main historical events were happening at that time?	
2. What is the writer's main purpose?	
3. What key points does the writer make?	
4. What is the theme of the work? (Synthesize the key points you listed in #3.)	
5. What rhetorical devices are employed? Give four examples from the text.	**a.**
	b.
	c.
	d.
6. What makes this document significant? Does it have both historical and literary significance? Explain.	

Name _____ Date _____ Selection _____

Analyzing Historical Documents

Answer the questions in the graphic organizer to analyze a historical document.

Selection: ....

1. When was the document written? What main historical events were happening at that time?	
2. What is the writer's main purpose?	
3. What key points does the writer make?	
4. What is the theme of the work? (Synthesize the key points you listed in #3.)	
5. What rhetorical devices are employed? Give four examples from the text.	**a.**
	b.
	c.
	d.
6. What makes this document significant? Does it have both historical and literary significance? Explain.	

Name _____ Date _____ Selection _____

Analyzing Historical Documents

Answer the questions in the graphic organizer to analyze a historical document.

Selection: ....

1. When was the document written? What main historical events were happening at that time?	
2. What is the writer's main purpose?	
3. What key points does the writer make?	
4. What is the theme of the work? (Synthesize the key points you listed in #3.)	
5. What rhetorical devices are employed? Give four examples from the text.	**a.**
	b.
	c.
	d.
6. What makes this document significant? Does it have both historical and literary significance? Explain.	

Name _____ Date _____ Selection _____

Analyzing Historical Documents

Answer the questions in the graphic organizer to analyze a historical document.

Selection: ....

1. When was the document written? What main historical events were happening at that time?	
2. What is the writer's main purpose?	
3. What key points does the writer make?	
4. What is the theme of the work? (Synthesize the key points you listed in #3.)	
5. What rhetorical devices are employed? Give four examples from the text.	**a.**
	b.
	c.
	d.
6. What makes this document significant? Does it have both historical and literary significance? Explain.	

For use with Informational Text 9

Name _____ Date _____ Selection _____

Analyzing Historical Documents

Answer the questions in the graphic organizer to analyze a historical document.

Selection: ....

1. When was the document written? What main historical events were happening at that time?	
2. What is the writer's main purpose?	
3. What key points does the writer make?	
4. What is the theme of the work? (Synthesize the key points you listed in #3.)	
5. What rhetorical devices are employed? Give four examples from the text.	**a.**
	b.
	c.
	d.
6. What makes this document significant? Does it have both historical and literary significance? Explain.	

F

Informational Text 10

> 10. By the end of grade 12, read and comprehend literary nonfiction at the high end of the grades 11–CCR text complexity band independently and proficiently.

Explanation

Works of literary nonfiction vary widely in their **complexity**, or how difficult they are to understand. The factors that contribute to the complexity of a text vary. The level of vocabulary may be high, the writer's style may be challenging, or the subject matter may require special background or technical knowledge. However, you can comprehend even the most complex texts by employing a variety of reading strategies. Examples of the best nonfiction reading strategies are given below.

Examples

- **Preview the text:** Previewing or scanning a text before reading it can give you a basic understanding of what the text is about. Pay close attention to the title, subheadings, and boldfaced words since they often give information about the text's main ideas. In addition, look over the visual features such as photos and informational graphics.

- **Monitor your comprehension:** Check your understanding of the text as you read. If you lose the thread of meaning, reread the confusing passages. Slow your reading pace as you reread, and use punctuation cues to break complex sentences into meaningful parts. If you still don't understand the passage, read ahead to see if the meaning is **clarified**.

- **Summarize:** A summary is a short statement that presents the key ideas and main points of a text. Summarizing helps you remember the key points of a text by focusing on the most important information. When reading nonfiction, stop about every five minutes and summarize what you've read. When summarizing, follow these steps: (1) Reread to identify main ideas. Jot them down. (2) Organize your points in order and cross out minor details that are not important for an overall understanding of the work. (3) Summarize by restating the major ideas in as few words as possible.

- **Use context clues:** *Context* is the text around a particular word. When you come upon unfamiliar words, use context clues like these to figure out the meaning: *synonyms* (words that mean the same as the unfamiliar word), *antonyms* (words with opposite meanings), *explanations* (words that give information about the word), and *sentence role* (the way the word is used).

Academic Vocabulary

complexity the degree to which a work is difficult to understand

clarify explain; make clearer

Apply the Standard

Use the worksheet that follows to help you apply the standard as you read informational text. Several copies of each worksheet have been provided for you.

- Comprehending Complex Texts

Name _____ Date _____ Selection _____

Comprehending Complex Texts

Explain what makes the literary nonfiction text you are reading complex. Then explain how you used reading strategies to understand the difficult parts of the text.

- Use the left-hand column of the graphic organizer to list specific examples of complex text.

- Use the right-hand column to identify reading strategies that you used and how they helped you.

Title: .... Writer: ....

What makes this selection complex?

....

....

....

Examples of Complex Text	Helpful Reading Strategies
1.	
2.	
3.	
4.	

A

Name _____ Date _____ Selection _____

Comprehending Complex Texts

Explain what makes the literary nonfiction text you are reading complex. Then explain how you used reading strategies to understand the difficult parts of the text.

- Use the left-hand column of the graphic organizer to list specific examples of complex text.

- Use the right-hand column to identify reading strategies that you used and how they helped you.

Title: ....   **Writer:** ....

What makes this selection complex?

....

....

....

Examples of Complex Text	Helpful Reading Strategies
1.	
2.	
3.	
4.	

For use with Informational Text 10

Name _____ Date _____ Selection _____

Comprehending Complex Texts

Explain what makes the literary nonfiction text you are reading complex. Then explain how you used reading strategies to understand the difficult parts of the text.

- Use the left-hand column of the graphic organizer to list specific examples of complex text.

- Use the right-hand column to identify reading strategies that you used and how they helped you.

Title: ....   **Writer:** ....

What makes this selection complex?

....

....

....

Examples of Complex Text	Helpful Reading Strategies
1.	
2.	
3.	
4.	

C

Name _____ Date _____ Selection _____

Comprehending Complex Texts

Explain what makes the literary nonfiction text you are reading complex. Then explain how you used reading strategies to understand the difficult parts of the text.

- Use the left-hand column of the graphic organizer to list specific examples of complex text.

- Use the right-hand column to identify reading strategies that you used and how they helped you.

Title: .... **Writer:** ....

What makes this selection complex?

....

....

....

Examples of Complex Text	Helpful Reading Strategies
1.	
2.	
3.	
4.	

For use with Informational Text 10

Name _____ Date _____ Selection _____

Comprehending Complex Texts

Explain what makes the literary nonfiction text you are reading complex. Then explain how you used reading strategies to understand the difficult parts of the text.

- Use the left-hand column of the graphic organizer to list specific examples of complex text.

- Use the right-hand column to identify reading strategies that you used and how they helped you.

Title: ....   **Writer:** ....

What makes this selection complex?

....

....

....

Examples of Complex Text	Helpful Reading Strategies
1.	
2.	
3.	
4.	

E

Name _____ Date _____ Selection _____

Comprehending Complex Texts

Explain what makes the literary nonfiction text you are reading complex. Then explain how you used reading strategies to understand the difficult parts of the text.

- Use the left-hand column of the graphic organizer to list specific examples of complex text.

- Use the right-hand column to identify reading strategies that you used and how they helped you.

Title: .... **Writer:** ....

What makes this selection complex?

....

....

....

Examples of Complex Text	Helpful Reading Strategies
1.	
2.	
3.	
4.	

F

Writing Standards

Writing 1

> 1. **Write arguments to support claims in an analysis of substantive topics or texts, using valid reasoning and relevant and sufficient evidence.**

Writing Workshop: Argument

When you develop an **argument** in writing, you present and support a claim. An argument is not just an expression of your personal opinion. Sound arguments are reasoned and supported with evidence. For example, if you are developing an essay about community service, you might present the claim, "Young people should commit to volunteering in their communities." Valid reasoning and evidence form the heart of that argument. If you support your claim with compelling reasons for volunteering and relevant, sufficient evidence—and make effective use of rhetorical techniques—your argument will be persuasive.

Assignment

Write a persuasive essay in which you take a position on an issue and include these elements:

✓ a claim, or brief statement that identifies an issue and clearly states your position

✓ evidence and reasoning to support your position or claim

✓ acknowledgement of opposing positions or claims, recognizing their strengths as well as pointing out their limitations

✓ effective and coherent organization

✓ use of rhetorical technique, including make effective choices for meaning or style and varying syntax for effect

✓ a formal style and objective tone

✓ correct use of language conventions

*Additional Standards

Writing

1. Write arguments to support claims in an analysis of substantive topics or texts, using valid reasoning and relevant and sufficient evidence.

1.a. Introduce precise, knowledgeable claim(s), establish the significance of the claim(s), distinguish the claim(s) from alternate or opposing claims, and create an organization that logically sequences claim(s), counterclaims, reasons, and evidence.

1.b. Develop claim(s) and counterclaims fairly and thoroughly, supplying the most relevant evidence for each while pointing out the strengths and limitations of both in a manner that anticipates the audience's knowledge level, concerns, values, and possible biases.

1.c. Use words, phrases, and clauses as well as varied syntax to link the major sections of the text, create cohesion, and

clarify the relationships between claim(s) and reasons, between reasons and evidence, and between claim(s) and counterclaims.

1.d. Establish and maintain a formal style and objective tone while attending to the norms and conventions of the discipline in which they are writing.

1.e. Provide a concluding statement or section that follows from and supports the argument presented.

Language

2. Demonstrate command of the conventions of standard English capitalization, punctuation, and spelling when writing.

3.a. Vary syntax for effect, consulting references (e.g., Tufte's Artful Sentences) for guidance as needed; apply an understanding of syntax to the study of complex texts when reading.

Prewriting/Planning Strategies

Choose a topic. Think carefully about issues that are important to you.

Be sure that you can develop a fully-reasoned argument on your topic.

Identify your claim. After choosing a topic, decide what position you will take on the issue. Begin by conducting research to learn more about the issue. Explore your feelings about the issue by taking notes on the information you gather. Write a sentence that clearly states the position you develop. That is your claim.

My Topic:	
....	

Source 1:	**Notes:**
....	

Source 2:	**Notes:**
....	

Source 3:	**Notes:**
....	

My Claim:
....

Define task, purpose, and audience. At all points of the writing process, consider your **task,** or what specifically you are writing; your **purpose,** or the effect you want your writing to have; and your **audience,** or the people you want to persuade.

Supporting a Claim

Develop compelling reasons. To support your claim, develop strong reasons that will grab readers' attention and hold their interest. For example, your claim might be that "Young people should commit to volunteering in their communities." One compelling reason supporting your claim is that students who do volunteer work are much more likely to win college scholarships.

As you develop reasons, be sure to consider both your purpose for writing and your audience. Use the chart below to help develop compelling reasons.

- Your reasons should clearly support your claim. You should be able to link each reason to your claim using the subordinating conjunction *because*.

- Under each reason, write how the reason grabs your **audience's** attention and helps achieve your **purpose.**

My Claim:	
....	
....	
Reason 1:	
....	
....	
Purpose:	Audience:
Reason 2:	
....	
....	
Purpose:	Audience:
Reason 3:	
....	
....	
Purpose:	Audience:

Drafting Strategies

Create a structure for your draft. Plan a strategy for presenting your ideas. Be sure to structure your persuasive essay in a way that helps you achieve your purpose and is easy to follow. Use the organizer below to plan the structure of your argument.

- Evaluate your reasoning and evidence. Are your reasons valid and compelling? Are they supported by relevant, sufficient evidence?

- Consider starting with a valid yet obvious reason—for example, "Volunteering helps improve our communities"—and building to your strongest, most compelling reason.

Introduction/Claim:

....

....

Background on your topic:

....

....

....

Reason 1:

....

....

Reason 2:

....

....

Reason 3:

....

....

Counterclaims:

....

....

....

Conclusion:

....

....

Develop your claim. Use the organizer below to develop your claim, gather and evaluate your evidence, and anticipate and respond to counterclaims.

1. Write your claim and reasons, using precise wording to state your position on the issue and to explain your reasoning.

2. Gather evidence to support your claim and reasons.

   • Record your evidence in the center of the organizer.

   • Evaluate your evidence to ensure it's both relevant and sufficient to support your claim.

3. Anticipate counterclaims and plan your responses. Strive to be fair as you respond to counterclaims, pointing out their strengths as well as their limitations.

My Claim:		
Reason 1:	**Reason 2:**	**Reason 3:**

My Evidence:
Is all of my evidence relevant?   Is my evidence sufficient to support my claim?

Counterclaims:	Addressing Counterclaims:

Style and Tone

Establish a formal style and an objective tone. A formal style is appropriate for a persuasive essay that will be read by a variety of people, such as an essay submitted for a class assignment. In addition, a formal style is suitable for writing about an important issue, such as community service. An objective tone communicates respect for your audience, including readers who disagree with your position.

Examples:

Informal Style: Community service shows people things that they might not find out about any other way. Young people who volunteer in their communities learn a lot about the real world.

Formal Style: Community service exposes volunteers to aspects of contemporary life that they might not experience otherwise. Young people who volunteer in their communities develop new understanding of the world in which they live.

Subjective Tone: I go to school, do homework, do my chores, and go to an afterschool job, just like my busiest classmates. I still find time for community service, however, and so can all of you.

Objective Tone: Between school, homework, household chores, and afterschool jobs, many of us are extremely busy already. However, most young people can spare a few hours a month for community service.

As you draft your persuasive essay, choose words and phrases carefully to maintain a formal style and an objective tone.

Use words, phrases, and clauses to create cohesion. Link the sections of your persuasive essay by using transitional words, phrases, and clauses. Transitions improve your writing by helping your audience follow your claim, reasoning, and evidence.

- Linking your claim to your reasoning: *because, for these reasons*

- Linking reasons to each other: *also, in addition, what's more, more importantly*

- Linking reasoning to evidence: *for example, in this case, specifically*

- Linking your claim to counterclaims: *although, while, however*

Include transitions to clarify the relationships between your claim and your reasoning, between your reasons and your evidence, and between your claim and any counterclaims. Here are some examples:

- Young people should commit to volunteering in their communities *because* the experience offers them new perspectives and enriches their lives.

- Community service can help young people establish firm foundations for their futures. *Specifically*, volunteer work helps to develop skills that will be crucial in the workplace.

Conclusion

Include a powerful conclusion. Your persuasive essay should end with a compelling and persuasive conclusion. A powerful conclusion follows from and supports your argument, while reaching your audience in a new and dramatic way. The examples below illustrate strategies for writing a powerful conclusion.

- Take a forceful stand on your issue: *Each of us is an important part of our community. Our communities shape our lives, and what happens to us affects our communities in turn. Given how important our communities are, we should place the highest of values on community service. Whatever our age, we all owe this much to the people and places that make us who we are.*

- Return to your claim and offer a final, personal example to support it: *Every young person should commit to volunteering in their communities. Community service can be more rewarding than you can imagine. I know, because I volunteer each week at a nursing home in my town. The hours I have spent there are among the most important and valuable in my life so far.*

- Urge your audience to take action: *Young people who volunteer in their communities reap concrete benefits and gain valuable experiences. Furthermore, community service organizations need volunteers to help carry out their missions. It's time for every one of us to commit to doing his or her part. Together, we can make our communities and our own lives richer.*

My Conclusion
....
....
....
....
Describe the strategy you used to write your conclusion:
....
....

Evaluating My Conclusion	
❑ Does my conclusion follow from my argument?	❑ Is my conclusion powerful? Explain.
❑ Does it support my claim, reasoning, and evidence?	....
❑ Did I maintain an appropriately formal style and objective tone?	....
❑ Does it offer a memorable analogy or final reason?	....

Revising Strategies

Put a checkmark beside each question as your address it in your revision.

	Questions to Ask as You Revise
Writing Task	❏ Have I fulfilled my task? ❏ Does my writing contain the elements of a persuasive essay? ❏ Did I begin with a claim that identifies an issue and takes a clear position on the issue? ❏ Did I address alternative or opposing arguments? ❏ Did I include valid reasoning and relevant, sufficient evidence?
Purpose	❏ Is my argumentative essay persuasive? ❏ Are my reasons compelling? ❏ Is there enough evidence to support my argument? ❏ What reasons and evidence in my essay helped me achieve my purpose? .... ❏ Should I add more evidence? If so, list below: .... ❏ Have I included a powerful conclusion?
Audience	❏ Have I addressed my audience's knowledge? Have I addressed their concerns? ❏ Will my reasoning grab my audience's attention and hold their interest? ❏ Is my style of writing and tone suited to my audience? If not, what words and phrases need revision? .... ❏ Will my audience be able to follow my persuasive essay? ❏ What transitions should be added to link sections of my essay, create cohesion, and clarify relationships between ideas?
	....

Revising

Revise to make effective choices for meaning or style. The choices you make as you write and revise affect both the meaning of your persuasive essay and its style. The meanings of similar words are often different in small but important ways. In addition, one choice can be formal and another casual.

Choices that Affect Meaning
Original: Community service can be difficult, but the rewards of volunteering are unlimited. **Revised:** Community service can be **challenging,** but the rewards of volunteering are **immeasurable.**
Choices that Affect Style
Original: Teens who volunteer in their communities learn a lot from the experience. **Revised:** **Young people** who volunteer in their communities learn a **great deal** from the experience.

To revise word choices, follow these steps:

1. Read through your draft carefully. Sentences with word choices that are not effective will stand out.

2. Using a thesaurus or the "synonyms" function of your word processing software, search for synonyms of any words in your essay that are not effective.

3. Rewrite the sentences, choosing words that more effectively communicate your meaning or maintain a formal style.

Revise to vary syntax. Syntax describes the ways in which words and phrases are organized into sentences. If too many sentences have the same or similar structures, your persuasive essay will not be interesting to read. To vary syntax, change repetitive structures by rewriting and combining sentences.

Original: Community service organizations help many people. They provide important services. Our communities need these organizations. The organizations need volunteers. Young people can meet that need.

Revised: Community service organizations help many people by providing important services. Our communities need these organizations, and in turn, the organizations need volunteers. Young people can meet that need.

Revision Checklist

❏ Are there words that do not convey your intended meaning effectively?

❏ Are there words that create an inappropriately casual style?

❏ Are there paragraphs in which the syntax is unvaried, or many sentences have the same or similar structures?

Editing and Proofreading

Review your draft to correct errors in capitalization, spelling, and punctuation.

Focus on Capitalization: Review your draft carefully to find and correct capitalization errors. If you make reference to or cite information from newspapers, magazine articles, journals, books, or other sources, be sure that you have capitalized the titles correctly.

Incorrect capitalization:	**Correct capitalization**
the *Hilldale county gazette*	the *Hilldale County Gazette*
"Community Service And You"	"Community Service and You"

Focus on Spelling: A persuasive essay that includes spelling errors loses its authority to convince. Check the spelling of each word. Look for words that you frequently misspell and make sure they are correct. If you have typed your draft on a computer, use the spell-check feature to double-check for error. Carefully review each suggested change before accepting the spell-check's suggestions. Also note that spell-check features will not catch all errors. Proofread carefully even after running a spell-check.

Focus on Punctuation: Titles and Quotations Proofread your writing to find and address punctuation errors. In particular, look for places in your writing where you include the titles of articles, newspapers and magazines, and books. Also, look for places where you have included quotations.

Rule: Use quotation marks for the titles of short works. The titles of articles, essays, short stories, short poems, and other short works should be enclosed in quotation marks.

Rule: Use italics for the titles of periodicals and long works. The titles of newspapers, magazines, journals, books, plays, long poems, and other long works should be italicized.

> **Example:** The article "Community Organizations Call for Volunteers" appeared in *News for Students* magazine.

Rule: Use quotation marks for direct quotations. Enclose a source's exact words in quotation marks. Commas and periods that end quotations are placed within the quotation marks.

> **Example:** "Organizations around the country are desperately in need of committed volunteers," explains the article.

Publishing and Presenting

Consider one of the following ways to present your writing:

Create a Web site. Create a Web site focusing on the issue you address in your persuasive essay. Explain the issue and identify your position on your Web site's home page. Create links to pages that detail each of your reasons and present your evidence. You may wish to create links to related Web sites, including sites you used in your research.

Record an audio documentary. Use your persuasive essay as the basis for an audio documentary. Record your explanation of the issue you addressed in your essay and a brief presentation of your claim and argument. Then, record other students discussing their positions on the issue. You may wish to include music as well. Play your audio documentary for your class.

Rubric for Self-Assessment

Find evidence in your writing to address each category. Then, use the rating scale to grade your work. Circle that score that best applies for each category.

Evaluating Your Argument	not very					very
Focus: How clearly has your claim been stated?	1	2	3	4	5	6
Organization: How effectively and coherently have you organized your argument?	1	2	3	4	5	6
Style: How well have you maintained a formal, objective tone throughout your argument?	1	2	3	4	5	6
Support/Elaboration: How valid, sufficient, and suited to your audience is your evidence?	1	2	3	4	5	6
Conventions: How free of errors in grammar, usage, spelling, and punctuation is your argument?	1	2	3	4	5	6

Writing 2

> **2. Write informative/explanatory texts to examine and convey complex ideas, concepts, and information clearly and accurately through the effective selection, organization, and analysis of content.**

Writing Workshop: Expository Essay

When you write an **expository essay**, your task is to inform your audience and provide them with accurate and persuasive information. In a specific form of the expository essay known as a cause-and-effect essay, you examine the relationship between two or more events by explaining how one event causes or influences another. As with other types of informative text, the first paragraph of a cause-and-effect essay must clearly identify the connection between specific causes and effects in a thesis sentence. In the body of the essay, you should fully develop that analysis by supporting it with facts, quotations, concrete details, and other relevant information.

Assignment

Write an expository essay that focuses on a cause-and-effect relationship in history, in current events, in your school, in your community, or in the wider world. Include these elements:

✓ a clear statement of the relationship between or among cause(s) and effect(s)

✓ an organization with formatting that helps make the cause(s) and effects clear

✓ graphics or multimedia, if they are useful for exploring cause(s) and effect(s)

✓ explanation, sufficient facts, quotations, concrete details, and other development specific to your purpose and audience

✓ appropriate transitional words and phrases

✓ precise language and techniques such as metaphor, simile, and analogy

✓ a logical and effective conclusion

✓ correct use of language conventions and a formal style and objective tone

*Additional Standards

2.a. Introduce a topic; organize complex ideas, concepts, and information so that each new element builds on that which precedes it to create a unified whole; include formatting (e.g., headings), graphics (e.g., figures, tables), and multimedia when useful to aiding comprehension.

2.b. Develop the topic thoroughly by selecting the

most significant and relevant facts, extended definitions, concrete details, quotations, or other information and examples appropriate to the audience's knowledge of the topic.

2.c. Use appropriate and varied transitions and syntax to link the major sections of the text, create cohesion, and clarify the relationships among complex ideas and concepts.

2.d. Use precise language, domain-specific vocabulary, and techniques such as metaphor, simile, and analogy to manage the complexity of the topic.

2.e. Establish and maintain a formal style and objective tone while attending to the norms and conventions of the discipline in which students are writing.

2.f. Provide a concluding statement or section

that follows from and supports the information or explanation presented (e.g., articulating implications or the significance of the topic).

Language

1. Demonstrate command of the conventions of standard English grammar and usage when writing or speaking.

2.a. Observe hyphenation conventions.

Name _____ Date _____ Assignment _____

Prewriting/Planning Strategies

List phenomena, events, and trends. Make a list of scientific phenomena, historic events, or popular trends that you find interesting, important, startling, or amazing. Look over your list to find a topic you would like to explore in an essay.

Scan newspapers and magazines. Review print or online articles, looking for stories or ideas that grab your attention or make you ask "Why?" Jot down possible topics, then focus on the one topic that most stimulates your curious.

Narrow your topic. If the topic you choose is too broad, you will not be able to analyze it in depth. The best analyses tend to be tightly focused on a specific topic—that is, they begin with a relatively narrow topic and develop it in detail. The funnel organizer below helps show this progression from a topic that is too broad to one that is appropriately narrow. For example:

> **Broad:** *Exercise brings benefits.*
>
> **Less Broad:** *Exercise can boost your performance at school.*
>
> **Narrow:** *Regular aerobic exercise can boost your performance at school.*

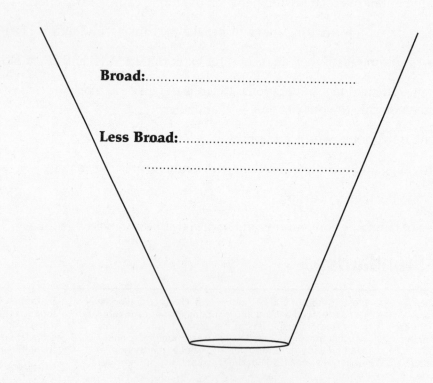

Broad:..

Less Broad:..

....

Narrow: ....

Name _____ Date _____ Assignment _____

Developing a Topic

Explore the cause(s) and effect(s). To develop your topic, list the causes and effects as well as concrete details about each cause and effect. Depending on your topic, add or delete boxes and arrows from this diagram as needed.

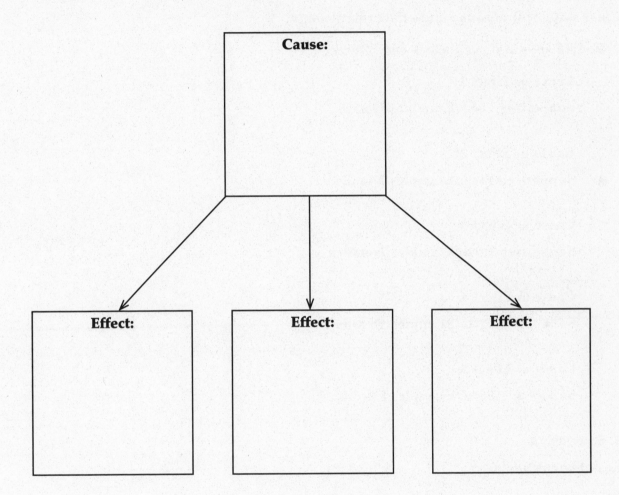

Name _____ Date _____ Assignment _____

Organizing Ideas

Outline your essay. Use an informal outline to begin developing the major parts of your essay. Follow the structure of the model provided below.

1. Introduction

Opening hook:

Clear statement of cause-and-effect relationship:

2. Body: Exploration of Causes and Effects

    Cause or Effect 1:

    Supporting Facts/Examples/Details:

    Cause or Effect 2:

    Supporting Facts/Examples/Details:

    Cause or Effect 3:

    Supporting Facts/Examples/Details:

    Cause or Effect 4:

    Supporting Facts/Examples/Details:

    Cause or Effect 5:

    Supporting Facts/Examples/Details:

3. Conclusion

Restatement/Summary:

Closure:

Name _____ Date _____ Assignment _____

Choose a logical organization for the body of your essay. The structure of your body paragraphs depends on the information you are conveying to your readers.

- **Chronological order.** Arranging your main ideas in chronological order makes sense for cause-and-effect essay. You can start with a cause and then continue by describing its effects over time, or you could start with the effect, and then work back through time to discuss its causes. Keep in mind, however, that a time-order relationship is not in itself proof of a cause and effect relationship between events.

- **Order of importance.** This method of organization works well if you are describing multiple causes. You can either begin with your most important cause, or you can save the most important cause for last.

In the organizer below, arrange your causes and their effect(s) in chronological order or by order of importance. Cross out or add a box or boxes if you need to.

1. [   ]

▼

2. [   ]

▼

3. [   ]

▼

4. [   ]

▼

5. [   ]

Using Transitions

Use appropriate and varied transitions. Link the ideas in your writing by using transitional words, phrases, and clauses such as the following:

as a result	*for this reason*	*so that*
because	*if … then*	*therefore*
because of	*since*	*thus*
consequently	*so*	*why*
for		

To help your audience move easily from one sentence or paragraph to the next, you may use transitions that suggest time order, such as *first, second, then,* and *last,* or order of importance, such as *first, next, more important,* and *most important.*

You might also link the final sentence of one paragraph with the opening sentence of the next paragraph by means of repetition:

> **Paragraph 1 ends:** . . . are the major causes of <u>criticism</u> aimed at for-profit colleges.

> **Paragraph 2 begins:** Perhaps the most common <u>criticism</u> is . . .

Create coherence. Just as repetition can form an effective link between paragraphs by causing them to cohere, or "hang together," repetition can also be used successfully within a paragraph to create coherence. In addition, other elements such as clear pronoun-antecedent agreement, transitional language that links ideas and sentences, and words that qualify or intensify meaning also help a block of prose "flow" as a unified whole.

In the writing example below, identify each boldfaced word as a transitional word or phrase, a pronoun with a clear antecedent, a repeated word, or word and phrases that qualify or intensify meaning.

> Exercise **results in** neurogenesis, the creation of **neurons** in the **learning** center of the **brain. It** is **also** believed to initiate responses that protect already existing **neurons** and to promote the plasticity of the **brain.** These **effects** potentially translate to benefits for **learners** in the **classroom.** Studies conducted with people between the ages of 18 and 24 have shown that **effects** of **exercise** may include better **abilities** to plan, to schedule, and to remember. **All of these abilities** are crucial for **classroom** success.

Include formatting, graphics, or multimedia. Depending on the information you are trying to convey to your audience, you may want to use formatting options such as headings and bulleted points. You may also want to include tables, graphs, charts, and other figures. These can help you provide a more comprehensive analysis or help relay information in the most effective manner, and they also help to engage or sustain an audience's interest.

Drafting a Conclusion

Write an effective conclusion. The task of informing an audience is usually a formal one. For that reason, you should follow a conventional essay structure and include a formal conclusion. That conclusion must support the information and explanation you have provided in the thesis and body of your essay. To create an effective conclusion, synthesize, summarize, or restate your main ideas in a fresh way that re-emphasizes your thesis and the significance of the topic. Then provide a satisfying sense of closure by leaving your reader with a sense of the greater significance of implications of your topic. One effective way to do this is with a final question or a prediction about the future. Other techniques include placing the discussion in a larger or global context, or referring back to what one of your quoted experts or sources might say in summary.

Evaluating Language

Check for precise language. If the cause you are presenting is "fast food contributes to childhood obesity," your statement might be accurate, but you are not precise. To be precise, you must be concrete and support your argument with specific details and information. For example, you might add details such as the following: *children who eat fast food are less likely to consume the recommended numbers of fruits and vegetables, they increase their caloric intake by approximately 190 calories per day, and they are likely to gain 6 more pounds per year than children who do not eat fast food.* When you are revising your essay, general, imprecise, or overused words and phrases should be deleted or replaced with more precise and concrete language.

Check for technological or topic-specific language. Suppose that the effects you are analyzing include the effects of exercise on the brain. If so, you should include technical or topic-specific language such as *neurogenesis, neurons,* and *endorphins* if they help explain effects. If you are writing for a general audience, briefly define these terms as you introduce or first use them. Alternatively, you might include an illustration to help illustrate and explain certain technical concepts to your reader or audience.

Replace everyday explanation with literary techniques. A metaphor, simile, or analogy can be every bit as powerful in nonfiction writing as it can be in a work of literature. You may also find that such techniques help to keep your audience interested, as well as help you to achieve your writing purpose. To create a metaphor, you might say "fast food is a magnet" or, for a simile, that "fast food is like a magnet." You might even develop that figurative language by noting that people are always drawn to it or that they cannot get enough of it.

Evaluating Your Writing Style and Tone

Evaluate your tone. When you are writing an expository essay, aim for an objective tone. To create an objective tone, eliminate any friendly, chatty language. Never use sarcasm, and be wary of making any statement that implies disrespect or condescension toward your reader or toward an opposing point of view. You should also avoid the first or second person, except in cases where a personal anecdote is both relevant and persuasive. Instead, create a little distance between your audience and yourself by using the tone and language of textbooks or other credible, authoritative sources.

Evaluate your style. A large part of your style is created through tone, but you most also make other style choices to ensure that your writing is appropriate to your purpose and audience. For example, you should use standard English and avoid slang and informal wording. Avoid fragments except where they are rhetorically appropriate, such as for dramatic effect or emphasis. You should also avoid punctuation choices such as unwarranted exclamation marks, and revise to edit out contractions. Also, craft your sentences for pleasing variety and rhythm, and create formal grace through the use of parallelism.

In the following writing example, examine the tone and style choices that are printed in bold. Decide why each is inconsistent with the task, purpose, and the audience, and suggest replacements in the blanks that follow the example.

A keyword search **(1) thru** the school paper shows that an unforeseen result of cutting the activities budget six years ago was a **(2) pretty** dramatic increase in absenteeism. When students **(3) couldn't** play sports after school, they **(4) just plain (5)** didn't show up some days, or they **(6) cut out** early **(7) !** **(8) Ditto for students in the music program. (9) Kids** who found their identity in the band or jazz group were suddenly left without a compelling reason to come to school. Administrators who were **(10) bent out of shape** by the rise in absenteeism during those years seem to have forgotten all about it now.

1. .... 6. ....
2. .... 7. ....
3. .... 8. ....
4. .... 9. ....
5. .... 10. ....

Name _____ Date _____ Assignment _____

Revising Strategies

Using the checklist below, put a checkmark beside each question as you address it in your essay revision.

	Questions To Ask as You Revise
Task	❏ Have I written a cause-and-effect essay? ❏ Is there a clear relationship between each cause and each relationship that I present?
Purpose	❏ Have I presented a clear cause-and-effect relationship beginning with my introduction? ❏ Have I fully developed each cause and effect with sufficient facts, statistics, quotations, concrete details, examples, or other forms of development? ❏ Have I sufficiently explained and supported my major points? ❏ Are all of the details I've included relevent to my explanation of cause and effect? ❏ Have I provided a formal and effective conclusion?
Audience	❏ Will my audience understand the relationship between each cause and effect? ❏ Do I need to add, delete, or adjust any details to suit them better to my audience's interest, knowledge, or experience? ❏ Have I adequately explained technical or topic-specific or technical language? ❏ Have I maintained an objective tone throughout? ❏ Is my style and tone specific to my audience? ❏ Have I included appropriate graphics, headings, or multimedia as needed to help my audience understand and follow causes and effects? ❏ Have I used transitions, clear pronoun references, and other connectors so that my audience can easily follow my ideas?

Revising

Revise for pronoun-antecedent agreement. Pronouns are words that take the place of nouns, such as *him, her, them,* or *it.* Antecedents are the nouns that the pronouns refer to, such as *Dr. Miller, Sharon, the listeners,* or *the committee.*

Identifying errors in pronoun-antecedent agreement In your writing, check to be sure each pronoun agrees with its antecedent in number (singular or plural), person (first person, second person, or third person), and gender (masculine, feminine, or neuter).

Use a plural personal pronoun with two or more antecedents joined by *and.*

> **Incorrect:** In separate papers, <u>Cohen and Wu</u> came to the same conclusion in *his* research.

> **Correct:** In separate papers, <u>Cohen and Wu</u> came to the same conclusion in *their* research.

Use a singular personal pronoun with two or more antecedents joined by *or* or *nor.*

> **Incorrect:** Neither <u>an 8-year-old nor a 40-year-old</u> should increase *their* intake by 180 calories per day.

> **Correct:** Neither <u>an 8-year-old nor a 40-year-old</u> should increase *his or her* intake by 180 calories per day.

Fixing Pronoun-Antecedent Agreement Errors

To correct a pronoun and antecedent that do not agree, choose the pronoun that expresses the correct number, person, and gender.

1. Identify the number, person, and gender of the antecedent.

2. Choose a pronoun with the same number, person, and gender. Be sure you choose the right pronoun case: nominative, objective, or possessive.

Revision Checklist

❑ Does every pronoun I used clearly refer back to an antecedent?

❑ Does each pronoun agree with its antecedent in number, person, and gender?

❑ Does each pronoun agree in sentences in which compound subjects are joined by *and, or,* or *nor*?

Editing and Proofreading

Review your draft to correct errors in capitalization, spelling, and punctuation.

Focus on Usage Errors: Check your writing for commonly confused words. Remember that *then* is often used for time and that *than* is used for comparisons. Use *since* to refer to a previous time, not to mean *because*. If you are unsure about a word, consult a dictionary or usage guide.

Focus on Capitalization: Review your draft carefully to find and correct capitalization errors. Capitalize all proper adjectives.

Incorrect capitalization: Recent statistics show that 30% of american children, 24% of mexican children, and 23% of british children are obese.

Correct capitalization: Recent statistics show that 30% of American children, 24% of Mexican children, and 23% of British children are obese.

Focus on Spelling: As you read, circle any words that you are not sure how to spell, frequently misspell, or seldom use. Then, use reference resources such as a dictionary or thesaurus to confirm the correct spelling. Follow these steps to find spellings in a dictionary:

- **Check the first letters of a word.** Think of homophones for that sound.

- **Check the other letters.** Once you spell the first sound correctly, try sounding out the rest of the word. Look for likely spellings in the dictionary. If you do not find your word, look for more unusual spellings of the sound.

Focus on Punctuation: Hyphens in Compounds Proofread your writing to find and address punctuation errors. In particular, look for compound words that may need hyphens, or pairs or groups of words that form temporary compounds. Be sure you use hyphens correctly.

Rule: Use hyphens with year-old: *Shouldn't a three-year-old be eating foods selected and prepared by his or her own family?*

Rule: Use a hyphen in compound nouns using *self-* or *vice-*. *Vandals frequently have low self-esteem.*

The vice-principal was concerned about recent acts of vandalism.

Rule: Use a hyphen in temporarily formed compound adjectives before a noun. *She led a fact-finding session to isolate causes of vandalism.*

Publishing and Presenting

Consider one of the following ways to present your writing:

Give a class presentation. Use your essay as the basis of a class presentation. Use photographs, charts, tables, or other graphics to help make the cause-and-effect relationship clear. Practice combining visuals with your oral presentation, deciding when you will show each visual as you share ideas from your essay.

Use e-mail. Share your writing electronically. Type the essay using word processing software. Attach the essay to an e-mail to a friend or relative. Save a printout of the essay and any responses in your portfolio.

Rubric for Self-Assessment

Find evidence in your writing to address each category. Then, use the rating scale to grade your work. Circle the score that best applies for each category.

Evaluating Your Expository Essay	not very					very
Focus: How clearly have you stated the cause-and-effect relationship?	1	2	3	4	5	6
Organization: How effectively have you organized your essay, especially body paragraphs that analyze the cause(s) and effect(s)?	1	2	3	4	5	6
Support/Elaboration: How effectively is your topic developed with significant and relevant facts, concrete details, and other information appropriate to your audience's knowledge of the topic?	1	2	3	4	5	6
Style: How effectively have you created a formal style and objective tone that are appropriate to your task, purpose, and audience?	1	2	3	4	5	6
Conventions: How free is your essay from errors in grammar, spelling, and punctuation?	1	2	3	4	5	6

Writing 3

> 3. Write narratives to develop real or imagined experiences or events using effective technique, well-chosen details, and well-structured event sequences.

Writing Workshop: Narrative

When you write a **narrative,** you task is to tell a story that grabs and holds your audience's interest from the first detail to the last. The elements of the type of narrative called the short story, which include characters, a point of view, a setting, a conflict, rising action, a climax, and a resolution, can arise solely out of your imagination or be based, to a large or small degree, on real people and events. Successful short stories rely on a carefully plotted and effectively paced series of events that move realistic or otherwise compelling characters from a state of conflict to a state of resolution.

Assignment

Write a short story from any genre, including realistic fiction, historical fiction, mystery, fantasy, or science fiction. Include these elements:

✓ a effective single or multiple point of view

✓ characters, a setting, and an inciting incident

✓ a conflict that precipitates the rising action until the action reaches a climax

✓ a clear sequence of events that builds toward a particular tone and outcome

✓ narrative techniques, including natural dialogue, reflection or interior monologue, multiple plot lines, and appropriate pacing

✓ precise words, telling details, and sensory language

✓ a satisfying conclusion narrative

✓ correct use of language conventions

*Additional Standards

Writing

3.a. Engage and orient the reader by setting out a problem, situation, or observation and its significance, establishing one or multiple point(s) of view, and introducing a narrator and/or characters; create a smooth progression of experiences or events.

3.b. Use narrative techniques, such as dialogue, pacing, description, reflection, and multiple plot lines, to develop experiences, events, and/or characters.

3.c. Use a variety of techniques to sequence events so that they build on one another to create a coherent whole and build toward a particular tone

and outcome (e.g, a sense of mystery, suspense, growth, or resolution).

3.d. Use precise words and phrases, telling details, and sensory language to convey a vivid picture of the experiences, events, setting, and/or characters.

3.e. Provide a conclusion that follows from and

reflects on what is experienced, observed, or resolved over the course of the narrative.

Language

2. Demonstrate command of the conventions of standard English capitalization, punctuation, and spelling when writing.

Name _____ Date _____ Selection _____

Prewriting/Planning Strategies

Try out an idea in a story map. Use the story map below to record ideas for a short story with the following parts:

- **Exposition.** Introduce the characters, setting, and basic situation.

- **Inciting incident.** Introduce the main conflict.

- **Rising action.** Develop the conflict.

- **Climax.** Bring the conflict to a high point of interest or suspense.

- **Falling action.** Wind down the conflict.

- **Resolution.** Provide a general insight or change in the characters.

Exposition
Characters **Settitng** **Basic Situation**
Conflict and Inciting Incident
Rising Action
Event 1 **Event 2** **Event 3**
Climax
Falling Action
Resolution

Name _____ Date _____ Selection _____

Introducing Characters, Conflict, and Setting

Develop ideas for characters. Use the chart to jot down ideas for important characters or antagonists.

	Character 1: _____	Character 2: _____
Personality		
Habits		
Key Strengths		
Key Weaknesses/Flaws		
Appearance/Gestures/ Movements		

Name _____ Date _____ Selection _____

Develop a setting. Establish a time and a place for your story. Also, record details that relate to environmental factors, such as the weather, the light, and the ambient sounds. Determine the mood you are aiming to create, such as gloom, excitement, or fear.

Time:
Place:
Environment:
Mood:

Creating Point of View

Select a point of view. Use the chart below to develop ideas for different narrators. Recall that narrators may know all, or they may observe or understand only part of what happens. Then choose a single point of view, or, perhaps, use multiple points of view by telling your story first from one point of view and then from another.

	Relationship to Conflict and Main Character	Knows	Doesn't Know
Narrator 1: _____			
(or) **Narrator 2:** _____			
(or) **Narrator 3:** _____			

Name _____ Date _____ Selection _____

Organizing the Narrative

Structure your plot. In addition to using chronological or time order, you might integrate a flashback or foreshadowing. Alternatively, consider flashing forward to a future time. Other options include starting at the middle or end of the story and then going back to the beginning.

Climax: _____

Rising Action

Falling Action

Exposition:
_____
_____
_____
_____
_____
_____
_____
_____
_____

Resolution:
_____
_____
_____
_____
_____
_____
_____
_____
_____

Using Narrative Techniques

Move the plot along with dialogue. Dialogue is one of your best choices for communicating events to the reader. You can and should use it to create rising action and to increase narrative tension. Furthermore, you can develop characters through dialogue. Characteristic speech patterns may help distinguish, for example, the old man at the café, who perhaps speaks formally, from the young woman who finds out about his life, perhaps as she speaks in the language of text messages and online chat.

Follow these guidelines for writing natural sounding, effective dialogue:

- **Use real-life, informal language.** Real conversations usually proceed in brief bits and fragments. Characteristics include contractions, hesitations, unfinished sentences, informal language, and limited vocabulary.

- **Incorporate dialect and jargon.** Dialect can help you show the background of your character or the region he or she lives in or comes from. Jargon can make your characters and the action more real; for example, a computer scientist is going to use specialized terms that range from *bitmap* to *refresh rate.*

- **Don't overuse dialogue.** Keep in mind that dialogue is just one tool in your writer's toolbox; don't rely on it to tell the whole story.

Employ interior monologue. You can balance your use of dialogue with monologue. An interior monologue reveals a character's inner thoughts and feelings, and may take the form of an unbroken reflection on events, the past, or another character.

Pace your narrative. Recall the skewed-pyramid structure of fiction, and pace your narrative to reflect its shape and proportion. That is, introduce the characters, establish the setting, and lay out the basic situation without haste. Get the action going with an inciting incident, and build, as if you were up heading up the pyramid toward its apex, event by event, from that incident to a high point of tension. Structure your narrative so that most of it is devoted to everything that leads up to the climax. After you reach that high point of excitement, then you can move far more quickly as you present the falling action and the resolution.

Build toward a particular tone or outcome. All your details must combine to present a unified whole. Although you may incorporate surprises or reversals in your plot, your details, in the main, should build toward a particular tone, such as humorous, sarcastic, celebratory, playful, or vengeful. Similarly, the final outcome must spring organically from the details that have preceded it.

Using Descriptive and Sensory Language

Use sensory language. Sensory details are a key to developing the setting and mood of your story. Also use them to help the readers see your characters and experience the conflict and action. In selecting sensory language, prefer just the right word to a pileup of sights, sounds, colors, textures, tastes, and smells. If the aroma of camellias is the trigger that takes the character back in time to the evening when she first met the stranger, there is no need to also mention the flavor of gum she was chewing at the time.

Use descriptive language. In addition to using sensory language, make your settings, characters, and actions more lifelike and vivid through a combination of these techniques:

- **Open your mind's eye.** Imagine the character is in the room with you and record what you sense about that person's appearance, such as heft or slightness; hair or baldness; pleasing smile or grimace; squared, upright posture or stooped roundedness. Then select the most revealing or suggestive details, the trait or traits that will best help the reader understand the character in relation to the conflict and events.

- **Choose exact nouns and verbs.** Favor concrete, specific nouns over abstract or vague ones; for example, prefer, "the small and gloomy looking Victorian with peeling paint" to "the house." Similarly, choose precise verbs instead of general ones, such as *flap, flit, flutter,* and *sail* to *fly.*

- **Describe with phrases and clauses.** Effective description requires more than adding adjectives to nouns. In addition to using adjectives, also use adjective and adverb phrases, as well as participles, and participial phrases. Clauses can also modify. Notice how much more descriptive it is to write "Claudia could not finish reading the e-mail, which was full of accusations" than to write "Claudia could not finish reading the e-mail."

- **Use figurative language.** Similes, metaphors, and personification are often powerful and creative ways to reveal characters, events, and the setting.

Writing and Evaluating a Conclusion

Resolve the conflict. Your conclusion must tie your story together, which means it must relate to the central conflict. That doesn't mean that a surprising event couldn't occur, or that you couldn't present a final twist, but neither can you depart entirely from what you've already written. Consider showing the ending through a main character's action, such as coming over the finish line in a big race, locking the gate, or returning the journal to the old chest—as long as that action relates to the conflict.

Evaluate your ending. Be sure you have ended with a satisfying sense of closure. Ask a peer reader to help you determine how well your story ends and what qualities it has that make it effective.

Name _____ Date _____ Selection _____

Revising Strategies

Put a checkmark beside each question as your address it in your revision.

	Questions To Ask as You Revise
Task	❏ Have I written a short story? ❏ Have I included the following elements of a short story: characters, setting, and inciting incident; conflict; rising action; climax; and resolution?
Purpose	❏ Have I created an effective and consistent point of view, or have I effectively and clearly used multiple points of view? ❏ Have I used dialogue to move the plot along? ❏ Have I paced my story to lead slowly to the climax and more quickly from the climax to the resolution? ❏ Have I varied narrative techniques, such as by including reflection or interior monologue, or by incorporating one or more additional plot lines? ❏ Have I sequenced events in an interesting, effective, and clear manner?
Audience	❏ Have I engaged my readers from start to finish? ❏ Have I used precise words, telling details, and sensory language to create interest? ❏ Do I need to add, delete, or adjust any details to make the characters or setting more interesting, more convincing, or more appropriate to the conflict and events? ❏ Do I need to add, delete, or adjust any details to make the events clearer, more interesting, or easier to follow in sequence? ❏ Have I provided my readers with a conclusion that relates clearly to the conflict and follows from the story events?

For use with Writing 3

Developing Your Style

Use punctuation in dialogue. Dialogue shows what people say, and the punctuation in dialogue often helps to show how they say it. Punctuation at the end of a speaker's line helps to create the tone of that line. Other forms of punctuation help readers to hear the rhythms and pauses of natural speech.

Rule	Example
Use commas to indicate short pauses.	"Well, yeah, it's no problem."
Use an ellipsis to show a longer pause or hesitation. An ellipsis can also show a voice trailing off.	"Yes . . . I guess I could do that." "I thought she said . . . "
Use a dash to indicate a sudden stop, such as an interruption.	"But what if—."
Use italics to emphasize a word or phrase.	"*You* may think that's a great idea, but I sure don't."
Use apostrophes to show dropped letters in dialect.	"I'll be sayin' the same thing till the day I die."

Apply It to Your Writing

To improve dialogue in your story, follow these steps:

1. Read each line aloud. Listen for whether or not it sounds natural. Consider adding punctuation to indicate natural pauses in your character's voice.

2. Decide whether there is more than one possible reading the line. For important lines, consider adding italics to show which word or words the character emphasizes.

3. Be careful not to overuse special punctuation such as ellipsis points, dashes, and italics. Limit exclamation points as well—they are more effective when used sparingly. Reread all of the dialogue in your story, paying attention to the balance of punctuation.

Revision Checklist

❏ Have I used punctuation to help show the natural pauses, stops and starts, and other rhythms and emphases of everyday speech?

❏ Have I used commas for short pauses, dashes for sudden stops, ellipses for longer pauses or trailing off, italics for emphasis, and apostrophes to show the dropped letters or sounds of dialect or informal speech?

❏ Have I refrained from overusing punctuation, especially exclamation points, dashes, ellipses, and italics?

Editing and Proofreading

Review your draft to correct errors in capitalization, spelling, and punctuation.

Focus on Capitalization: Review your draft carefully to find and correct capitalization errors. Capitalize the first word in each new bit of dialogue.

Incorrect capitalization: "what's up with you and Mai?" Tom asked.
Correct capitalization: "What's up with you and Mai?" Tom asked.

Capitalize the first word in dialogue that is interrupted by speaker tag if the words that follow form a complete sentence.

Incorrect capitalization: "Nothing," Dylan said, adding as an afterthought, "don't even ask."
Correct capitalization: "Nothing," Dylan said, adding as an afterthought, "Don't even ask."

Focus on Spelling: To add *-ing, -ish,* or *-ist* to words that end in *y*, keep the *y* and add the suffix. For example, *comply* becomes *complying, yellow* becomes *yellowish,* and *hobby* becomes *hobbyist.*

Focus on Punctuation: Use punctuation to set off nonrestrictive/parenthetical elements. Proofread your writing to find phrases and clauses that are not essential to the meaning of the sentence. Be sure you have used the correct punctuation before and after these elements.

Rule: Use commas to set off nonrestrictive information.
The subsystems, which Steve programmed, did not all default to the secure setting.
Steve, who had set up many systems, should have known better.

Rule: Use dashes to set off nonrestrictive information, especially when it interrupts the established train of thought.
The new system—the very first to use "defense in depth"—was installed last year.

Rule: Use parentheses to set off nonrestrictive or extra information.
The new system (installed in 2010) is based on automatic theorem proving.

Name _____ Date _____ Selection _____

Publishing and Presenting

Consider one of the following ways to present your writing:

Make an audio recording. Set your story to a soundtrack. Manipulate the song you choose as needed to work with a dramatic reading of your story. Play the recording for your classmates.

Videotape a scene. Gather props and a camera, and with classmates, practice and act out a single scene from your story. Post the tape on line for others to view.

Rubric for Self-Assessment

Find evidence in your writing to address each category. Then, use the rating scale to grade your work. Circle the score that best applies for each category.

Evaluating Your Narrative	not very				very	
Focus: How clear and consistent are the point of view, the characters, the setting, the inciting incident, and the conflict?	1	2	3	4	5	6
Organization: How well is the narrative sequenced in a clear and effective manner? How well have you used appropriate pacing, dialogue, and other narrative techniques to help move the plot along and reach a satisfying ending?	1	2	3	4	5	6
Support/Elaboration: How effectively are details used to show the characters, the conflict, and the sequence of events?	1	2	3	4	5	6
Style: How effectively have you engaged the reader with an interesting conflict, precise words that create a vivid picture of the characters and their experiences, and an apt conclusion?	1	2	3	4	5	6
Conventions: How free of errors in grammar, usage, spelling, and punctuation is your narrative?	1	2	3	4	5	6

Writing 4

> 4. **Produce clear and coherent writing in which the development, organization, and style are appropriate to task, purpose, and audience.**

Explanation and Examples

Clarity and coherence are essential goals for all writers, but producing writing that is appropriate for your particular writing situation—your task, purpose, and audience—is important as well.

Your **task** is the specific reason you are writing—anything from writing a research report for English class to writing a story just for fun. Your **purpose** for writing is related to your task. It is the goal you want your writing to achieve, such as persuading people, explaining a topic, or entertaining readers. The person or people who will read what you write are your **audience.** Consider each of these elements as you develop and organize your writing and select an appropriate style.

- **Development:** Develop your argument, topic, or narrative by selecting information, evidence, and details that are appropriate for your specific writing situation. For example, if you are writing a persuasive essay on the issue of mass transit, present your argument by showing that a lack of public transportation is a problem in your community. Build your case for a new bus system with evidence and rhetorical devices that appeal to your audience. One effective rhetorical device is parallelism, the use of similar grammatical structures to express similar ideas (buses can save more fuel, carry more commuters, and build more communities than automobiles ever could).

- **Organization:** Use transitional words, phrases, and clauses to show how your ideas are related to each other. For example, if you are writing a research report on the effects of the Industrial Revolution in Britain, *consequently, as a result,* and other transitions can help establish causal links. Also, sequence your ideas and information—or the events in a narrative—appropriately for your writing situation. In a personal narrative, for example, chronological order will help readers follow events.

- **Style:** The language and tone in your writing should be appropriate for your task, purpose, and audience. Most academic writing requires a formal style and an objective tone, while a book or movie review can be less formal and more subjective. For a personal narrative, use a conversational style, a friendly tone, and precise words and descriptive details.

Academic Vocabulary

development the use of information, evidence, and details in writing to build an argument, present a topic, or unfold a narrative

organization the way ideas, information, and other elements are arranged and connected in writing

style the language and tone used by a writer to communicate clearly and engage readers

Apply the Standard

Use the worksheet that follows to help you apply the standard as you write. Several copies of the worksheet have been provided for you to use with different assignments.

Name _____ Date _____ Assignment _____

Writing for a Specific Task, Purpose, and Audience

Identify your writing task, your purpose for writing, and your audience. Then, use the organizer to plan a development, organization, and style appropriate for your writing situation.

Task: ....

Purpose: ....

Audience: ....

DEVELOPMENT	**Argument, Topic, or Narrative:** .... **Appropriate Information/Evidence/Detail:** ....

ORGANIZATION	**Sequencing:** ....

STYLE	**Describe Appropriate Style:** .... **Describe Appropriate Tone:** ....

For use with Writing 4

Name _____ Date _____ Assignment _____

Writing for a Specific Task, Purpose, and Audience

Identify your writing task, your purpose for writing, and your audience. Then, use the organizer to plan a development, organization, and style appropriate for your writing situation.

Task: ....

Purpose: ....

Audience: ....

DEVELOPMENT	**Argument, Topic, or Narrative:** .... **Appropriate Information/Evidence/Detail:** ....

ORGANIZATION	**Sequencing:** ....

STYLE	**Describe Appropriate Style:** .... **Describe Appropriate Tone:** ....

Name _____ Date _____ Assignment _____

Writing for a Specific Task, Purpose, and Audience

Identify your writing task, your purpose for writing, and your audience. Then, use the organizer to plan a development, organization, and style appropriate for your writing situation.

Task: ....

Purpose: ....

Audience: ....

DEVELOPMENT	**Argument, Topic, or Narrative:** .... **Appropriate Information/Evidence/Detail:** ....

ORGANIZATION	**Sequencing:** ....

STYLE	**Describe Appropriate Style:** .... **Describe Appropriate Tone:** ....

Name _____ Date _____ Assignment _____

Writing for a Specific Task, Purpose, and Audience

Identify your writing task, your purpose for writing, and your audience. Then, use the organizer to plan a development, organization, and style appropriate for your writing situation.

Task: ....

Purpose: ....

Audience: ....

DEVELOPMENT	**Argument, Topic, or Narrative:** .... **Appropriate Information/Evidence/Detail:** ....

ORGANIZATION	**Sequencing:** ....

STYLE	**Describe Appropriate Style:** .... **Describe Appropriate Tone:** ....

Name _____ Date _____ Assignment _____

Writing for a Specific Task, Purpose, and Audience

Identify your writing task, your purpose for writing, and your audience. Then, use the organizer to plan a development, organization, and style appropriate for your writing situation.

Task: ....

Purpose: ....

Audience: ....

DEVELOPMENT	**Argument, Topic, or Narrative:** .... **Appropriate Information/Evidence/Detail:** ....

ORGANIZATION	**Sequencing:** ....

STYLE	**Describe Appropriate Style:** .... **Describe Appropriate Tone:** ....

E

Name _____ Date _____ Assignment _____

Writing for a Specific Task, Purpose, and Audience

Identify your writing task, your purpose for writing, and your audience. Then, use the organizer to plan a development, organization, and style appropriate for your writing situation.

Task: ....

Purpose: ....

Audience: ....

DEVELOPMENT	**Argument, Topic, or Narrative:** .... **Appropriate Information/Evidence/Detail:** ....

ORGANIZATION	**Sequencing:** ....

STYLE	**Describe Appropriate Style:** .... **Describe Appropriate Tone:** ....

F

Writing 5

> 5. **Develop and strengthen writing as needed by planning, revising, editing, rewriting, or trying a new approach, focusing on addressing what is most significant for a specific purpose and audience.**

Explanation and Examples

The writing process starts before you draft your introduction and continues after you write the conclusion. The steps you take before and after writing are as essential as writing your first draft.

- Before you begin, **develop** your writing by generating ideas and gathering information.
- After completing a draft, strengthen your writing by reviewing and making changes to improve it.

Develop and strengthen your writing by planning before you write and **revising** and **editing** after you finish a draft. As you plan, revise, and edit, focus on addressing your purpose, or the goal you want to achieve. Consider also what is significant for your audience.

Planning Look for ideas and information that will help you achieve your purpose. For example, if you are planning a persuasive essay about renewable sources of energy, you might choose to take the position that more funding is needed. To achieve your purpose, gather information about renewable energy projects that will persuade your audience to agree with you.

Revising Review what you have written, focusing on what is most significant for your purpose and audience. For example, when revising an expository essay about England during William Shakespeare's lifetime, ask yourself: Did I include enough information for my audience to understand what life was like? Is my style appropriately academic and formal? Be prepared to add, delete, or change ideas, details, sentences, and paragraphs to address your writing purpose and audience.

Editing After you have revised, edit for errors in grammar, spelling, usage, and punctuation. For example, if you are editing a personal narrative, make sure readers can easily find the antecedents to which pronouns refer.

If your writing still does not achieve its purpose or meet the audience's needs, consider trying a new approach to your task and rewriting your narrative or essay. For example, with a persuasive essay, try rewriting your piece by including additional evidence for your case.

Academic Vocabulary

develop present and build an argument, topic, or narrative in writing with information, evidence, and details

editing checking a piece of writing and correcting errors in grammar, spelling, usage, and punctuation

revising reviewing and making changes to a piece of writing to better address the purpose and audience

Apply the Standard

Use the worksheet that follows to help you apply the standard as you write. Several copies of the worksheet have been provided for you to use with different assignments.

Name _____ Date _____ Assignment _____

Strengthening Your Writing

Use the checklists below to strengthen your writing as you revise and then edit your work.

Your Purpose for Writing: ....

Your Audience: ....

Writing Stage	Questions to Ask and Answer
Revising	❑ Will my claim, topic, or subject be clear to my audience? ❑ Do the ideas in my writing help to achieve my purpose? ❑ Will my ideas appeal to my audience? ❑ Does the information in my writing help to achieve my purpose? ❑ Have I included enough information for my audience? ❑ Is my style appropriate for my purpose and audience? ❑ Does my draft address what is most significant for my purpose? ❑ Does my draft meet the needs of my audience? To better address my purpose and meet the needs of my audience, I should add: .... I should delete: .... I should change: .... Do I need to rewrite or try a new approach? Yes .... No .... If "yes," describe the new approach. ....
Editing	❑ Have I used verb tenses consistently? ❑ Are there sentence fragments or run-on sentences? ❑ Have I introduced and punctuated quotations correctly? ❑ Are my pronoun references clear? ❑ Have I checked for other errors in grammar, spelling, and punctuation?

A

For use with Writing 5

Name _____   Date _____   Assignment _____

Strengthening Your Writing

Use the checklists, below, to strengthen your writing as you revise and then edit your work.

Your Purpose for Writing: ....

Your Audience: ....

Writing Stage	Questions to Ask and Answer
Revising	❑ Will my claim, topic, or subject be clear to my audience? ❑ Do the ideas in my writing help to achieve my purpose? ❑ Will my ideas appeal to my audience? ❑ Does the information in my writing help to achieve my purpose? ❑ Have I included enough information for my audience? ❑ Is my style appropriate for my purpose and audience? ❑ Does my draft address what is most significant for my purpose? ❑ Does my draft meet the needs of my audience? To better address my purpose and meet the needs of my audience, I should add: .... I should delete: .... I should change: .... Do I need to rewrite or try a new approach? Yes .... No .... If "yes," describe the new approach. ....
Editing	❑ Have I used verb tenses consistently? ❑ Are there sentence fragments or run-on sentences? ❑ Have I introduced and punctuated quotations correctly? ❑ Are my pronoun references clear? ❑ Have I checked for other errors in grammar, spelling, and punctuation?

For use with Writing 5

Name _____ Date _____ Assignment _____

Strengthening Your Writing

Use the checklists, below, to strengthen your writing as you revise and then edit your work.

Your Purpose for Writing: ....

Your Audience: ....

Writing Stage	Questions to Ask and Answer
Revising	❑ Will my claim, topic, or subject be clear to my audience? ❑ Do the ideas in my writing help to achieve my purpose? ❑ Will my ideas appeal to my audience? ❑ Does the information in my writing help to achieve my purpose? ❑ Have I included enough information for my audience? ❑ Is my style appropriate for my purpose and audience? ❑ Does my draft address what is most significant for my purpose? ❑ Does my draft meet the needs of my audience? To better address my purpose and meet the needs of my audience, I should add: .... I should delete: .... I should change: .... Do I need to rewrite or try a new approach? Yes .... No .... If "yes," describe the new approach. ....
Editing	❑ Have I used verb tenses consistently? ❑ Are there sentence fragments or run-on sentences? ❑ Have I introduced and punctuated quotations correctly? ❑ Are my pronoun references clear? ❑ Have I checked for other errors in grammar, spelling, and punctuation?

C

For use with Writing 5

Name _____ Date _____ Assignment _____

Strengthening Your Writing

Use the checklists, below, to strengthen your writing as you revise and then edit your work.

Your Purpose for Writing: ....

Your Audience: ....

Writing Stage	Questions to Ask and Answer
Revising	❑ Will my claim, topic, or subject be clear to my audience? ❑ Do the ideas in my writing help to achieve my purpose? ❑ Will my ideas appeal to my audience? ❑ Does the information in my writing help to achieve my purpose? ❑ Have I included enough information for my audience? ❑ Is my style appropriate for my purpose and audience? ❑ Does my draft address what is most significant for my purpose? ❑ Does my draft meet the needs of my audience? To better address my purpose and meet the needs of my audience, I should add: .... I should delete: .... I should change: .... Do I need to rewrite or try a new approach? Yes .... No .... If "yes," describe the new approach. ....
Editing	❑ Have I used verb tenses consistently? ❑ Are there sentence fragments or run-on sentences? ❑ Have I introduced and punctuated quotations correctly? ❑ Are my pronoun references clear? ❑ Have I checked for other errors in grammar, spelling, and punctuation?

For use with Writing 5

Strengthening Your Writing

Use the checklists, below, to strengthen your writing as you revise and then edit your work.

Your Purpose for Writing: ....

Your Audience: ....

Writing Stage	Questions to Ask and Answer
Revising	❑ Will my claim, topic, or subject be clear to my audience? ❑ Do the ideas in my writing help to achieve my purpose? ❑ Will my ideas appeal to my audience? ❑ Does the information in my writing help to achieve my purpose? ❑ Have I included enough information for my audience? ❑ Is my style appropriate for my purpose and audience? ❑ Does my draft address what is most significant for my purpose? ❑ Does my draft meet the needs of my audience? To better address my purpose and meet the needs of my audience, I should add: .... I should delete: .... I should change: .... Do I need to rewrite or try a new approach? Yes .... No .... If "yes," describe the new approach. ....
Editing	❑ Have I used verb tenses consistently? ❑ Are there sentence fragments or run-on sentences? ❑ Have I introduced and punctuated quotations correctly? ❑ Are my pronoun references clear? ❑ Have I checked for other errors in grammar, spelling, and punctuation?

Name _____ Date _____ Assignment _____

Strengthening Your Writing

Use the checklists, below, to strengthen your writing as you revise and then edit your work.

Your Purpose for Writing: ....

Your Audience: ....

Writing Stage	Questions to Ask and Answer
Revising	❏ Will my claim, topic, or subject be clear to my audience? ❏ Do the ideas in my writing help to achieve my purpose? ❏ Will my ideas appeal to my audience? ❏ Does the information in my writing help to achieve my purpose? ❏ Have I included enough information for my audience? ❏ Is my style appropriate for my purpose and audience? ❏ Does my draft address what is most significant for my purpose? ❏ Does my draft meet the needs of my audience? To better address my purpose and meet the needs of my audience, I should add: .... I should delete: .... I should change: .... Do I need to rewrite or try a new approach? Yes .... No .... If "yes," describe the new approach. ....
Editing	❏ Have I used verb tenses consistently? ❏ Are there sentence fragments or run-on sentences? ❏ Have I introduced and punctuated quotations correctly? ❏ Are my pronoun references clear? ❏ Have I checked for other errors in grammar, spelling, and punctuation?

F

Writing 6

> **6. Use technology, including the Internet, to produce, publish, and update individual or shared writing products in response to ongoing feedback, including new arguments or information.**

Explanation

Today's technology provides writers with many powerful tools. For example, you can use technology—including the Internet—to produce, publish, and update your writing in response to **ongoing feedback,** continuing comments on your work. With your teacher's guidance, you can create a **blog** on your school's Web site where classmates can read and comment on your writing. You can also receive and respond to such feedback through an e-mail exchange with classmates.

Examples

Following are examples of a blog post on Shakespeare's *Macbeth,* ongoing feedback in response to the post, and the writer's updating of the original post.

- **Original Post** Macbeth's tragic flaw is his desperate ambition. That he wants to be king of Scotland at any cost is evident from the beginning of the play. In Act I, Scene iii, Macbeth meets the three witches for the first time and looks surprised and frightened when the Third Witch says he will "be King hereafter!" He is fearful because the witch has discovered his secret ambition

- **Ongoing Feedback** I disagree with your suggestion that Macbeth is entirely defined by his ambition. Note, for example, the doubts about the prospective assassination that he expresses in the soliloquy at the beginning of Act I, Scene vii. He realizes that Duncan is "here in double trust: / First, as I am his kinsman and his subject, / . . . then, as his host . . ."

- **Updated Post:** The soliloquy you cite actually proves the original point, that Macbeth is driven by ambition. If you read it carefully, you will see that he is not so much concerned with the morality of what he plans to do as with the practical consequences of the deed. He is afraid that it will encourage others to assassinate him: ". . . that we but teach / Bloody instructions, which, being taught, return / To plague the inventor . . ."

Academic Vocabulary

blog short for "Web log," a popular online format that generally includes entries from writers as well as comments from readers.

ongoing feedback continuing comments on a piece of writing

post to publish a piece of writing online (verb); also, an entry on a blog (noun)

Apply the Standard

Use the worksheet that follows to help you apply the standard as you write. Several copies of the worksheet have been provided for you to use with different assignments.

- Using Technology to Publish and Revise Writing

Name _____ Date _____ Assignment _____

Using Technology to Publish and Revise Writing

In the left column of the organizer, below, note the ongoing feedback in response to your writing. In the right column, explain how you will respond to new arguments and information presented in these responses. Then, answer the question at the bottom of the page.

Subject/date of original post or e-mail: ....

Format: Blog Post   E-mail   Other: ....

ONGOING FEEDBACK	RESPONDING TO FEEDBACK
Summarize feedback from blog comments or emails:	**Summarize your response to feedback:** ....
Describe any new arguments:	**How you will respond to new arguments:** ....
Describe any new information:	**How you will respond to new information:** ....

Describe how you used technology and the Internet to receive and respond to ongoing feedback.

....

....

....

....

....

For use with Writing 6

Name _____ Date _____ Assignment _____

Using Technology to Publish and Revise Writing

In the left column of the organizer, below, note the ongoing feedback in response to your writing. In the right column, explain how you will respond to new arguments and information presented in these responses. Then, answer the question at the bottom of the page.

Subject/date of original post or e-mail: ....

Format: Blog Post   E-mail   Other: ....

ONGOING FEEDBACK	RESPONDING TO FEEDBACK
Summarize feedback from blog comments or emails:	**Summarize your response to feedback:**
Describe any new arguments:	**How you will respond to new arguments:**
Describe any new information:	**How you will respond to new information:**

Describe how you used technology and the Internet to receive and respond to ongoing feedback.

....

....

....

....

....

For use with Writing 6

Name _____ Date _____ Assignment _____

Using Technology to Publish and Revise Writing

In the left column of the organizer, below, note the ongoing feedback in response to your writing. In the right column, explain how you will respond to new arguments and information presented in these responses. Then, answer the question at the bottom of the page.

Subject/date of original post or e-mail: ....

Format: Blog Post   E-mail   Other: ....

ONGOING FEEDBACK	RESPONDING TO FEEDBACK
Summarize feedback from blog comments or emails:	**Summarize your response to feedback:** ....
Describe any new arguments:	**How you will respond to new arguments:** ....
Describe any new information:	**How you will respond to new information:** ....

Describe how you used technology and the Internet to receive and respond to ongoing feedback.

....

....

....

....

....

C

Name _____ Date _____ Assignment _____

Using Technology to Publish and Revise Writing

In the left column of the organizer, below, note the ongoing feedback in response to your writing. In the right column, explain how you will respond to new arguments and information presented in these responses. Then, answer the question at the bottom of the page.

Subject/date of original post or e-mail: ....

Format: Blog Post   E-mail   Other: ....

ONGOING FEEDBACK	RESPONDING TO FEEDBACK
Summarize feedback from blog comments or emails:	**Summarize your response to feedback:** ....
Describe any new arguments:	**How you will respond to new arguments:** ....
Describe any new information:	**How you will respond to new information:** ....

Describe how you used technology and the Internet to receive and respond to ongoing feedback.

....

....

....

....

....

D

For use with Writing 6

Name _____ Date _____ Assignment _____

Using Technology to Publish and Revise Writing

In the left column of the organizer, below, note the ongoing feedback in response to your writing. In the right column, explain how you will respond to new arguments and information presented in these responses. Then, answer the question at the bottom of the page.

Subject/date of original post or e-mail: ....

Format: Blog Post   E-mail   Other: ....

ONGOING FEEDBACK	RESPONDING TO FEEDBACK
Summarize feedback from blog comments or emails:	**Summarize your response to feedback:** ....
Describe any new arguments:	**How you will respond to new arguments:** ....
Describe any new information:	**How you will respond to new information:** ....

Describe how you used technology and the Internet to receive and respond to ongoing feedback.

....

....

....

....

....

Name _____ Date _____ Assignment _____

Using Technology to Publish and Revise Writing

In the left column of the organizer, below, note the ongoing feedback in response to your writing. In the right column, explain how you will respond to new arguments and information presented in these responses. Then, answer the question at the bottom of the page.

Subject/date of original post or e-mail: ....

Format: Blog Post   E-mail   Other: ....

ONGOING FEEDBACK	RESPONDING TO FEEDBACK
Summarize feedback from blog comments or emails:	**Summarize your response to feedback:**
Describe any new arguments:	**How you will respond to new arguments:**
Describe any new information:	**How you will respond to new information:**

Describe how you used technology and the Internet to receive and respond to ongoing feedback.

....

....

....

....

....

For use with Writing 6

Writing 7

> 7. Conduct short as well as more sustained research projects to answer a question (including a self-generated question) or solve a problem; narrow or broaden the inquiry when appropriate; synthesize multiple sources on the subject, demonstrating understanding of the subject under investigation.

Explanation and Examples

Research projects vary in scope. Short research projects focus on narrow subjects and involve only a few sources. Complex subjects require more **sustained research** involving in-depth investigation and multiple sources. Be prepared to narrow or broaden your **inquiry,** as appropriate for the scope of your research.

Narrowing an Inquiry: Narrow a broad question or problem for a short research project. For example, if you are researching William Shakespeare, the question "How does Shakespeare use language?" is too broad. Narrow your inquiry to focus on language in Shakespeare's sonnets. If the question is still too broad for a short project, narrow it again: "In Sonnet 106, how does Shakespeare use words and images referring to the Middle Ages?"

Broadening an Inquiry: Broaden a narrow question or problem for a more sustained research project. For example, the problem of installing new computers in your school's computer lab might be too narrow for a sustained project. Consider broadening your inquiry to focus on securing funds for upgrading your school's computers or on devising a new computer science program for your school.

Develop an understanding of your subject by gathering ideas and information from multiple sources, rather than only one or two. Then, **synthesize,** or combine, information from your sources, drawing your own conclusions. When you present the results of your research, demonstrate your understanding of the subject under investigation by supporting your answer or solution with relevant information from several different sources. Be sure to properly credit the sources you use.

Academic Vocabulary

inquiry process of looking for information to answer questions about a topic or to solve a problem

sustained research in-depth investigation or inquiry involving multiple sources

synthesize combine information from different sources to reach your own conclusion

Apply the Standard

Use the worksheets that follow to help you apply the standard as you write. Several copies of each worksheet have been provided for you to use with different assignments.

- Researching to Answer Questions or Solve Problems

- Synthesizing Information from Different Sources

Name _____ Date _____ Assignment _____

Researching to Answer Questions or Solve Problems

First, narrow or broaden your inquiry, as appropriate. Then, use the chart, below, to list your sources and summarize the ideas and information that you gather.

Subject: ....

Scope of Research Project: ....

Initial Question or Problem ....

....

Narrow Inquiry   Broaden Inquiry

Narrowed/Broadened Question or Problem:

....

....

RESEARCH
List your sources:
....
....
....
....
....
Summarize ideas and information from your sources:
....
....
....
....
....

Name _____ Date _____ Assignment _____

Researching to Answer Questions or Solve Problems

First, narrow or broaden your inquiry, as appropriate. Then, use the chart, below, to list your sources and summarize the ideas and information that you gather.

Subject: ....

Scope of Research Project: ....

Initial Question or Problem ....

....

Narrow Inquiry   Broaden Inquiry

Narrowed/Broadened Question or Problem:

....

....

RESEARCH
List your sources:
Summarize ideas and information from your sources:

Name _____ Date _____ Assignment _____

Researching to Answer Questions or Solve Problems

First, narrow or broaden your inquiry, as appropriate. Then, use the chart, below, to list your sources and summarize the ideas and information that you gather.

Subject: ....

Scope of Research Project: ....

Initial Question or Problem ....

....

Narrow Inquiry   Broaden Inquiry

Narrowed/Broadened Question or Problem:

....

....

RESEARCH
List your sources:
....
....
....
....
....
Summarize ideas and information from your sources:
....
....
....
....
....

Name _____ Date _____ Assignment _____

Synthesizing Information from Different Sources

List your subject and sources. Then, use the chart to synthesize information from these sources in order to reach your own conclusion. Support your conclusion with information from multiple sources. Then, answer the questions at the bottom of the page.

Subject: ....

Information from Source 1:

....

....

Information from Source 2:

....

....

Information from Source 3:

....

....

Information from Source 4:

....

....

SYNTHESIS
Your Conclusion:
Support 1:
Support 2:

Which sources provide the information you used to support your conclusion?

....

....

Have you demonstrated understanding of the subject under investigation?   Yes   No

Explain why or why not:

....

....

A

Name _____ Date _____ Assignment _____

Synthesizing Information from Different Sources

List your subject and sources. Then, use the chart to synthesize information from these sources in order to reach your own conclusion. Support your conclusion with information from multiple sources. Then, answer the questions at the bottom of the page.

Subject: ....

Information from Source 1:

....

....

Information from Source 2:

....

....

Information from Source 3:

....

....

Information from Source 4:

....

....

SYNTHESIS
Your Conclusion:
Support 1:
Support 2:

Which sources provide the information you used to support your conclusion?

....

....

Have you demonstrated understanding of the subject under investigation? Yes   No

Explain why or why not:

....

....

Name _____ Date _____ Assignment _____

Synthesizing Information from Different Sources

List your subject and sources. Then, use the chart to synthesize information from these sources in order to reach your own conclusion. Support your conclusion with information from multiple sources. Then, answer the questions at the bottom of the page.

Subject: ....

Information from Source 1:

....

....

Information from Source 2:

....

....

Information from Source 3:

....

....

Information from Source 4:

....

....

SYNTHESIS
Your Conclusion:
Support 1:
Support 2:

Which sources provide the information you used to support your conclusion?

....

....

Have you demonstrated understanding of the subject under investigation? Yes   No

Explain why or why not:

....

....

For use with Writing 7

Writing 8

> **8.** Gather relevant information from multiple authoritative print and digital sources, using advanced searches effectively; assess the strengths and limitations of each source in terms of the task, purpose, and audience; integrate information into the text selectively to maintain the flow of ideas, avoiding plagiarism and overreliance on any one sourc and following a standard format for citation.

Writing Workshop: Research Report

When you write a **research report**, your task is to conduct sustained and focused research in order to present your own analysis and perspective on a topic. First, gather enough information about a topic to arrive at a thesis; then develop, refine, and support that thesis as you continue to research.

Your report must have a clear beginning, body, and conclusion, and ideas must be smoothly integrated. Also, a research report requires an ongoing process of documentation. From the moment you consult your first source, you should be recording bibliographic information.

Assignment

Write a historical investigation report about a literary work. That is, investigate an issue that helps to form the literary context of the work, such as the closing of theaters in Elizabethan England, the Long Parliament, the Civil Wars, the Corn Laws or Poor Laws, or the new warfare of World War I. Include these elements:

✓ a sufficiently narrow topic that you can cover in satisfying depth

✓ a clear thesis that serves as the unifying statement of your paper

✓ supported body paragraphs that relate to your thesis

✓ substantial support from a variety of respected and authoritative sources

✓ your own clarifications, explanations, and insights

✓ organized paragraphs that integrate source material and your commentary

✓ complete parenthetical citations or notes and a bibliography or Works Cited list

*Additional Standards

Writing
1.d. Establish and maintain a formal style and objective tone while attending to the norms and conventions of the discipline in which students are writing.

7. Conduct short as well as more sustained research projects to answer a question (including a self-generated question) or solve a problem; narrow or broaden inquiry when appropriate; synthesize multiple sources on the subject, demonstrating understanding of the subject under investigation.

9. Draw evidence from literary or informational texts to support analysis, reflection, and research.

Language
2. Demonstrate command of the conventions of standard English capitalization, punctuation, and spelling when writing.

Name _____ Date _____ Selection _____

Prewriting/Planning Strategies

Review your textbooks and notebooks. Review school notebooks, textbooks, and writing journals to list the topics that interest you. Also review selections from your literature textbook, and consider topics related to the historical context of your favorite works. Frame your favorite topic ideas as research questions. That is, focus them by thinking of an aspect of the era or context that you would like to explore and asking about what you want to learn.

Do a research preview. When you have two or three good research questions, spend ten to fifteen minutes researching each topic on the Internet or at the library. Seek out both primary and secondary sources. This quick research preview will help you identify how much information is readily available on each topic. Look for both primary sources, such as letters, diaries, interviews, and eyewitness accounts, as well as secondary sources, such as encyclopedias, nonfiction books, and articles.

Freewrite to find your focus. If your topic can be divided into significant subheads, each with its own focus, it is probably too broad. Using what you already know or have learned in preliminary research, write freely on your topic for two or three minutes. Review your writing and circle the most important or interesting idea. Continue this process until you arrive at a topic that is narrow enough for your paper.

Identify your audience. If your audience is not specified, decide who would be most interested by your topic or most likely to benefit by learning about it. Then, whether assigned or imagined, think about what your audience already knows about your topic and what their expectations might be for a paper on that topic:

Audience:
Audience's Prior Knowledge:
Audience's Possible Expectations:

For use with Writing 8

Draft a working thesis statement. Your research report must develop a worthy thesis. This controlling idea cannot be a simple or obvious fact. To go beyond simple fact, strive for something a bit more complex as you write your thesis. For example, think of an original comparison or contrast, state a cause and effect, or classify an idea or phenomenon within a larger context.

Do not worry if you are not precisely sure of what your thesis will be at this point. Instead, regard your working thesis as a kind of a signpost to a far off destination. As you do more research and reading, and as your own understanding of your topic becomes clearer and more developed, you can and should revisit this thesis and rework it appropriately. In fact, it is good to aim to revisit and revise or fine-tune your thesis at several stages in the writing process.

Researching From Print and Digital Sources

Do the research. Use both library and Internet resources to locate information. Because information is the basis of a successful research report, you must be discriminating in the information you choose. Furthermore, even if you are using the best sources, it will only be through systematic and careful research, reading, and notetaking that you will succeed in producing a compelling and high-quality research report.

Work systematically. To enlarge the overview of your topic that you began in the research preview, as well as to learn new aspects of it, begin the formal research process with general reading in encyclopedias and reference books. That is, look for specialized encyclopedias or references, such as those that index topics in British literature, or eras in history. Many of these resources are available online with a public library card. You may have to visit a library to find others on the shelves of the reference section. You can also access high-quality overview documents on the Internet, using search words that specify the literary work and the era in history. Of course, before use, you must check any and every source for its validity and reliability, being especially careful with Internet sources.

Do advanced searches. Because the first search results returned by most search engines are based on advertising revenue for the search engine company, advanced searches are particularly important when you are searching the Internet. You can also use them effectively with your library catalog and specific database searches.

- **Internet advanced searches.** Look for the "Advanced Search" link on the home page of your favorite search. Typically, it will allow you to limit your search to documents with some words but not others, as well as by the domain. For example, you can limit your search to government publications only by specifying the domain .gov or to institutions, such as the British Museum, by specifying the domain .org. (The address of the British Library does not follow this pattern; it is www.bl.uk.)

- **Library catalog advanced searches.** To use the advanced search function in a library catalog, look for a link on the catalog home page. An advanced search in a library catalog might allow you to limit your results to the material type (print book, e-book, DVD, periodical, software, and so on); to the collection type (adult or children's); to the language, and to the publication date. You might also be able to order your search results by relevance, by date, or by other criteria.

- **Database advanced searches.** Each database will have its own methods for conducting advanced searches, but the effect of using the advanced search will be the same: you will more quickly and easily arrive at the specific information you want or need.

Use primary sources. When you are writing about literature, the literary work or works on which you base your paper are the primary source; also, any sources on which the literary work was based are primary. Therefore, if lines from a Shakespeare play first appeared in Ovid, Ovid's work is also primary. Such works are often at the heart of a historical research report that is based on literature. To investigate and analyze the historical context in which a work is set, or its specific historical references, consult other primary sources, which are original or firsthand accounts of events.

Use a variety of other sources. Among the most valuable sources for research are databases, which index magazines, newspapers, general and specialized encyclopedias, and scholarly journals. You can access databases from terminals in your local library. To access them from home, you usually need a library card number. Other sources you might consult include almanacs, atlases, microfiche, and even government documents such as records of proceedings in Parliament. A good research paper is based on a variety of appropriate sources and avoids overreliance on any single source.

Re-evaluate your topic and thesis. One of the many possible stopping points for evaluating and refining your thesis is after conducting initial research. Sometimes, you might find that the topic is actually a problem. Remember that it is better to abandon or revise a bad topic now, during the prewriting stage of the writing process, than to plow forward heedlessly.

Name _____ Date _____ Selection _____

Evaluating Credibility and Usefulness of Your Sources

Evaluate Web sites. To evaluate a Web site, begin by analyzing the URL. This may help you determine whether a search result is even worth clicking on. Check the domain name, such as *.com*, *.org*, *.gov*, and *.edu*. Do not assume that a site with an *.edu* domain is either authoritative or reliable. If the domain *.edu* is followed by a slash and then a designation of faculty, it is probably more reliable than a student page. Still, keep in mind that what appears on a faculty site is not necessarily edited or reliable either. Sometimes a Web site will include a country extension, such as *.de* for Germany or *.uk* for the United Kingdom.

The URL may contain hints as to who created the site and whether it is a personal page, a special interest site, a news site, or a site intended to sell a product or service. If you cannot determine this information based on the URL, visit the site to decide its purpose.

In the end, the most important factor in assessing the worth of a site is its author or the sponsoring institution. Look for authorities on your topic, as well as documentation of sources on the site. Also consider how current the site is and its potential bias(es).

URL and analysis of URL:
Author/Sponsor:
Documentation:
Dates created and last updated:
Bias(es):

For use with Writing 8

Name _____ Date _____ Selection _____

Evaluate Other Sources. You must evaluate every source you use relative to your task, purpose, and audience. Use a form or questions such as the following for this purpose:

Source (with complete bibliographic information):	
Criterion	**My Evaluation**
Writing task *Is the source authoritative and credible? What are the author's or editor's qualifications? Is he or she an authority on the subject?*	
Timeliness *Is the source sufficiently current in relation to the information I am seeking? Would a work published later be more up-to-date on the latest scholarship?*	
Reliability and Validity *Who is the publisher? Is this a well-edited, respected publication or publisher such as a scholarly journal or university press? Is there a bias? If so, does that bias affect the quality of the information I am using? How well documented is this source?*	

Recording Information

Taking notes. For every source you consult, make a source card. On the source card for a book, record the name of the author, editor, and or translator; the title of the work; the publisher and city of publication; and the copyright date. If the source is a Web site, your source card should list the name and Web address of the site, the author and sponsoring institution if available, and the date you accessed the site. To create source cards for other types of sources, refer to the style guide you are using, such as the Modern Language Association (MLA) handbook or the American Psychological Association (APA) style guide. Determine the types of information your will need to cite the work in a list at the end of the paper, such as the volume and issue number of a journal, and record that information on your source card. Label each source you create with a letter, beginning with A, or a number, beginning with 1.

Make notecards. Create a separate notecard for every bit of information you take from your sources. Number or letter each source card or listing in the upper right hand corner with the number or letter you assigned to the source on your source card. Then record any useful or interesting information.

Avoid plagiarism. Plagiarism is using the words or ideas of others as if they were your own. Plagiarism is a serious legal and ethical offense. Furthermore, it inhibits your progress as a writer if you shirk the responsibility for doing your own thinking. There are many ways to avoid plagiarism. Be sure to use all of them beginning with the very first source you consult.

- **Avoid copying and pasting.** It is greatly tempting to copy and paste information from a Web site into your notes or into a paper, but this method can easily lead to plagiarism. You may forget to properly credit your source, or every detail you use from your source. You may also let the Web site's author do your thinking for you.

- **Paraphrase as much as possible.** As you take notes, use your own words whenever you can. This interaction with the topic will help you understand your source material better as well as help you avoid plagiarism.

- **Credit summaries.** If you distill large chunks or even many pages of text into your own words, remember that you still have to credit your summary.

- **Quote sparingly and with care.** Quote only when the words of the source are particularly important or potentially memorable. Be sure to enclose those words in quotation marks on your notecard. If you omit anything from the quoted material, use an ellipsis to show that omission.

Name _____ Date _____ Selection _____

Organizing and Drafting Your Report

Establish your organizational plan. Decide whether you will present conclusions about your sources as part of your introduction or build toward your conclusions throughout your paper. Use one these organizational plans and try it out with details specific to your topic in the organizer below:

- **Plan 1.** Present the historical context and your thesis in the introduction. That is, draw a conclusion at the outset. Then use your body paragraphs to present, analyze, and compare your sources: that is, to prove your conclusion. Then summarize in your formal closing.

- **Plan 2.** Use your introduction to present the historical context and establish the issue in your thesis statement. Then use your body paragraphs to present, analyze, and compare your sources in order to lead up to a conclusion. Draw the conclusion in your formal closing.

Plan 1	Plan 2
Context: **Thesis/Conclusion:**	**Context:** **Thesis/Issue:**
Support/Proof:	**Analysis/Support:**
Summary:	**Draw Conclusion:**

Organize paragraphs effectively. Even if you select an overall organizational strategy such as chronological order, you should still use other methods where they help clarify relationships or otherwise prove effective. For example, you might structure entire paragraphs, or significant portions of paragraphs, in any of these ways:

- **Chronological order.** Discuss events in time order.

- **Cause and effect.** Analyze the causes and/or effects of an event.

- **Problem and solution.** Identify a specific problem or conflict and tell how it was resolved.

- **Parts-to-whole order.** Relate elements of a single event or topic to a whole.

- **Order of importance.** Present your support from most to least important, or from least to most important.

- **Compare and contrast.** When comparing two topics, discuss their similarities and then their differences, or discuss each topic separately.

Place topic sentences effectively. Each of your body paragraphs should contain a topic sentence and supporting details. Remember that the topic sentence can appear as the first sentence, the last sentence, or anywhere else in the paragraph. Place it where it is most effective.

Write a powerful introduction. Consider your readers, and include background information they may need to understand your topic, such as the time, the place, and relevant political and social conditions and issues. An effective introduction will create interest at the same time that it provides the audience with necessary information.

Create a serious tone and formal style. Strive to sound as reasonable and objective as you can. Throughout your paper, choose formal words and phrases and standard usages. Avoid contractions, exclamation points, and fragments—unless fragments are absolutely crucial for creating rhetorical effect.

Providing Elaboration

Handle your sources well. When you present your sources, use a mix of mainly paraphrases or summaries and well-chosen quotations. Do not string quotations together without interpretation. Instead, frame your quotations so that your reader understands why you chose them. One way to frame a quotation is by describing your source. You can also provide an analysis of whether a particular source agrees or disagrees with other sources, accounting for differences that occur. If a writer's perspective is unique, explain it, if possible, by analyzing the writer's circumstances and motives.

Integrate source material smoothly. You must create other logical, smooth connections between ideas as well. Be sure to use transitional words and phrases to create links between your quoted, paraphrased, or summarized information and your thesis and analysis. One way to create links or coherence is to introduce quoted and paraphrased material with a transitional word or phrase, such as "[Author's name] notes," "According to…," or "In [title of work]." You should also make use of transitional words and phrases such as the following:

above all	*aside from*	*however*	*on the whole*
accordingly	*because*	*in other words*	*otherwise*
alternatively	*consequently*	*instead*	*particularly*
although	*for example*	*likewise*	*similarly*
as a result	*for that reason*	*on the contrary*	*therefore*
as well as	*furthermore*	*on the other hand*	*usually*

Similarly, keep in mind that whatever you quote or paraphrase may not only need explanation to relate it to your topic sentence and thesis, but it may also need to be clearly connected to the ideas that follow it. In some cases, you may need to insert a sentence or more to explain the significance of the cited information. In fact, don't waste this precious opportunity to express your own thinking and to relate your source material to your controlling idea.

Citing Sources

Provide appropriate citations. You must cite the sources for the information and ideas you use in your report. In the body of the paper, include a footnote, an endnote, or a parenthetical citation that identifies the sources of facts, quotations, summaries, and paraphrases. At the end of your paper, provide a bibliography or Works Cited list, a list of all the sources you cite. Follow the format your teacher recommends, such as the MLA or APA style, for both your notes or parenthetical citations and your bibliography or Works Cited List.

Decide what to cite. A general fact that can be found in three or more sources is probably common knowledge and does not have to be cited. For example, common knowledge about William Butler Yeats includes his dates of birth and death, the names of his poems, and the fact that he was Irish. Words from Yeats's letters, however, are not common knowledge, no matter how many sources you find them in. You must cite all facts and opinions that are not common knowledge.

Revising

Define jargon or specialized vocabulary. Almost all topics have some form of specialized vocabulary or jargon. You should not assume that such terms do not belong in your research paper. For one thing, it may be hard to delve thoroughly into your topic without them. For another, you may need to use such terms to maintain an appropriate level of sophistication. You must be careful to clearly and simply explain or define specialized vocabulary at its first point of use, however.

Original: Phosgene proved far more potent than chlorine.
Revised: Phosgene, a type of gas developed after chlorine, proved far more potent than its predecessor had been.

In some cases, you will find that specialized vocabulary or jargon, or certain selected bits of jargon, are not appropriate to your task, your purpose, or your audience. In those cases, you will need to replace the jargon with simpler language.

Original: Although the Germans were the first to use gas successfully, the French fired xylyl bromide against the Germans during the first weeks of the war.
Revised: Although the Germans were the first to use gas successfully, the French fired tear gas against the Germans during the first weeks of the war.

Revising for Word Choice

When you revise for appropriate or inappropriate jargon, follow these steps:

1. Review your work and identify specialized vocabulary or jargon that may be unfamiliar to your intended audience.

2. If you judge the use of the jargon to be appropriate to your purpose and audience, check to see whether you defined it as clearly and simply as possible the first time you used it.

3. If you judge the use of jargon to be inappropriate to your purpose and audience, replace it with simpler, more accessible language.

Revision Checklist

❏ Are all my uses of specialized vocabulary or jargon necessary?

❏ If I have used specialized vocabulary, have I made its meaning clear to my intended audience?

Name _____ Date _____ Selection _____

Revising Strategies

Put a checkmark beside each question as your address it in your revision.

	Questions To Ask as You Revise
Task	❏ Have I presented a historical investigation? ❏ Have I chosen a topic that is appropriate to the assignment requirements? ❏ Have I consistently used one style manual for all citations and correctly given credit to every source I used? ❏ Have I formatted my paper according to the assignment specifications or according to standard conventions for a research report?
Purpose	❏ Have I presented a worthy thesis or drawn a conclusion that is more than a statement of simple fact? ❏ Have I fully developed my thesis by presenting relevant, in-depth information from a variety of valid sources? ❏ What details, if any, do not relate to my purpose and should be deleted? ❏ Where do I need to add more support or explanation to achieve my purpose?
Audience	❏ Is my thesis or conclusion immediately recognizable to my reader? ❏ Will my audience be able follow the development of my thesis throughout the paper? ❏ Have I used a logical overall method of organization, as well as effective paragraph-by-paragraph organization? ❏ Have I provided enough information to link my support to my thesis? Have I introduced and analyzed that support? ❏ Is my tone appropriately objective? ❏ Have I limited myself to formal and standard word choices? Have I clearly defined or replaced any jargon? ❏ Can my audience follow the sources of all my ideas?

For use with Writing 8

Editing and Proofreading

Review your draft to correct errors in format, capitalization, spelling, and punctuation.

Focus on Format: Prepare the final copy of your research report according to your teacher's requirements. These requirements often include the following:

- Use 12-point type. It is also best to choose a clean, professional looking font, such as one you would find on the front page of a newspaper or on the pages of a respected journal. Examples of these fonts include Times Roman and Courier.

- Leave one-inch margins on the top, bottom, and sides of every page.

- Double-space the body of the paper and the entries on the Works Cited list.

Focus on Capitalization: Make sure you have capitalized all proper nouns and proper adjectives correctly. Capitalize the names of historical events and eras according to a respected style handbook by consulting the conventions their use as both proper nouns and proper adjectives. You may need to look up correct capitalization for choices such as *Tudor era, Stuart period, Medieval scholar, the Great War, Edwardian fashion,* and *Darwinian principles.*

Focus on Spelling: Follow this spelling rule: for adjectives that end in *-ent,* such as the words *dependent, delinquent,* and *competent* use *c* in place of *t* to form parallel forms, as in *dependence, delinquency,* and *competence.*

Focus on Punctuation: Colons to Introduce List and Long Quotations Proofread your writing to find places where you have introduced lists or long quotations.

Rule: Use a colon before a list of items following an independent clause: *Poison gas was the most controversial weapon used during World War I: it was deadly, it could be used even when an attack was not occurring, and it left its victims to suffer for days and weeks before they died.*

Rule: Use a colon to introduce a formal quotation or a long quotation that follows an independent clause. *"In Dulce et Decorum Est," Wilfred Owen may well have referred to a gas attack like this one reported by* The New York Times *in April, 1915:*

> *"[The vapors from the poison gas] settled to the ground like a swamp mist and drifted toward the French trenches on a brisk wind. Its effect on the French [soldiers] was a violent nausea and faintness, followed by an utter collapse. . . ."*

Name _____ Date _____ Selection _____

Publishing and Presenting

Consider one of the following ways to present your writing:

Present an oral historical investigation report. Deliver your paper as an oral report. Be sure to rehearse well, focusing clear diction and accessible syntax. Also practice using slight modulations in pacing, volume, and pitch to help sustain interest.

Submit your paper for publication. Identify a magazine or Web site that publishes student writing or that covers your research topic. Revise your paper as needed for your new intended audience. Then submit it for publication.

Rubric for Self-Assessment

Find evidence in your writing to address each category. Then, use the rating scale to grade your work. Circle the score that best applies for each category.

Evaluating Your Historical Investigation Report	not very				very	
Focus: Have you maintained a focus on a clear, specific thesis throughout your report, or have you led smoothly and logically to a reasonable conclusion? Have you avoided plagiarism?	1	2	3	4	5	6
Organization: Have you organized your paper with a clear introduction, body paragraphs, and a conclusion? Do your paragraphs employ logical patterns of organization?	1	2	3	4	5	6
Support/Elaboration: Is your support from multiple authoritative, reliable, and varied print and digital sources? Have you smoothly integrated information into the text to maintain the flow of ideas? Have you used your own thinking and insights to elaborate on source material?	1	2	3	4	5	6
Style: Have you used a formal style and a serious tone that are appropriate to your task, your purpose, and your audience? Have you followed a single, standard format for all your parenthetical citations and your Works Cited list or bibliography?	1	2	3	4	5	6
Conventions: Is your research report free from errors in grammar, spelling, and punctuation? Does it use appropriate manuscript conventions for a research report?	1	2	3	4	5	6

Writing 9a

> **9. Draw evidence from literary or informational texts to support analysis, reflection, and research.**
>   - **Apply *grades 11–12 Reading standards* to literature (e.g., "Demonstrate knowledge of eighteenth-, nineteenth- and early-twentieth-century foundational works of American literature, including how two or more texts from the same period treat similar themes or topics").**

Explanation and Examples

To demonstrate your understanding of literature, you might compare how two works from the same period reflect similar topics, **themes,** styles, or other literary elements. For a course in British literature, a comparison of British works would be appropriate.

Here is how to proceed with such a comparison:

- Determine the basis for comparing the two works, whether it be similarly motivated main characters, similar settings, or related themes.

- Decide on the significance of the comparison. For example, does the comparison reveal a certain type of British colonial officer in the late Victorian Era? Does it help to show the individualism, or alienation, of the modern person in the post-World War I era?

- Plan your thesis statement, noting the titles of the two works and the basis on which you will compare them.

- Incorporate the significance of your comparison into your thesis statement.

- Gather evidence from both works to support your thesis. Choose the best examples. A few clear comparisons are better than many shaky ones.

- Clearly link the exact lines or ideas from each work to the specific points you are making in support of your thesis.

Academic Vocabulary

theme central idea, concern, or insight explored by a literary work

Apply the Standard

Use the worksheet that follows to help you apply the standard as you write. Several copies have been provided for you to use with different assignments.

- Comparing Works of Literature

Name _____ Date _____ Assignment _____

Comparing Works of Literature

Use the chart, below, to develop a thesis and record evidence for your comparison.

Works to Compare:
Basis for Comparison:
Significance of Comparison:
Thesis:

Evidence in Support of Thesis:	
Work 1	**Work 2**

For use with Writing 9a

Name _____ Date _____ Assignment _____

Comparing Works of Literature

Use the chart, below, to develop a thesis and record evidence for your comparison.

Works to Compare:	
Basis for Comparison:	
Significance of Comparison:	
Thesis:	

Evidence in Support of Thesis:	
Work 1	**Work 2**

Name _____ Date _____ Assignment _____

Comparing Works of Literature

Use the chart, below, to develop a thesis and record evidence for your comparison.

Works to Compare:
Basis for Comparison:
Significance of Comparison:
Thesis:

Evidence in Support of Thesis:

Work 1	**Work 2**

C

Writing 9b

> 9. Draw evidence from literary or informational texts to support analysis, reflection, and research.
>
> • Apply *grades 11–12 Reading standards* to literary nonfiction (e.g., "Delineate and evaluate the reasoning in seminal U.S. texts, including the application of constitutional principles and use of legal reasoning [e.g., in U.S. Supreme Court Case majority opinions and dissents] and the premises, purposes, and arguments in works of public advocacy [e.g., *The Federalist*, presidential addresses]").

Explanation

Two main types of reasoning are used in argumentation. **Inductive reasoning** is based on observations. For example, a writer might observe that a particular highway is always jammed during rush hour. From these observations, the writer draws the conclusion that the town needs to build more roads. Inductive reasoning is more likely than deductive reasoning to be illogical or to be characterized by fallacies, or errors in reasoning.

A writer using **deductive reasoning,** however, begins with a generalization or **premise,** then presents a specific situation, and provides facts and evidence that leads to a logical conclusion. For example, a writer might argue: "Fruit is nutritious food. Blueberries are a type of fruit. They provide healthy antioxidants. Eating blueberries is good for me."

Thomas Jefferson uses deductive reasoning in the Declaration of Independence. He asserts that God gives people the right to be free, and that people have an obligation to claim that right (by overthrowing a government that denies that freedom, if necessary). He concludes that people have a duty to overthrow the government of George III.

When you evaluate an argument, look not only at the reasoning, but also at the quality of evidence or support. For example, in the Declaration of Independence, Jefferson lists the many tyrannies George III has visited on "these States" as support for his assertions.

Academic Vocabulary

deductive reasoning a writer arrives at a conclusion by applying a general principle to a specific situation

inductive reasoning a writer draws a general or broad conclusion from specific observations

premise a statement that proposes; a proposition

Apply the Standard

Use the worksheet that follows to help you apply the standard as you complete your writing assignments. Several copies of the worksheet have been provided for you.

• Evaluating Reasoning

Name _____ Date _____ Selection _____

Evaluating Reasoning

Use the organizer to evaluate the reasoning in an argument.

Observations or Premises
1.
2.
3.
Conclusion:
Type of Reasoning:
Reason(s) why the conclusion is/is not logical/valid:
Reason(s) why the support is/is not logical or sufficient:

A

For use with Writing 9b

Name _____ Date _____ Selection _____

Evaluating Reasoning

Use the organizer to evaluate the reasoning in an argument.

Observations or Premises
1.
2.
3.

Conclusion:

Type of Reasoning:

Reason(s) why the conclusion is/is not logical/valid:

Reason(s) why the support is/is not logical or sufficient:

B

For use with Writing 9b

Name _____ Date _____ Selection _____

Evaluating Reasoning

Use the organizer to evaluate the reasoning in an argument.

Observations or Premises
1.
2.
3.
Conclusion:
Type of Reasoning:
Reason(s) why the conclusion is/is not logical/valid:
Reason(s) why the support is/is not logical or sufficient:

C

For use with Writing 9b

Writing 10

> 10. **Write routinely over extended time frames (time for research, reflection, and revision) and shorter time frames (a single sitting or a day or two) for a range of tasks, purposes, and audiences.**

Explanation

Writing is a routine part of every student's life. Some writing tasks, such as essays or research reports, may require a week or more to complete. Other writing activities can be finished in one class period or over a day or two. A cover letter is an example of writing that can be completed in a shorter time frame.

A cover letter is a formal letter in which the writer asks to be considered for a job. It usually accompanies or "covers" a completed job application, a résumé, or both.

Prewriting:

- Carefully study the job ad or listing. Underline or highlight key words.

- Note how your interests, experiences, and education match the job requirements.

Drafting:

- Create a consistent format such as block format or modified block format.

- Include the six main business letter parts: heading, inside address, salutation, body, closing, and signature. In the heading, write your phone number and e-mail address on separate lines after your city, state, and zip code.

- State the position you are applying for in the first sentence.

- Use your **voice** to express a high level of interest in the position. Find sophisticated, formal ways to say, "I *really* want this job!"

- Explain what makes you a good fit for the job, but do not repeat your résumé. Stress your most relevant skills and experience.

Revising and Editing:

- Check that you have consistently and correctly formatted your letter.

- Evaluate your voice: Have you created a professional first impression?

Academic Vocabulary

voice the writer's distinctive "sound" or way of "speaking" on the page

Apply the Standard

Use the worksheet that follows to help you apply the standard as you complete your writing assignments.

- Writing a Cover Letter

Name _____ Date _____ Assignment _____

Writing a Cover Letter

Use the organizer during prewriting to plan what you will say in your cover letter.

Key Requirements in the Job Ad	How My Experience, Interests, and Education Match the Key Requirements
1.	1.
2.	2.
3.	3.
Ways I Can Communicate My Interest	

A

Writing 10

> 10. Write routinely over extended time frames (time for research, reflection, and revision) and shorter time frames (a single sitting or a day or two) for a range of tasks, purposes, and audiences.

Explanation

A memo is an example of writing that usually can be completed in one class period. A memo—short for *memorandum*—is a brief written message that may focus on completing tasks, policy changes, or other updates. Effective memos are clear and focused, using a formal style and a professional tone.

Prewriting

- Determine who the audience for your memo will be.

- Write a clear, succinct subject line that accurately conveys your purpose.

- If you're planning a longer memo, map out the opening statement, paragraphs or bullet points, and a closing point or reminder.

Drafting

- Start with a conventional memo heading, which features these elements, each on a separate line: TO, FROM, DATE, and **Re** or SUBJECT.

- Begin the body of the memo with an opening statement. Then explain major points that develop the purpose stated in the subject line.

- Use a **block format,** and use paragraphs and bullet points as needed for clarity.

Revising and Editing

- Is your subject line clear and accurate? Is the memo focused on your purpose?

- Check for inappropriate word choices or unprofessional comments.

Academic Vocabulary

block format each part of the memo begins at the left margin, and a double space is used between paragraphs

Re Latin for "about"; may be used instead of "Subject" in conventional memo heading

Apply the Standard

Use the worksheet that follows to help you apply the standard as you complete your writing assignments.

- Writing a Memo

Name _____ Date _____ Assignment _____

Writing a Memo

Use the organizer to plan a memo.

Audience:

Purpose:

Subject/Re Line:

Body	**Information and Details**
First Sentence/Statement of Purpose:	
Paragraphs or Bullet Points:	
•	
•	
•	
Closing/Final Instruction/Reminder:	

Writing 10

> **10. Write routinely over extended time frames (time for research, reflection, and revision) and shorter time frames (a single sitting or a day or two) for a range of tasks, purposes, and audiences.**

Explanation

A reflective essay is an example of writing that can be completed in one or two class periods or over a day or two. A reflective essay expresses a writer's life-changing personal experience in order to move an audience. Effective reflective essays are written in the first person and use concrete language, vivid imagery, and a personal style.

Prewriting

- Choose an experience or event that affected you deeply and that you can interpret in a meaningful way for an audience. List details and images related to your topic.

- In your notes, link the experience and a key insight you learned, or a new belief.

Drafting

- Identify and describe your experience or event.

- **Elaborate** by describing your thoughts and feelings, and by including concrete details and sensory images that make your writing vivid and interesting.

- Establish an appropriate and effective tone. Your subject matter may require a serious tone; on the other hand, humor or irony may be appropriate.

- End with an insight or a belief that you gained from the event or experience.

Revising and Editing

- Have you emphasized your insight, as well as the experience or event itself?

- Check for language: Have you used concrete language and vivid imagery? Can you vary sentence lengths and structures to create interest?

Academic Vocabulary

elaborate extend ideas and statements by adding explanation, details, or images

Apply the Standard

Use the worksheet that follows to help you apply the standard as you complete your writing assignments.

- Writing a Reflective Essay

Name _____ Date _____ Assignment _____

Writing a Reflective Essay

Use the organizer to plan a reflective essay.

Experience/Event:

↓

Details of the Experience/Event	Insights/Beliefs
1.	
2.	
3.	**Broader Themes**
4.	

What tone is appropriate for your reflective essay?

....

....

A

Writing 10

> **10. Write routinely over extended time frames (time for research, reflection, and revision) and shorter time frames (a single sitting or a day or two) for a range of tasks, purposes, and audiences.**

Explanation

A letter to the editor is an example of writing that can be completed in a shorter time frame. A letter to the editor is a type of persuasive writing that comments on an issue or responds to a news story or an editorial. For example, you might write a letter to the editor to take issue with how a news article depicted your community. Effective letters to the editor are brief, clear, specific, and supported with evidence.

Prewriting

- Choose an issue, news story, or editorial about which you have a strong opinion.

- Write a thesis that states your opinion clearly and confidently.

- Gather factual evidence to support your argument.

Drafting

- Begin by clearly identifying the issue, story, or editorial to which you are responding. For stories or editorials, include the date and title in parentheses.

- Present your argument, supporting it with facts and other evidence. Keep your letter concise; many letters to the editor are shortened for publication.

- State your qualifications if they help your argument. For example, if you are arguing for a new soccer field, being a soccer player is a qualification.

- Establish and maintain a polite tone.

- Avoid *ad hominem* attacks.

Revising and Editing

- Replace vague words and clichés with powerful, well-chosen, and precise words.

- Check your evidence: Do you need to add facts or other evidence?

Academic Vocabulary

ad hominem attacking a person associated with a policy, rather than the policy itself

Apply the Standard

Use the worksheet that follows to help you apply the standard as you complete your writing assignments.

- Writing a Letter to the Editor

Speaking and Listening Standards

Speaking and Listening 1

1. **Initiate and participate effectively in a range of collaborative discussions (one-on-one, in groups, and teacher-led) with diverse partners on grades 11–12 topics, texts, and issues, building on others' ideas and expressing their own clearly and persuasively.***

Workshop: Deliver a Research Presentation

Research presentations present, interpret, and analyze information gathered through comprehensive study of a subject. Creating a research presentation is a good way to learn about a topic that is outside your own experience.

Assignment

Present a research report on a topic of your choosing. Include these elements:

- ✓ a specific thesis statement
- ✓ supporting details and evidence
- ✓ a logical organization of details and ideas
- ✓ graphics and media elements to help illuminate important points
- ✓ appropriate eye contact, adequate volume, and clear pronunciation
- ✓ language that is formal and precise and that follows the rules of Standard English

*Additional Standards

Speaking and Listening
1. Initiate and participate effectively in a range of collaborative discussions (one-on-one, in groups, and teacher-led) with diverse partners on grades 11–12 topics, texts, and issues, building on others' ideas and expressing their own clearly and persuasively.

1.a. Come to discussions prepared, having read and researched material under study; explicitly draw on that preparation by referring to evidence from texts and other research on the topic or issue to stimulate a thoughtful, well-reasoned exchange of ideas.

1.b. Work with peers to promote civil, democratic discussions and decision-making, set clear goals and deadlines, and establish individual roles as needed.

1.c. Propel conversations by posing and responding to questions that probe reasoning and evidence; ensure a hearing for a full range of positions on a topic or issue; clarify, verify, or challenge ideas and conclusions; and promote divergent and creative perspectives.

1.d. Respond thoughtfully to diverse perspectives; synthesize comments, claims, and evidence made

on all sides of an issue; resolve contradictions when possible; and determine what additional information or research is required to deepen the investigation or complete the task.

4. Present information, findings, and supporting evidence, conveying a clear and distinct perspective, such that listeners can follow the line of reasoning, alternative or opposing perspectives are addressed, and the organization, development, substance, and style are appropriate to purpose, audience, and a range of formal and informal tasks.

5. Make strategic use of digital media (e.g., textual, graphical, audio, visual, and interactive elements) in presentations to enhance understanding of findings, reasoning, and evidence and to add interest.

6. Adapt speech to a variety of contexts and tasks, demonstrating command of formal English when indicated or appropriate.

Language
1. Demonstrate command of the conventions of standard English grammar and usage when writing or speaking.

Name _____ Date _____ Assignment _____

Plan Your Report

A research report can provide information on any topic under the sun. As a result, choosing a topic can be challenging. But finding and refining your topic is the first step in creating an effective research report.

Choose your topic. Consult with a partner to brainstorm ideas for your topic. Consider topics from other disciplines that interest you, such as history or math. Jot down ideas in a notebook. You may also wish to review newspaper and magazine articles for topics that you find intriguing. For example, you might consider researching the history behind a story that is currently in the news. Determine what you already know about the topic and what you would like to learn. Remember that the topic you choose should be complex and multifaceted so that you will have sufficient information for your research. Use a chart like the one below to organize your thoughts:

What I Know	What I Want to Know

Collaborate and decide. Next, consult with a small group to help make your choice. Ask students for feedback about your ideas, including whether the topic is too narrow or too broad. Listen for good suggestions about your ideas, and offer your thoughts about other students' ideas. Respond to and ask questions of the group to help clarify your main idea.

For use with Speaking and Listening 1

Name _____ Date _____ Assignment _____

Research Your Topic

Conduct research. Gather a variety of sources to learn about your topic. Seek out both primary and secondary sources. Keep careful notes so that you can accurately cite them.

Take notes to capture or identify the most useful information you find in each source. Conduct further research to settle any discrepancies you find among your sources. Be sure to consider the reliability of sources as you plan. Evaluating sources is especially important on the Internet. Some Web pages may include information that is unreliable, invalid, or inaccurate. The most reliable Web sites tend to have URLs ending in **.edu** and **.gov.**

Use the graphic organizer to help you research and take notes.

Source	Main Point It Supports	Where to Include It and How to Introduce It
(Name, type, author, date)		Is this source ❏ useful? ❏ current? ❏ accurate? ❏ free from bias?
(Name, type, author, date)		Is this source ❏ useful? ❏ current? ❏ accurate? ❏ free from bias?
(Name, type, author, date)		Is this source ❏ useful? ❏ current? ❏ accurate? ❏ free from bias?
(Name, type, author, date)		Is this source ❏ useful? ❏ current? ❏ accurate? ❏ free from bias?

For use with Speaking and Listening 1

Name _____ Date _____ Assignment _____

Organize Your Speech

Write a thesis. Review your notes and researched materials. Write a thesis—one clear statement that will express the focus of your presentation. All aspects of your presentation, from script to visuals, graphics, audio, and charts, should support this main idea.

Thesis Statement: ....

....

Choose a structure. Choose an organizational pattern that matches the content and purpose of your writing. Consider these options.

- **Chronological order** offers information in the sequence in which it happened.
- **Cause-and-effect** analyzes the causes and/or effects of an event.
- **Part-to-whole** order examines how categories affect a larger subject.
- **Order of importance** presents information in order of increasing or decreasing importance.
- **Comparison-and-contrast** presents similarities and differences between two topics.

To select an appropriate organization, use the graphic organizer to review the patterns and consider their pros and cons. For example, chronological order can present a sequence of events clearly, but may not establish the importance of a particular event. Choose the overall organizational method that best supports your thesis statement.

Chronological Order	Cause-and-Effect	Part-to-Whole	Order of Importance	Comparison-and-Contrast
Pros: Cons:	Pros: Cons:	Pros: Cons:	Pros: Cons:	Pros: Cons:
Which organizational structure will best support your purpose? Explain.				

Name _____ Date _____ Assignment _____

Draft Your Script

Write a draft. Use the following graphic organizer to arrange your presentation so that your thesis and main points follow a logical progression. Make sure to support each point with detailed evidence that you gathered through your research. As you prepare, remember that you must end your presentation with a strong conclusion. The conclusions should restate your main idea and one or two of your main supporting details. Build in time to answer your classmates' questions.

I. Introduction
A. Interesting Opening: ....
....

B. Thesis Statement: ....

II. Point 1
A. Topic Sentence: ....

B. Supporting Evidence: ....
....

C. Supporting Evidence: ....
....

III. Point 2
A. Topic Sentence:...

B. Supporting Evidence: ....
....

C. Supporting Evidence: ....
....

IV. Point 3
A. Topic Sentence: ....

B. Supporting Evidence: ....
....

C. Supporting Evidence: ....
....

V. Conclusion
A. Restatement of Thesis:...

B. Memorable Closing: ....
....

Name _____ Date _____ Assignment _____

Presentation techniques

The way you deliver your research report is just as important as what you say in it. Practice your presentation in front of a mirror or for family and friends so that you can present your information smoothly and with confidence.

Use presentation techniques. Use these tips to help you practice your delivery:

- **Eye contact:** Maintain eye contact with your audience so that listeners feel as though you are speaking directly to them rather than at them.

- **Speaking rate:** Speak slowly when explaining new concepts and pause to emphasize important ideas or for effect when appropriate. Do not rush.

- **Volume:** Project your voice so everyone in your audience can hear you and increase or decrease your volume for dramatic effect.

- **Enunciation:** Pronounce words clearly, especially words that are unfamiliar to your audience, so that listeners can understand what you are saying.

- **Purposeful gestures:** Use gestures to illustrate ideas and emphasize important points, but be aware of movements that may be distracting.

- **Language conventions:** Use formal language and follow conventions of Standard English to ensure that your audience can understand you.

Use visual displays and multimedia components. Work with a small group to brainstorm ideas for visuals and multimedia to use in your presentation. Remember to choose a few strong elements that clearly support your main ideas. Try to use them throughout the presentation, instead of clustering their use at one point.

Visual Element or Multimedia Component	Main Idea or Evidence it Supports	Where to Include It

Name _____ Date _____ Assignment _____

Discuss and Evaluate

After you have completed your research presentation, take time to participate in a group discussion of the content and delivery of your speech.

Discuss and evaluate the research presentation.

Hold a discussion with a group of classmates to determine what worked well in your presentation and what did not. Each member of the group should identify where explanations need to be clarified or where your evidence and support were insufficient. Try to reach a consensus, and if a consensus cannot be reached, then summarize the points of agreement and disagreement among group member. Refer to the Guidelines below to ensure that your discussion is productive.

Guidelines for Discussion

In order to prepare for the discussion, review the rubric for evaluating a research presentation below.

- Help the group set goals for the discussion and assign roles, such as leader and note-taker, as applicable.

- Ask questions and answer others' questions and clarify, verify, or challenge ideas and conclusions.

- Be open to new ideas suggested by others and change your own thinking to take such ideas into account when appropriate.

- Make sure all group members have a chance to participate and express his or her views.

Guidelines for Group Discussion

Discussion Rubric	Notes
❑ Did everyone participate in the discussion? ❑ Was each group member able to freely express his or her opinion?	
❑ Was a leader guiding the discussion? ❑ Did someone take notes for everyone to share at the end of the discussion?	
❑ Did people in the group ask questions and answer those posed by others? ❑ Did group members' questions and answers stay focused on the topic?	
❑ Did participants accept comments from others? ❑ Were participants open to new ideas or perspectives suggested by others?	

Name _____ Date _____ Assignment _____

Self-Assessment

After you've completed your presentation, you should reflect on your speech. Ask yourself how well you thought it went. Was your speech organized and logical? Was your delivery effective? Did you clearly define any unfamiliar terms and phrases for your audience? Did you integrate visual and multimedia elements effectively? Consider how your classmates reacted to your presentation and whether or not the group discussions helped you to realize anything about your speech.

Using a rubric for self-assessment. Combine your self-evaluation with what you learned from your classmates' response to your speech. Then, apply those insights as you fill in the rubric below. Use the rating scale to grade your work, and circle the score that best applies to each category.

Self-Assessment Rubric

Criteria for Discussion	Rating Scale					
	not very				very	
Focus: How clear was my thesis, and did all of my details and support focus on the topic of my speech?	1	2	3	4	5	6
Organization: How well-organized was my presentation so that listeners could easily follow it?	1	2	3	4	5	6
Support/Elaboration: How well did I support main idea with examples and detailed evidence, using visual displays and multimedia components where appropriate?	1	2	3	4	5	6
Delivery: How effectively did I create a relaxed but formal tone, making eye contact with listeners, maintaining an adequate volume, and speaking clearly?	1	2	3	4	5	6
Conventions: How free was my presentation from errors in grammar, spelling, and punctuation?	1	2	3	4	5	6

Speaking and Listening 2

2. Integrate multiple sources of information presented in diverse formats and media (e.g., visually, quantitatively, orally) in order to make informed decisions and solve problems, evaluating the credibility and accuracy of each source and noting any discrepancies among the data.

Explanation

When you have a problem to solve or a decision to make, a good first step is to find useful information. Check a variety of print and non-print sources, such as newspapers, Web sites, documentary films, and recorded political speeches.

Once you have found several sources of information, you must **evaluate** their **credibility** and accuracy. As you evaluate each source, consider the author's, sponsor's, or creator's interests or bias, the intended audience and purpose, and the date of the source.

To share your findings, **integrate** information from all your sources and create a cohesive, convincing multimedia presentation. Be sure to select the appropriate media to support each point.

Examples

- **Gather Information** Gather multiple sources to learn about a topic or issue. Then, decide which sources can help you. For example, a newspaper article about local traffic patterns could help identify solutions to traffic problems in your town. However, a book on traffic regulations throughout America would be too general.

- **Note Discrepancies** Sources sometimes contradict one another. When they do, conduct research to resolve the discrepancy.

- **Evaluate Sources** Is a source accurate? Is it credible? Evaluating the credibility of sources is especially important when you use the Internet. The most reliable Web sites are usually those with URLs ending in *.edu* and *.gov*. However, in using college or university sites with an *.edu* suffix, be sure you are not relying solely on information posted by a student.

- **Integrate Information** Weave together information presented in diverse formats and media, recognizing that written text is not the only source of valuable facts.

Academic Vocabulary

credibility power or ability to inspire belief or confidence

evaluate judge or assess value or usefulness

integrate bring together parts to create a coherent whole

Apply the Standard

Use the worksheet that follows to help you apply the standard. Several copies of the worksheet have been provided for you to use with different assignments.

- Integrating Multiple Sources of Information

Name _____ Date _____ Selection _____

Integrating Multiple Sources of Information

Use the chart, below, to take notes on your sources and evaluate the information in each. Then, explain how the sources support your decision, viewpoint, or solution.

Topic or Issue: ....

Source	What information does this source provide?	Is this source credible and accurate? Explain.
Source: Media Type: Format: ❑ Visual ❑ Quantitative ❑ Oral		
Source: Media Type: Format: ❑ Visual ❑ Quantitative ❑ Oral		
Source: Media Type: Format: ❑ Visual ❑ Quantitative ❑ Oral		

Perspective, Decision, or Solution: ....

....

....

How do your sources support your decision, viewpoint, or solution? ....

....

....

Integrating Multiple Sources of Information

Use the chart, below, to take notes on your sources and evaluate the information in each. Then, explain how the sources support your decision, viewpoint, or solution.

Topic or Issue: ....

Source	What information does this source provide?	Is this source credible and accurate? Explain.
Source: Media Type: Format: ❑ Visual ❑ Quantitative ❑ Oral		
Source: Media Type: Format: ❑ Visual ❑ Quantitative ❑ Oral		
Source: Media Type: Format: ❑ Visual ❑ Quantitative ❑ Oral		

Perspective, Decision or Solution: ....

....

....

How do your sources support your decision, viewpoint, or solution? ....

....

....

Name _____ Date _____ Selection _____

Integrating Multiple Sources of Information

Use the chart, below, to take notes on your sources and evaluate the information in each. Then, explain how the sources support your decision, viewpoint, or solution.

Topic or Issue: ....

Source	What information does this source provide?	Is this source credible and accurate? Explain.
Source: Media Type: Format: ❏ Visual ❏ Quantitative ❏ Oral		
Source: Media Type: Format: ❏ Visual ❏ Quantitative ❏ Oral		
Source: Media Type: Format: ❏ Visual ❏ Quantitative ❏ Oral		

Perspective, Decision or Solution: ....

....

....

How do your sources support your decision, viewpoint, or solution? ....

....

....

For use with Speaking and Listening 2

Speaking and Listening 3

> **3. Evaluate a speaker's point of view, reasoning, and use of evidence and rhetoric, assessing the stance, premises, links among ideas, word choice, points of emphasis, and tone used.**

Explanation

Evaluating a speech or presentation involves identifying and assessing a number of elements. One is the speaker's **tone,** or attitude towards a subject. Another is the premise, or underlying belief, of the speaker and how that **premise** is supported. In addition, speakers can:

- appeal to emotion by arousing an audience's feelings, and

- appeal to authority by claiming that experts support an idea.

It is also important to assess a speaker's use of **rhetorical devices** to persuade an audience:

- *alliteration:* repeating the same initial sound in nearby words

- *parallelism:* using the same grammatical structure to express related ideas

- *rhetorical questions:* asking a question with a self-evident answer

Example

In evaluating a presentation on the need to build an animal shelter for stray cats and dogs, you might jot down notes like these:

- point of view — pressing need for such a shelter

- expressed premise — morality of avoiding needless suffering of animals

- tone — serious and urgent

- words with an emotional appeal — *poor creatures*

- logical support — argument showing shelter will save money in the long run

- evidence — financial report of nearby town that built such a shelter

- rhetorical device — alliteration (". . . pets that were abused and abandoned . . .")

Academic Vocabulary

premises expressed or implied assumptions behind an argument

tone attitude toward a subject

rhetorical device specific use of language to persuade

Apply the Standard

- Evaluating Elements of a Speech

- Evaluating a Speaker's Use of Evidence

Name _____ Date _____ Assignment _____

Evaluating Elements of a Speech

Use the chart, below, to evaluate a speaker's point of view, reasoning, and persuasive appeals. Then, assess the speaker's word choice and tone and their effects on the audience.

Topic and speaker	
Audience	
Speaker's point of view	
Speaker's reasoning	
Persuasive appeals	❏ appeal to emotion Example: ❏ appeal to authority Example:
Rhetorical Devices and Word Choice	Examples: Effect on Audience:
Tone	Description of Tone: Effect on Audience:
How well did the presentation convey and support the argument? Explain.	

A

Name _____ Date _____ Assignment _____

Evaluating Elements of a Speech

Use the chart, below, to evaluate a speaker's point of view, reasoning, and persuasive appeals. Then, assess the speaker's word choice and tone and their effects on the audience.

Topic and speaker	
Audience	
Speaker's point of view	
Speaker's reasoning	
Persuasive appeals	☐ appeal to emotion Example: ☐ appeal to authority Example:
Rhetorical Devices and Word Choice	Examples: Effect on Audience:
Tone	Description of Tone: Effect on Audience:
How well did the presentation convey and support the argument? Explain.	

Name _____ Date _____ Assignment _____

Evaluating Elements of a Speech

Use the chart, below, to evaluate a speaker's point of view, reasoning, and persuasive appeals. Then, assess the speaker's word choice and tone and their effects on the audience.

Topic and speaker	
Audience	
Speaker's point of view	
Speaker's reasoning	
Persuasive appeals	❑ appeal to emotion Example: ❑ appeal to authority Example:
Rhetorical Devices and Word Choice	Examples: Effect on Audience:
Tone	Description of Tone: Effect on Audience:
How well did the presentation convey and support the argument? Explain.	

For use with Speaking and Listening 3

Name _____ Date _____ Assignment _____

Evaluating a Speaker's Use of Evidence

Use the chart, below, to evaluate the evidence a speaker uses.

Topic and speaker	
Speaker's Point of View	
Supporting Evidence	**Example:** **Was the evidence** ❏ relevant? ❏ of good quality? ❏ credible? ❏ persuasive? ❏ exaggerated or distorted? **Example:** **Was the evidence** ❏ relevant? ❏ of good quality? ❏ credible? ❏ persuasive? ❏ exaggerated or distorted? **Examples of exaggerated or distorted evidence:**
How well did the evidence support the speaker's reasoning? Explain.	

For use with Speaking and Listening 3

Name _____ Date _____ Assignment _____

Evaluating a Speaker's Use of Evidence

Use the chart, below, to evaluate the evidence a speaker uses.

Topic and speaker	
Speaker's Point of View	
Supporting Evidence	**Example:** **Was the evidence** ☐ relevant? ☐ of good quality? ☐ credible? ☐ persuasive? ☐ exaggerated or distorted? **Example:** **Was the evidence** ☐ relevant? ☐ of good quality? ☐ credible? ☐ persuasive? ☐ exaggerated or distorted? **Examples of exaggerated or distorted evidence:**
How well did the evidence support the speaker's reasoning? Explain.	

Name _____ Date _____ Assignment _____

Evaluating a Speaker's Use of Evidence

Use the chart, below, to evaluate the evidence a speaker uses.

Topic and speaker	
Speaker's Point of View	
Supporting Evidence	**Example:** **Was the evidence** ❏ relevant? ❏ of good quality? ❏ credible? ❏ persuasive? ❏ exaggerated or distorted? **Example:** **Was the evidence** ❏ relevant? ❏ of good quality? ❏ credible? ❏ persuasive? ❏ exaggerated or distorted? **Examples of exaggerated or distorted evidence:**
How well did the evidence support the speaker's reasoning? Explain.	

Speaking and Listening 4

> **4. Present information, findings, and supporting evidence, conveying a clear and distinct perspective, such that listeners can follow the line of reasoning, alternative or opposing perspectives are addressed, and the organization, development, substance, and style are appropriate to purpose, audience, and a range of formal and informal tasks.**

Explanation

First identify your purpose, audience, and task to determine how much depth to go into and how to adapt your argument. Then identify your **perspective** on the topic and how you will address opposing perspectives. Identifying and refuting opposing arguments will help persuade your audience that your perspective is correct.

Make sure your line of reasoning is focused and coherent, and your findings and **evidence** are strong. To develop and present your ideas clearly, consider using one of these organizational patterns:

- *Order of importance:* Present your ideas and evidence from most to least important, or from least to most important.

- *Cause-and-effect:* Analyze the cause of an event or problem and its effect or effects.

- *Problem/solution:* Identify a specific problem and tell how it might be solved.

Examples

- Address opposing perspectives. For example, your perspective is that litter is creating an unsafe environment in your town, and a community clean-up day should be mandatory for all students. To address and refute opposing perspectives, you might say: "Some students might argue that they didn't create the mess. However, they will benefit from a cleaner town, so they should take part in the clean-up."

- Consider which organizational structure will best highlight your ideas and make them clear and easy to follow. For example, a problem-and-solution organization would work well for the issue of how to handle litter in your community.

Academic Vocabulary

evidence support or proof of something

perspective a way of regarding a topic or situation

Apply the Standard

Use the worksheets that follow to help you apply the standard. Several copies of each worksheet have been provided for you to use with different assignments.

- Presenting a Speech Effectively

- Addressing Other Perspectives

Name _____ Date _____ Assignment _____

Presenting a Speech Effectively

Use the chart below to help you plan and deliver your presentation clearly and effectively

Topic	
Intended Audience	
Purpose	
Task	The task is ❑ formal. ❑ informal. **Explain:**
Purpose	
Supporting Evidence	
Audience	The presentation ❑ meets the needs of the audience. ❑ meets the needs of the purpose. ❑ meets the needs of the task. ❑ conveys a clear perspective. ❑ uses effective supporting evidence.

Name _____ Date _____ Assignment _____

Presenting a Speech Effectively

Use the chart below to help you plan and deliver your presentation clearly and effectively

Topic	
Intended Audience	
Purpose	
Task	**The task is** ❏ formal. ❏ informal. **Explain:**
Purpose	
Supporting Evidence	
Audience	**The presentation** ❏ meets the needs of the audience. ❏ meets the needs of the purpose. ❏ meets the needs of the task. ❏ conveys a clear perspective. ❏ uses effective supporting evidence.

Name _____ Date _____ Assignment _____

Presenting a Speech Effectively

Use the chart below to help you plan and deliver your presentation clearly and effectively

Topic	
Intended Audience	
Purpose	
Task	The task is ☐ formal. ☐ informal. Explain:
Purpose	
Supporting Evidence	
Audience	The presentation ☐ meets the needs of the audience. ☐ meets the needs of the purpose. ☐ meets the needs of the task. ☐ conveys a clear perspective. ☐ uses effective supporting evidence.

Name _____ Date _____ Assignment _____

Addressing Other Perspectives

After you have completed a rough draft of a speech, use the chart below to help you make sure that you address any possible questions and opposing perspectives.

Topic:..

My Perspective:	
My Argument:	
Possible questions: 1. 2. 3.	**My answers:** 1. 2. 3.
Possible objections: 1. 2. 3.	**Ways to minimize or refute them:** 1. 2. 3.

A

For use with Speaking

Name _____ Date _____ Assignment _____

Addressing Other Perspectives

After you have completed a rough draft of a speech, use the chart below to help you make sure that you address any possible questions and opposing perspectives.

Topic:..

My Perspective:	
My Argument:	

Possible questions:	**My answers:**
1.	1.
2.	2.
3.	3.
Possible objections:	**Ways to minimize or refute them:**
1.	1.
2.	2.
3.	3.

For use with Speaking

Name _____ Date _____ Assignment _____

Addressing Other Perspectives

After you have completed a rough draft of a speech, use the chart below to help you make sure that you address any possible questions and opposing perspectives.

Topic:..

My Perspective:	
My Argument:	
Possible questions: 1. 2. 3.	**My answers:** 1. 2. 3.
Possible objections: 1. 2. 3.	**Ways to minimize or refute them:** 1. 2. 3.

For use with Speaking

Speaking and Listening 5

> 5. Make strategic use of digital media (e.g., textual, graphical, audio, visual, and interactive elements) in presentations to enhance understanding of findings, reasoning, and evidence and to add interest.

Explanation

Making **strategic** use of digital media is an important part of creating a good multimedia presentation. Digital media include a variety of formats.

- **Textual elements,** such as titles, captions, and bulleted lists

- **Graphical elements,** such as charts, maps, and diagrams

- **Audio elements,** such as music, recorded interviews, and sound effects

- **Visual elements,** such as still photographs and video clips

- **Interactive elements,** such as message boards and games

Choose only those that have a clear meaning and relevance to the presentation.

Examples

- To add interest, pace your use of digital media elements. For example, in a presentation on rain forests, include photographs, audio clips, and video clips at various points throughout the presentation. Avoid clustering media elements together at either the beginning or end. That will prevent your audience from absorbing the information the media convey.

- Use media elements that complement one another. For example, photographs of birds that live in rain forests can be accompanied by recordings of their calls. By creating interplay among media elements, you can avoid repeating in words what other media elements have already communicated in sounds or visuals.

- Create a varied, rich experience for your audience. Avoid overusing any one form of media. For example, images of rain forest plants and insects may become repetitive. Add variety by including a recording of rainforest sounds.

Academic Vocabulary

strategic integral or essential to a carefully made plan

Apply the Standard

Use the worksheet that follows to help you apply the standard.

- Using Digital Media

Name _____ Date _____ Assignment _____

Using Digital Media

Use this chart to help you plan which digital media elements to use in your presentation. After your presentation, evaluate your use of digital media elements by answering the questions at the bottom of the page.

Textual Element(s):	**How element(s) enhance understanding:** .... **Location in Presentation:** ....
Graphical Element(s):	**How element(s) enhance understanding:** .... **Location in Presentation:** ....
Audio Element(s):	**How element(s) enhance understanding:** .... **Location in Presentation:** ....
Visual Element(s):	**How element(s) enhance understanding:** .... **Location in Presentation:** ....
Interactive Element(s):	**How element(s) enhance understanding:** .... **Location in Presentation:** ....

How did the digital media elements in your presentation enhance your audience's understanding of findings, reasoning, and evidence? ....

....

How did the digital media elements add interest? ....

....

Speaking and Listening 6

> **6. Adapt speech to a variety of contexts and tasks, demonstrating command of formal English when indicated or appropriate.**

Explanation

To effectively present a speech, it is important to first identify the **context** and the audience—be it a formal presentation in class or a group discussion with peers. Identifying your task, or purpose, is another key factor. Are you aiming to persuade, to share information, to entertain, or to offer a solution to a problem?

With your context and task in mind, determine how to **adapt** your presentation to appeal to your particular audience, focusing on delivery techniques. Speak each word clearly and precisely and vary the tone of your voice as needed. Remember to make eye contact with members of the audience and vary the pace of your delivery using appropriate body language to stress key points.

When you deliver a presentation, use formal English to communicate your ideas. Formal English shows that you respect both your subject and your audience. Avoid using casual, everyday language and slang when speaking.

Examples

- The context and task of a presentation should determine its level of formality and its tone. For example, if you were giving a presentation about a local sporting event, informal language may be appropriate. However, a speech about the death of a famous political leader would call for formal language and a serious, solemn tone.

- Observe your command of formal English in presentations that require you to use it. Avoid common usage problems, including incorrect verb tenses. "She rung the doorbell three times," is incorrect. It should be "She rang the doorbell three times."

- Avoid using filler words and phrases, which interrupt the flow of a presentation. These words include *um, like, you know,* and *I mean.*

Academic Vocabulary

adapt change to suit a new purpose or different conditions

context circumstance or situation that determines interpretation

Apply the Standard

Use the worksheets that follow to help you apply the standard. Several copies of each worksheet have been provided for you.

- Adapting a Speech

- Using Appropriate Language

Name _____ Date _____ Selection _____

Adapting a Speech

Use this chart to help you adapt a speech to the appropriate context, audience, and, task.

Topic: ....

What is the context, or situation?
Who is your audience?
What is your task, or purpose?

↓

Adaptations I Will Make	Reasons for Changes
1.	
2.	
3.	

For use with Speaking and Listening 6

Name _____ Date _____ Selection _____

Adapting a Speech

Use this chart to help you adapt a speech to the appropriate context, audience, and, task.

Topic: ....

What is the context, or situation?
Who is your audience?
What is your task, or purpose?

↓

Adaptations I Will Make	**Reasons for Changes**
1.	
2.	
3.	

Name _____ Date _____ Selection _____

Adapting a Speech

Use this chart to help you adapt a speech to the appropriate context, audience, and, task.

Topic: ....

What is the context, or situation?
Who is your audience?
What is your task, or purpose?

↓

Adaptations I Will Make	Reasons for Changes
1.	
2.	
3.	

C

Name _____ Date _____ Selection _____

Using Appropriate Language

Before you give a speech, use the checklist to evaluate your use of language.

Audience: ....

Context: ....

Speaking Task: ....

	Speech Checklist
Language	❏ Is my language appropriate for the context and speaking task? ❏ Have I avoided making common usage errors? ❏ Is my language and word choice precise and engaging enough to keep the listeners interested? ❏ Have I avoided using filler words?
Sentences	❏ Are my sentences varied enough? ❏ Can I change sentences lengths to vary my pace and tempo? ❏ Have I avoided using fragments and run-on sentences?
Verbs	❏ Am I using the correct form of irregular verbs? ❏ Are my verbs vivid and precise?

A

Name _____ Date _____ Selection _____

Using Appropriate Language

Before you give a speech, use the checklist to evaluate your use of language.

Audience: ....

Context: ....,...................

Speaking Task: ....

	Speech Checklist
Language	❑ Is my language appropriate for the context and speaking task? ❑ Have I avoided making common usage errors? ❑ Is my language and word choice precise and engaging enough to keep the listeners interested? ❑ Have I avoided using filler words?
Sentences	❑ Are my sentences varied enough? ❑ Can I change sentences lengths to vary my pace and tempo? ❑ Have I avoided using fragments and run-on sentences?
Verbs	❑ Am I using the correct form of irregular verbs? ❑ Are my verbs vivid and precise?

For use with Speaking and Listening 6

Name _____ Date _____ Selection _____

Using Appropriate Language

Before you give a speech, use the checklist to evaluate your use of language.

Audience: ....

Context: ....

Speaking Task: ....

	Speech Checklist
Language	❏ Is my language appropriate for the context and speaking task? ❏ Have I avoided making common usage errors? ❏ Is my language and word choice precise and engaging enough to keep the listeners interested? ❏ Have I avoided using filler words?
Sentences	❏ Are my sentences varied enough? ❏ Can I change sentences lengths to vary my pace and tempo? ❏ Have I avoided using fragments and run-on sentences?
Verbs	❏ Am I using the correct form of irregular verbs? ❏ Are my verbs vivid and precise?

C

Language Standards

Language 1a

> **1a. Demonstrate command of the conventions of standard English grammar and usage when writing or speaking.**
>   • **Apply the understanding that usage is a matter of convention, can change over time, and is sometimes contested.**

Explanation

Throughout your school career, you have studied the rules of **standard English** grammar and usage. People are expected to demonstrate a strong command of these rules in their formal writing and speaking. Grammar and usage rules are **conventions,** or agreements, accepted by most speakers and writers. These conventions often change over time and are sometimes contested, or challenged. To succeed in society, however, you need to understand and consistently apply the conventions of standard English that are accepted at any given time.

Examples

Over time, the conventions of standard English usage can change. Up until very recently, for example, commas were used to separate only the first and second in a series of items. For example: *Suzanne brought her guitar, her harmonica and her accordion.* Now the convention is to separate all three items in a series: *Suzanne brought her guitar, her harmonica, and her accordion.* However, because this convention shifted only fairly recently, many people still follow the old rule.

It is important to have command of the current conventions of standard English grammar and usage. The table below summarizes some of the most important conventions.

Convention	Errors	Corrections
A present-tense verb must agree with its subject.	One of these games are difficult. The expressions on her face changes often. Jen want a new phone.	**One** of these games **is** difficult. The **expressions** on her face **change** often. **Jen wants** a new phone.
A pronoun must agree with its antecedent in person and gender.	One of the men lost their voice. Athletes need to build your stamina.	One of the men lost **his** voice. Athletes need to build **their** stamina.
Place a modifier as close as possible to the word it modifies.	Torn to shreds, I tried to repair my math paper.	I tried to repair my math paper, **which was torn to shreds.**
Use verbs in the active voice, unless you want to emphasize the receiver of the action or the doer of the action is unknown or unimportant.	The ball was hit over the outfield fence by Deion.	**Deion hit** the ball over the outfield fence.

Name _____ Date _____ Assignment _____

Apply the Standard

A. Circle the correct or best word in parentheses to complete each sentence.

1. The poems of the Romantic Period (is, are) well known.

2. One of the qualities that people admire in Romantic poems (is, are) an emphasis on emotions.

3. Equally admired (is, are) the subject matter of the poetry.

4. William Wordsworth's poems are known for (its, their) celebration of nature.

5. The poet Lord Byron is most remembered for (his, its) creation of a figure known as the "Byronic hero."

6. Wordsworth, one of the most famous poets of this period, (was, were) from the Lake District.

7. An area in northwestern England, (it, they) was a place where he spent much time in his youth.

8. Both of Wordsworth's parents (died, were dead) before he left to pursue his education at Cambridge University.

9. The approaches of the different Romanic poets (is, are) different in many respects.

10. After becoming caught up in the French Revolution, Wordsworth (return, returned) to England a changed man.

B. Each sentence contains one or more errors in standard English grammar and usage. Circle the errors, and write the sentences correctly on the lines.

1. A controversial character, people were shocked by Lord Byron.

   ....

2. A gloomy, mysterious outcast, the Byronic hero feels no satisfaction in their accomplishments.

   ....

3. One of the most famous lines in English poetry were created by John Keats in its poem "Ode on a Grecian Urn."

   ....

4. "The Rime of the Ancient Mariner," the best-known of Samuel Taylor Coleridge's poems, is remembered for their vivid imagery and spooky mood.

   ....

5. Mary Shelley, the wife of poet Percy Bysshe Shelley, is remembered for his famous novel, *Frankenstein*.

   ....

For use with Language 1a

Language 1b

1b. Demonstrate command of the conventions of standard English grammar and usage when writing or speaking.

   • **Resolve issues of complex or contested usage, consulting references (e.g., *Merriam-Webster's Dictionary of English Usage, Garner's Modern American Usage*) as needed.**

Explanation

When usage conventions are complicated or contested, even professional editors are not always sure which word is considered correct in a certain context. To resolve usage issues, writers and editors turn to reliable reference books, such as an up-to-date college dictionary or usage handbook.

Examples

The **comparative** form of an adjective or adverb is used to compare two persons, places, or things. The **superlative** form is used to compare three or more. To form the comparative, you add *–er* to the modifier or use the word *more* before the modifier. To form the superlative, you add *–est* to the modifier or use the word *most* before it.

Modifier	Comparative Form	Superlative Form
smart	smarter	smartest
tiny	tinier	tiniest
narrow	narrower	narrowest
handsome	handsomer	handsomest
useful	more useful	most useful
interesting	more interesting	most interesting
quickly	more quickly	most quickly

Usage conventions once required using *more* and *most* with modifiers of two or more syllables. Today, however, many two-syllable modifiers have correct forms that end in *–er* and *–est*. For example, the comparative and superlative forms of *handsome* are *handsomer* and handsomest. If you look up *handsome* in an up-to-date dictionary, you will find these forms listed after the entry word.

If you look up other two-syllable adjectives such as *lonesome, helpful*, and *loyal*, however, you will not find any comparative or superlative forms listed. The absence of these comparative forms in the dictionary entry tells you that you must use *more* and *most* with these modifiers to form the comparative. If you are not sure of the correct comparative and superlative forms of a modifier, look up the word in a recently published dictionary. For other complex or contested usage issues, consult an authoritative usage guide such as *Webster's Dictionary of English Usage*.

Name _____ Date _____ Assignment _____

Apply the Standard

A. Circle the correct modifier in parentheses to complete each sentence. Use a dictionary if necessary.

1. Ebenezer Scrooge is the (more famous, most famous) character created by Charles Dickens.

2. As Scrooge becomes (wealthier, wealthiest), he becomes even (greedier, greediest) than he was as a young man.

3. He has no compassion for even the (needier, neediest) family in all of London.

4. After being visited by three ghosts, however, Scrooge becomes (generouser, more generous).

5. The (memorablest, most memorable) scene in *A Christmas Carol* is when Scrooge buys the (hugest, most huge) goose in the whole market for the Cratchit family.

6. One of the (popularest, most popular) novellas ever written, *A Christmas Carol* is now often performed as a drama.

7. The story has become one of the (more traditional, most traditional) representations of what Christmas spirit means.

8. *A Christmas Carol* is known (best, bestest) because of its brilliant characters, Scrooge and Bob Cratchit.

9. As Scrooge's (more miserable, most miserable) assistant, Bob Cratchit represents many of the poor, working-class people in England at that time.

10. Dickens's classic novella remains to this day one of the (more, most) frequently adapted works of all time.

B. Write the correct comparative or superlative form of the modifier to complete each sentence. Use an up-to-date college dictionary to check that you are using the currently accepted form.

1. My progress was .... than his. (steady)

2. Which of the three paths is the ....? (narrow)

3. Sandstone is .... than marble. (porous)

4. Jan's report was .... than Joe's. (timely)

5. That Chinese restaurant offers the .... service in town. (speedy)

6. What is the .... problem you have ever faced? (difficult)

7. Which of the three lakes is the ....? (shallow)

8. Snow is .... in December than it is in April. (welcome)

9. My dog is the .... member of my family. (loyal)

10. Your meal is .... than mine. (tasty)

For use with Language 1b

Language 2a

> **2a.** Demonstrate command of the conventions of standard English capitalization, punctuation, and spelling when writing.
> • Observe hyphenation conventions.

Explanation

In American standard English, hyphens are used with certain compound adjectives and compound nouns. They are also used to separate certain prefixes from the words that follow. Consult an up-do-date college dictionary or an authoritative usage guide if you are not sure whether to use a hyphen.

Examples

The table below summarizes current American standard English conventions for using hyphens.

Use a hyphen...	Rule	Examples
after a prefix	when the second word is capitalized.	mid-September
	when the second word is a number.	pre-1900
	when more than one word follows it.	pre-twentieth-century
	to distinguish a word from its homophone.	*repress* a memory, but *re-press* a shirt
	when the prefix *ex-* means "former"	ex-husband
in compound adjectives	when they come before a noun, unless the first word ends in -*ly*.	brown-eyed girl widely read magazine
in compound nouns	when they name numbers.	fifty-six
	when they name equally important functions.	poet-scholar
	when they include a prepositional phrase.	mother-in-law
	for *great* relatives and with *year-old*.	great-grandfather two-year-old
	when they begin with *self* or *vice*.	self-esteem vice-chairman

Name _____ Date _____ Assignment _____

Apply the Standard

A. Circle the words in each sentence that require a hyphen. Then write each hyphenated word correctly.

1. The month of March has thirty one days. ....

2. We saw a thought provoking video about pre Columbian architecture in Guatemala.

    ....

3. She was taking care of a high spirited four year old boy.

    ....

4. The vice president's mother in law is the well known architect engineer Rosa Gonzalez.

    ....

5. We are studying post 1917 Russian history. ....

6. My mother wants to recover the high backed chairs, using brightly colored paisley fabric.

    ....

7. The president announced a ten year plan for redeveloping the poverty stricken city.

    ....

8. Twenty five all American sports heroes received new state of the art video recorders.

    ....

B. Rewrite the paragraph below, adding hyphens where they are needed.

   The Polish born writer Joseph Conrad eventually became one of the masters of late nineteenth century British fiction. The son of a Polish nobleman nationalist, Conrad was orphaned at the age of eleven and fled his Russian occupied homeland when he was seventeen. He did not learn English until 1878 when, at the age of twenty one, he took a job on a British merchant ship. As a seaman, he made voyages to Asia, Africa, and South America, places that eventually became richly detailed settings in novels and stories such as *Lord Jim*, "The Secret Sharer," and "Heart of Darkness." His fiction can be read as adventures in which men face life threatening dangers, but also as voyages of self discovery, in which men face soul threatening isolation and moral dilemmas.

    ....

    ....

    ....

For use with Language 2a

Language 2b

> **2b. Demonstrate command of the conventions of standard English capitalization, punctuation, and spelling when writing.**
> • **Spell correctly.**

Explanation

Readers will not be convinced by your brilliant arguments or be swept up in your suspenseful story if they are stumbling over misspelled words. You can avoid spelling errors by learning a few spelling rules, consulting a dictionary when needed, and using spell-check cautiously as you write.

Examples

The tables below provide rules to help you avoid some common spelling errors. Notice which ones apply to you, and check those words carefully when you edit your writing.

TROUBLESOME SOUNDS

Many words contain similar sounds, yet have different spellings. Check a dictionary if you are unsure of the correct spelling.

Rule	Examples
The "seed" sound at the end of a word can be spelled *cede, ceed,* or *sede.*	precede, recede, concede, intercede exceed, proceed, succeed supersede
The "er" sound can be spelled many different ways: *ar, er, ear, ir, or, our, ur,* or *ure.*	calendar, verse, learn, first, neighbor, furniture, courage, pasture

ADDING SUFFIXES

Become familiar with the following rules for adding suffixes.

Rule	Examples
When adding *–ly* to form an adverb from an adjective ending in *–le,* first drop the *–le.*	reasonable + ly = reasonably intelligible + ly = intelligibly
When adding *–ing, -ish,* or *–ist* to words that end in *y,* keep the *y* at the end of the root word.	pity + ing = pitying essay + ist = essayist
The *shus* sound can be spelled with the suffix *-cious* or *-tious.* Check a dictionary to be sure of the correct spelling.	gracious, suspicious infectious, cautious
The *shun* sound is usually spelled with the suffix *-tion.* The *zhun* sound is usually the suffix *-sion.*	ration, mention confusion, decision

Name _____ Date _____ Assignment _____

Apply the Standard

A. Write the words described below. Be sure to spell them correctly. Check a dictionary if you are unsure of the correct spelling.

1. Write the word that means "a person who acts." ....

2. Add the suffix –*ly* to the word *remarkable*. ....

3. Write the word that means "to have success." ....

4. Write the word that begins with *re-* and means "to move back," like a tide or a hairline.

   ....

5. Add the suffix –*ist* to the word *hobby*. ....

6. Add the *shun* sound to the end of *prevent*. ....

7. Add the *zhun* sound to the end of *revise*. ....

8. Add the suffix –*ing* to the word *carry*. ....

9. Add the suffix –*ly* to the word *comfortable*. ....

10. Add the suffix –*ing* to the word *cry*. ....

B. Each sentence below contains one or more misspelled words. Circle each misspelled word, and write the correct spelling on the line. Use a dictionary if you are unsure of the correct spelling.

1. The spectaters at the fireworks display said that they saw a spectaculer presentation.

   ....

2. My parents praised me for behaving responsiblely and said they were no longer worrying about my futur or feeling suspishous about my decisions.

   ....

3. My cousin preceeded me up the circuler stairway.

   ....

4. To succede in life, you need to accept disappointment grashiously and proceed with confidence.

   ....

5. Some lobbyists may exceed the bounds of ethical behavier when dealing with legislaters such as senaters.

   ....

Language 3

> **3a.** Apply knowledge of language to understand how language functions in different contexts, to make effective choices for meaning or style, and to comprehend more fully when reading or listening.
>
> • Vary syntax for effect, consulting references (e.g., Tufte's *Artful Sentences*) for guidance as needed; apply an understanding of syntax to the study of complex texts when reading.

Explanation

To keep their readers interested, good writers use different kinds of sentences. Writers become experts in syntax—the different ways of arranging words in sentences. They vary the syntax of their sentences to create certain effects, such as suspense, surprise, or humor. By expanding your understanding of syntax, you can become a better writer and a more discerning reader.

Examples

To create dramatic effects and to prevent your writing from becoming monotonous, use a variety of sentence structures. Short sentences quicken the pace and create a sense of drama, while longer sentences cause the reader to slow down and reflect. Simple sentences focus the reader's attention on a single idea, while compound and complex sentences emphasize the relationships between ideas.

SENTENCE TYPES

Simple: a single independent clause	*I want to have a challenging career.*
Compound: Two or more independent clauses, joined by a comma and coordinating conjunction (*and, but, or*) or a semicolon	*I want to have a challenging career, but I don't want to sit at a desk all day.*
Complex: One independent clause and one or more subordinate clauses	*Because I like sports, I think athletic training is a career that I'd enjoy.*
Compound-Complex: Two or more independent clauses and one or more subordinate clauses	*Trainers earn a good living, and the job is never boring because it involves the drama of athletic competition.*

SENTENCE BEGINNINGS

Notice how you can express the same idea in five different ways, just by changing the beginning of a sentence.

Subject	*Many high school students* suddenly start planning their futures during their senior year.
Prepositional Phrase	*During their senior year,* many high school students suddenly start planning their futures.
Participle	*Starting* suddenly during their senior year, many high school students plan their futures.
Adverb	*Suddenly,* during their senior year, many high school students start planning their futures.
Subordinate Clause	*When they become seniors,* many high school students suddenly start planning their futures.

Name _____ Date _____ Assignment _____

Apply the Standard

A. Combine each group of sentences, using the sentence type indicated in parentheses.

1. Careers in health care are booming. Many of them pay quite well. (compound)

....

2. Some careers require many years of training. Others do not. (compound)

....

3. You may participate in an internship. You are going to school at the same time. (complex)

....

4. Physical therapy is a career. Many people find it rewarding. (complex)

....

5. Your college advisor will write recommendations. The placement office will help you find a job. They will do this when you are ready to graduate. (compound-complex)

....

....

B. Rewrite each sentence to begin as indicated in parentheses.

1. Representatives at the college fair greeted our high school seniors with information and advice. (prepositional phrase)

....

2. Dan, confused about his future, asked about many different areas of study. (participial phrase)

....

3. He gradually began to focus on the field of broadcast communications. (adverb)

....

4. He found a college with a great communications program when the fair was almost over. (subordinate clause)

....

5. When he got home, he talked to his parents about his plans. (subject)

....

Language 4a

> **4a.** Determine or clarify the meaning of unknown and multiple-meaning words and phrases based on grades 11–12 reading and content, choosing flexibly from a range of strategies.
>
> • Use context (e.g., the overall meaning of a sentence, paragraph or text; a word's position or function in a sentence) as a clue to the meaning of a word or phrase.

Explanation

To become a proficient reader of complex texts, you need to master the strategies for using **context clues**—the nearby words, phrases, and sentences. Context clues can help you determine and clarify the meaning of unknown words as well as words with multiple meanings. There are many different types of context clues, the most common of which are explained below.

Examples

Clues in Nearby Words Look for a nearby word or phrase that may have a meaning similar to, or the opposite of, the unknown word. Look, too, for examples that may clarify a word's meaning.

Similar meaning: Some animals take on the same look as their habit and change their <u>hue</u> as they change their surroundings.

(The context clues suggest that *hue* means "color.")

Opposite meaning: Samuel Johnson once said that authors can aspire to praise but lexicographers can only hope to escape <u>reproach</u>.

(The clue suggests that *reproach* means the opposite of *praise*, so it must mean "negative criticism.")

Examples: The <u>anatomy</u> of the frog resembles that of many aquatic animals, with lungs, heart, brain, and other organs.

(The examples suggest that *anatomy* means "the structures that make up a living creature.")

Clues in the Meaning of the Passage Look for the main idea of a sentence or passage. You can often use the main idea to figure out the meaning of an unknown word.

The soldiers divided their food into <u>rations</u> that would last the entire month. None were allowed to eat more than their daily portion.

(The general meaning of the passage suggests that *rations* means "limited amounts allowed during a shortage.")

Clues in the Word's Function in the Sentence Look at where the word falls in the sentence. Think about its job, or function. Does it follow an article or an adjective? Does it serve as a subject or as an object of a preposition? If so, it is a noun. Does it express action? If so, it is a verb. Use that information, plus any of the first two types of clues, to figure out the unknown word's meaning.

According the account by Thomas Malory, King Arthur smote Sir Mordred with a thrust of a spear.

(*Smote* comes after the subject *King Arthur* and appears to be acting as a verb. The clue words "with a thrust of his spear" suggest that *smote* means "attacked" or even "killed.")

Name _____ Date _____ Assignment _____

Apply the Standard

A. Use context clues in each sentence to determine or clarify the meaning of each underlined word. Write the probable meaning of each word on the line provided.

1. At Arthur's death, a number of ladies brought the dead corpse here and prayed me to <u>inter</u> him in this chapel. ....

2. King Arthur's servant asked the hermit if he might <u>abide</u> with him, fasting and saying prayers for the rest of his days. ....

3. Robbers <u>ransacked</u> the castle and took away all the goods that were left there, both the king's and those of the tenants. ....

4. At the funeral for the king, the <u>multitudes</u> from the surrounding villages came out to pay tribute to their beloved leader.

   ....

   ....

5. Few texts were as <u>scrutinized</u> and studied as those detailing the lives and triumphs of the kings who ruled in feudal times.

   ....

   ....

B. Think about the function of the underlined word and its position in the sentence. Use that information, plus any other context clues, to define the underlined word. Then write its meaning on the line.

1. Several knights on horses suddenly appeared before the castle and <u>brandished</u> their swords, demanding immediate entry. ....

2. The knight's <u>antagonist</u> in the jousting match was also his rival in the love of the king's fair daughter, Gwendolyn. ....

3. One first hears about Arthur, a High-King of Britain, from his <u>predecessor</u>, who had ruled the country in the years before Arthur first appeared. ....

4. At the time, the question of who would rule the country and who was to be the rightful heir cast Britain into <u>turmoil</u> that seemed as if it might never end. ....

5. The <u>specter</u> of his father, the previous king who was much beloved, continued to haunt the young prince who had so recently ascended to the throne. ....

Language 4b

> **4b.** Determine or clarify the meaning of unknown and multiple-meaning words and phrases based on grades 11–12 reading and content, choosing flexibly from a range of strategies.
>
> • Identify and correctly use patterns of word changes that indicate different meanings or parts of speech (e.g., *conceive, conception, conceivable.*)

Explanation

By adding suffixes to root words, you can change their meaning and part of speech. Many root words change their parts of speech in predictable ways. When you learn these patterns of word changes, you can figure out the meaning of related words by analyzing their root words and suffixes. You can also easily identify whether a word is acting as a noun, verb, or adjective in a sentence.

Examples

Many adjectives end in *–ent* or *–ant*. You can usually transform them into nouns by changing *–ent* to *–ence* and *–ant* to *–ance*:

- **adjectives:** persistent, omniscient, defiant, predominant
- **nouns:** persistence, omniscience, defiance, predominance

Many verbs have similar endings, such as those that end in the suffix *–ate*. These verbs can be changed into nouns by adding the suffix *–ation*:

- **verbs:** obliterate, intimidate, extenuate, exonerate,
- **nouns:** obliteration, intimidation, extenuation, exoneration

Many words also share Latin or Greek word parts. For example, a number of verbs that end in *-olve*. These verbs can be changed into nouns, following a predictable pattern:

- **verbs:** solve, absolve, resolve, revolve, evolve, dissolve
- **nouns:** solution, absolution resolution, revolution, evolution, dissolution

Verbs that end in *–ceive* also follow a predictable pattern, which includes two different adjective forms. Notice how the two adjective forms differ in meaning.

Verb	Noun	Adjective: able to	Adjective: able to be ....ed
deceive	deception	deceptive	deceivable
perceive	perception	perceptive	perceivable *or* perceptible
receive	reception	receptive	receivable
conceive	conception	....	conceivable

For verbs that end in *–ess*, add *–ion* to form a noun and *-ive* to form an adjective:

- **verbs:** impress, depress, express, transgress
- **nouns:** impression, depression, expression, transgression
- **adjectives:** impressive, depressive, expressive, transgressive

Name _____ Date _____ Assignment _____

Apply the Standard

A. Look at the suffix in each word. Then write the word's part of speech.

1. repression ....

2. confiscate ....

3. affluent ....

4. equivocation ....

5. revolve ....

6. perceptive ....

7. receivable ....

8. predominance ....

9. transgress ....

10. resolution ....

11. repressive ....

12. absolve ....

13. reliant ....

14. intimidation ....

15. unreceptive ....

16. obliterate ....

17. dominance ....

18. dissemination ....

19. believable ....

20. speculation ....

B. Fill in each blank with the correct form of the word in italics.

1. When you *deceive* someone, you are being a .... person.

2. When someone *absolves* you of blame, they are offering you ....

3. A .... person is one who likes to *defy* authority.

4. When you *exasperate* someone, that person feels the emotion of ....

5. If an idea can be *conceived,* it is a .... idea.

6. A *malevolent* person is spiteful. A person who demonstrates spitefulness shows his

....

7. A *perception* is something you ....

8. When something *evolves,* it undergoes an ....

9. A person who has a *transcendent* experience has a feeling of ....

10. *Vigilance* is a quality exhibited by .... people.

Language 4c

> **4c.** Determine or clarify the meaning of unknown and multiple-meaning words and phrases based on grades 11–12 reading and content, choosing flexibly from a range of strategies.
>
> • Consult general and specialized reference materials (e.g., dictionaries, glossaries, thesauruses), both print and digital, to find the pronunciation of a word or determine or clarify its precise meaning, its parts of speech, its etymology, or its standard usage.

Explanation

Use a **dictionary** to determine or clarify a word's precise meaning and part of speech. You can also check a dictionary to learn a word's **etymology,** or history, as well as whether it is considered standard English, colloquial (conversational English), or slang. Textbooks will often include a **glossary,** or alphabetical listing of important terms.

To vary the word choice in your writing, check a **thesaurus,** or book of synonyms. Many of the synonyms listed in a thesaurus have the same general meaning, but different connotations.

Examples

Sample Dictionary Entry

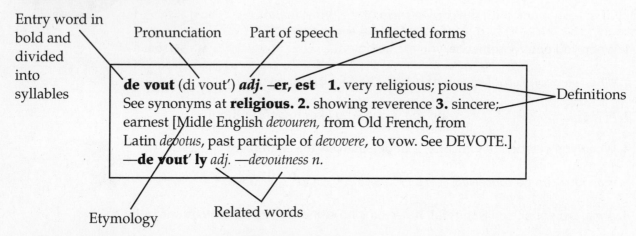

Entry word in bold and divided into syllables — Pronunciation — Part of speech — Inflected forms

de vout (di vout') *adj.* **–er, est   1.** very religious; pious See synonyms at **religious. 2.** showing reverence **3.** sincere; earnest [Midle English *devouren,* from Old French, from Latin *devotus,* past participle of *devovere,* to vow. See DEVOTE.] —**de vout' ly** *adj.* —*devoutness n.*

Definitions — Etymology — Related words

Usage Indicators: *Devout,* is considered standard English. For words that are not standard English, the dictionary entry will include a label before the definition, such as **colloq:** colloquial, conversational English (not to be used in formal writing).

Sample Thesaurus Entry

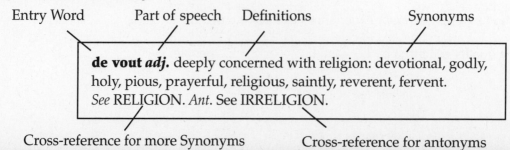

Entry Word — Part of speech — Definitions — Synonyms

de vout *adj.* deeply concerned with religion: devotional, godly, holy, pious, prayerful, religious, saintly, reverent, fervent. *See* RELIGION. *Ant.* See IRRELIGION.

Cross-reference for more Synonyms — Cross-reference for antonyms

Name _____ Date _____ Assignment _____

Apply the Standard

A. Use an up-to-date print or electronic dictionary to answer these questions.

1. Which syllable of the word *reciprocal* is accented when you pronounce the word?

....

2. Which word is a verb: *breath* or *breathe*?

....

3. Trace the path by which the word *khaki* entered the English language. What was the original meaning of the root from which the word comes?

....

4. Which definition of the word *wicked* is not considered standard English usage?

....

5. How do the words *showy* and *pretentious* differ in their connotative meanings?

....

B. Use a thesaurus to find five synonyms for each underlined word. Then use a dictionary to choose the best synonym to replace the underlined word in the context of the sentence.

1. In some typefaces, it is difficult to <u>discriminate</u> a capital letter *I* from a lowercase letter *l*.

synonyms: .... best synonym: ....

2. My mother finds it very <u>annoying</u> when telemarketers call at dinner time.

synonyms: .... best synonym: ....

3. The police officers were ordered not to <u>discharge</u> their weapons.

synonyms: .... best synonym: ....

4. The convicted criminal was <u>vindicated</u> when new evidence came to light.

synonyms: .... best synonym: ....

5. Two of the judges expressed their <u>dissent</u> from the majority opinion.

synonyms: .... best synonym: ....

Language 4d

> **4d. Determine or clarify the meaning of unknown and multiple-meaning words and phrases based on grades 11–12 reading and content, choosing flexibly from a range of strategies.**
>
> - **Verify the preliminary determination of the meaning of a word or phrase (e.g., by checking the inferred meaning in context or in a dictionary.**

Explanation

To infer the meaning of an unfamiliar word, you can analyze its word parts—prefix, root, suffix. You can also use **context clues**—other nearby words, phrases, and sentences. Sometimes the first inference you make about a word's meaning will not be exactly correct. As you read on, you can use more context clues to verify the meaning of the word. If you are still not sure of a word's exact meaning, check your understanding of the word by looking it up in a dictionary.

Examples

Unfamiliar terms In the following passage from Mary Wollstonecraft's *A Vindication of the Rights of Woman*, you may not be familiar with the word *frivolous*.

> The education of women has of late been more attended to than formerly; yet they are still reckoned a <u>frivolous</u> sex, and ridiculed or pitied by the writers who endeavor by satire or instruction to improve them.

Since the women are ridiculed and pitied, you may infer from the context that *frivolous* means "inferior." If you read on, however, you discover that *frivolous* has a more specific meaning:

> It is acknowledged that they spend many of the first years of their lives in acquiring a smattering of accomplishments; meanwhile strength of body and mind are sacrificed to . . . notions of beauty, . . . [W]hen they marry they act as such children may be expected to act— they dress, they paint, and nickname God's creatures.

Now you may infer that *frivolous* means "vain," "silly," or "not serious". To verify your inferences and confirm the word's meaning, look up *frivolous* in a dictionary, where you find this definition: "lacking in seriousness."

Multiple-meaning words Some of the puzzling words you encounter in your reading will be familiar, multiple-meaning words that are used in unfamiliar ways. When you infer their meaning in context, try replacing the word with the inferred meaning to see if it makes sense. For example, Wollstonecraft writes, "[C]ivilized women . . . are only anxious to inspire love, when they ought to cherish a nobler ambition, and by their abilities and virtues <u>exact</u> respect." Obviously, Wollstonecraft is not using the word *exact* as an adjective meaning "precise." Instead she is using at as a verb, meaning "demand." Try replacing the word *exact* with the word *demand* in the sentence. Then its meaning makes sense.

Name _____ Date _____ Assignment _____

Apply the Standard

Read this passage from *The Diary of Samuel Pepys*, in which Pepys describes the Great Fire of London. As you read, try to infer the meaning of each underlined word, using word analysis and context clues. Use additional context clues to verify whether your preliminary determination was correct. Then look up each word in a dictionary to confirm its meaning.

So I down to the waterside, and there got a boat and through bridge, and there saw a <u>lamentable</u> fire. Poor Michell's house, as far as the Old Swan, already burned that way, and the fire running farther, that in a very little time it got as far as the steel yard, while I was there. Everybody <u>endeavoring</u> to remove their goods, and flinging into the river or bringing them into <u>lighters</u> that lay off; poor people staying in their houses as long as till the very fire touched them, and then running into boats, or <u>clambering</u> from one pair of stairs by the waterside to another. And among other things, the poor pigeons, I perceive, were <u>loth</u> to leave their houses, but <u>hovered</u> about the windows and balconies till they were, some of them burned, their wings, and fell down. Having stayed, and in an hour's time seen the fire rage every way, and nobody, to my sight, endeavoring to <u>quench</u> it, but to remove their goods, and leave all to the fire . . . and everything, after so long a <u>drought,</u> proving <u>combustible,</u> even the very stones of churches, and among other things the poor steeple by which pretty Mrs. — lives, and <u>whereof</u> my old schoolfellow Elborough is parson, taken fire in the very top, and there burned till it fell down.

	Word	Inferred Meaning	Dictionary Meaning
1.			
2.			
3.			
4.			
5.			
6.			
7.			
8.			
9.			
10.			

Language 5a

5a. Demonstrate understanding of figurative language, word relationships, and nuances in word meanings.

- Interpret figures of speech (e.g., hyperbole, paradox) in context and analyze their role in the text.

Explanation

Writers use figurative language to express ideas in vivid, original, and memorable ways. **Figurative language** is writing or speech that is used imaginatively. Its meaning must be interpreted, rather than taken literally. Together, the many types of figurative language are known as **figures of speech.**

Examples

Figure of Speech	Definition	Example
simile	compares two unlike things, using *like* or *as*	Her eyes glowed like the moon.
metaphor	compares two unlike things; does **not** use *like* or *as*	He was a bulldozer running over all of her objections.
personification	gives human qualities to a nonhuman thing	The trees danced in the wind.
oxymoron	fuses two contradictory ideas in just a few words	Let's create a new tradition this holiday season.
paradox	states a idea that seems contradictory or impossible, but is actually true in some way	A coded message both increases communication and decreases communication.
hyperbole	exaggerates; overstates the truth	Not even Einstein could have passed that math test.
understatement	says less than is really meant	I was a just a tiny bit embarrassed when I tripped over my shoelaces as I walked across the stage.
verbal irony	says the opposite of what is really meant	I just love it when we have a pop quiz in math. My whole body tingles with excitement.

Name _____ Date _____ Assignment _____

Apply the Standard

A. Identify the type(s) of figurative language used in each sentence or passage.

1. The actress became just a little bit nervous when she forgot her lines. ....

2. It is so crowded here. Did you invite the entire school to this party? ....

3. As we grow older, we understand that change is the only constant in life.

   ....

4. Writer John Donne once said, "[A]ffliction is a treasure, and scarce any man hath enough of it."

   ....

5. The flowers are beckoning us to them. ....

6. The man's massive stone home was like a fortress. ....

7. Jonathan Swift once remarked, "Satire is a sort of glass, wherein beholders do generally discover

   everybody's face but their own." ....

8. I think I will order the jumbo shrimp. ....

9. She cried so hard she had to wear a raincoat. ....

10. Shakespeare is known for using moving language, as in this passage: "I think our country sinks
    beneath the yoke; / It weeps, it bleeds, and each new day a gash / Is added to her wounds."

   ....

B. Read the passage below. Identify examples of figurative language. Then explain how the figures of speech affect your understanding of the text and your emotional response to it.

Some persons of a desponding spirit are in great concern about that vast number of poor people, who are aged, diseased, or maimed, and I have been desired to employ my thoughts what course may be taken to ease the nation of so grievous an encumbrance. But I am not in the least pain upon that matter, because it is very well known, that they are every day dying, and rotting, by cold, and famine, and filth, and vermin, as fast as can be reasonably expected. And as to the younger laborers they are now in almost as hopeful a condition.

—Jonathan Swift

....

....

....

For use with Language 4d

Language 5b

Explanation

The **denotation** of a word is its basic meaning, while the **connotations** of a word are the feelings or ideas associated with it. Some synonyms with similar denotations convey different **nuances,** or slight differences in meaning. It is important to notice the nuances of word meanings as you read. When you write, it is important to choose words that have the connotations and nuances of meaning that you intend.

Examples

This chart shows words that are synonyms for *take.* Notice the different connotations and shades of meaning that each word conveys.

Word	Connotation/Nuance	Example Sentence
1. *grasp*	to take firm hold of something	*The gymnast* <u>grasped</u> *the parallel bars and began her routine.*
2. *clutch*	to take and anxiously hold on to a thing you fear losing	*She* <u>clutched</u> *her purse as she walked through the crowd.*
3. *snatch*	to take suddenly, without permission	*I* <u>snatched</u> *a cookie that had just come out of the oven.*
4. *seize*	to take someone or something by force	*The police* <u>seized</u> *the fugitive.*
5. *confiscate*	to seize something with official authority to do so	*The state* <u>confiscated</u> *the criminal's illegally obtained property.*

Name _____ Date _____ Assignment _____

Apply the Standard

A. Use a synonym for *took* to complete each sentence.

clutch   confiscate   grasp   seize   snatched

1. The kidnappers .... a wealthy man and held him for ransom.

2. She carefully .... the fragile eggs and walked across the kitchen.

3. He .... the handlebars of the bike as he made a left turn.

4. The stolen merchandise was .... by federal authorities.

5. Tanya .... my test paper while I wasn't looking.

B. Look up each pair of synonyms in a dictionary. Think about their different shades of meaning. Then use each word in a sentence that conveys the word's connotations.

1. anxiety/panic

....

....

2. donated/conferred

....

....

3. appreciate/cherish

....

....

4. divulge/expose

....

....

5. bashful/modest

....

....

Language 6

6. Acquire and use accurately general academic and domain-specific words and phrases, sufficient for reading, writing, speaking, and listening at the college and career readiness level; demonstrate independence in gathering vocabulary knowledge when considering a word or phrase important to comprehension or expression.

Explanation

Throughout your years in school, you have learned many **academic** and **domain-specific** vocabulary words and phrases.

- **Academic words** include words that you use every day at school to solve problems, analyze texts, express your ideas, and so on.
  Examples include *critique, clarify, refute, annotate,* and *debate.*

- **Domain-specific words** are words that are specific to a course of study. In a science course, examples include *inertia, radioactive,* and *catalyst.* In a social studies course, examples include *imperialism, assimilation,* and *parliamentary.*

Learning the meanings of academic and domain-specific words and using them frequently will help you to complete assignments effectively and express yourself clearly.

Examples

In many of your courses, you are asked to complete assignments based on specific academic words and phrases. On many tests, you are asked to write essays that fulfill directions containing academic words and phrases, such as the ones below.

Paraphrase the **thesis** of . . .	***Refute*** the **argument** that . . .
Debate the merits of . . .	***Clarify*** the meaning of . . .
Summarize the effects of . . .	***Categorize*** the different types of . . .

In a literature course, you learn and use many domain-specific words and phrases, as shown below. Make an effort to learn these domain-specific words in each of your courses.

caesura	*assonance*	*epic*	*legend*
frame story	*characterization*	*alliteration*	*allegory*

Name _____ Date _____ Assignment _____

Apply the Standard

A. Match each domain-specific word or phrase with its definition. Write the letter of the correct definition on the line provided.

.... **1.** caesura   **a.** long narrative poem about heroic deeds

.... **2.** assonance   **b.** narrative with both literal and symbolic meaning

.... **3.** epic   **c.** repeated vowel sounds

.... **4.** legend   **d.** technique for revealing character traits

.... **5.** frame story   **e.** traditional story inspired by real events

.... **6.** characterization   **f.** repeated initial consonant sounds

.... **7.** alliteration   **g.** pause in the middle of a line of poetry

.... **8.** allegory   **h.** story that brackets one or more other stories

B. Each statement includes one or more academic words or phrases. Circle the letter of the phrase that completes each statement.

1. When you **summarize** a text, you ....

     a. evaluate evidence   **c.** analyze its meaning

     b. classify concepts   **d.** tell the main ideas in your own words

2. When you **debate** the merits of a plan, you ....

     a. discuss its pros and cons   **c.** propose a new idea

     b. give step-by-step directions   **d.** annotate its sources

3. When you **refute** an **argument,** you ....

     a. provide reasons to support it   **c.** synthesize the pros and cons

     b. provide reasons to reject it   **d.** summarize its merits

4. When you **categorize** types of fiction, you ....

     a. evaluate their quality   **c.** sort them into related groups

     b. summarize their themes   **d.** tell why they are important

Performance Tasks

Name _____ Date _____ Assignment _____

Performance Task 1A

> **Literature 1** Cite strong and thorough textual evidence to support analysis of what the text says explicitly as well as inferences drawn from the text, including determining where the text leaves matters uncertain.

Task: Support Analysis of a Text

Write an essay in which you cite textual evidence to support your analysis of a literary text. In addition to including literal interpretation, provide strong and thorough textual support for any inferences you make. Identify instances of ambiguity, supporting all conclusions with evidence.

Tips for Success

Present a response to a literary selection you have read. In your essay, include these elements:

✓ a brief and objective summary of the work

✓ a thesis statement that clearly and concisely summarizes your analysis and interpretation of the work

✓ textual evidence that explicitly supports your interpretation, conclusions, and inferences

✓ evidence from the text that supports your analysis of ambiguities

✓ a formal style and objective tone appropriate for your audience and the genre

Rubric for Self-Assessment

Criteria for Success	not very					very
How effectively have you summarized the work?	1	2	3	4	5	6
How clear and concise is your thesis statement?	1	2	3	4	5	6
To what extent have you based your thesis on an in-depth analysis of the work?	1	2	3	4	5	6
How effectively have you used relevant quotes, facts, or examples from the text to support your thesis?	1	2	3	4	5	6
How well have you supported any inferences you made with explicit evidence from the text?	1	2	3	4	5	6
How well have you supported your analysis of ambiguities with textual references?	1	2	3	4	5	6
To what extent did you use a formal style and appropriate tone?	1	2	3	4	5	6

*Other standards covered include Writing 1, 1d, 2, 2b, 2e, 9; Speaking 1a, 1b, 1c, 1d, 4

For use with Speaking and Listening 1

Name _____ Date _____ Assignment _____

Performance Task 1B

Speaking and Listening 1 Initiate and participate effectively in a range of
   collaborative discussions (one-on-one, in groups, and teacher-led) with diverse
   partners on grade 11–12 topics, texts, and issues, building on others' ideas and
   expressing their own clearly and persuasively.

Task: Discuss the Responses to a Text

Participate in a group discussion in which you explain your analysis of a literary text and engage in
a thoughtful discussion about it. Deepen the discussion by building on the ideas of others.

Tips for Success

Participate in a discussion about an analysis of a literary text. As part of your participation, follow
these tips for success:

✓ read or re-read the literary text and take notes on your interpretation

✓ with the group, develop discussion guidelines that ensure equal and full
   participation for each person

✓ prepare questions that will evoke further discussion from participants

✓ formulate clear and full responses to questions asked by other group
   members

✓ locate passages from the text that support the points of view of other group
   members

✓ summarize the group's responses to the text

Rubric for Self-Assessment

Criteria for Discussion	not very				very	
To what extent did you prepare for the discussion?	1	2	3	4	5	6
How effectively did the guidelines established by the group ensure full and fair inclusion of ideas from all group members?	1	2	3	4	5	6
To what extent did you provide complete, but concise, responses to questions?	1	2	3	4	5	6
How successfully did you ask thoughtful questions that helped explore the points of view presented?	1	2	3	4	5	6
How effectively did you and other group members build on one another's ideas?	1	2	3	4	5	6
How well did the discussion summarize the main perspectives of the participants?	1	2	3	4	5	6

For use with Literature 1

Name _____ Date _____ Assignment _____

Performance Task 2A

> **Literature 2** Determine two or more themes or central ideas of a text and analyze their development over the course of the text, including how they interact and build on one another to produce a complex account; provide an objective summary of the text.

Task: Analyze Themes

Write an analytical essay in which you identify and analyze two or more themes in a literary work. Provide an objective summary of the text, and identify how the themes interact with one another to produce a complex story.

Tips for Success

Present an informative analysis of the themes in a literary selection and include these elements:

✓ a concise and objective summary of the work

✓ an analysis of two or more themes in the work

✓ a thesis about how the themes interact and relate to one another and how they influence the work

✓ evidence from the text that supports your interpretation

✓ a discussion of how the author integrates theme with other literary elements

✓ a formal style and objective tone appropriate for your audience and the genre

Rubric for Self-Assessment

Criteria for Success	not very					very
How concise and objective was your summary of the work?	1	2	3	4	5	6
How effectively have you analyzed the themes in the work?	1	2	3	4	5	6
How effectively have you described your premise about the interaction of themes in the work?	1	2	3	4	5	6
To what extent have you discussed the effect of this interaction on the overall work?	1	2	3	4	5	6
How effectively have you supported your analysis of the themes?	1	2	3	4	5	6
To what extent have you included examples from the text to show how the integration of themes creates a complex work?	1	2	3	4	5	6
To what extent have you used a formal style and appropriate tone for your audience?	1	2	3	4	5	6

* Other standards covered include Writing 1, 1d, 1e, 2, 2b, 2c, 2f, 4, 9; Speaking 1a, 1b, 1c, 3, 4

For use with Speaking and Listening 1d

Name _____ Date _____ Assignment _____

Performance Task 2B

> **Speaking and Listening 1d** Respond thoughtfully to diverse perspectives; synthesize comments, claims, and evidence made on all sides of an issue; resolve contradictions when possible; and determine what additional information or research is required to deepen the investigation or complete the task.

Task: Discuss the Themes in a Literary Work

With one or more classmates, participate in a discussion to compare and contrast your interpretations of how the author of a literary text uses themes to produce a complex work.

Tips for Success

Participate in a discussion about the themes of a literary text. Follow these tips for success:

✓ read or re-read the literary text and take notes to use in your discussion

✓ listen attentively to the points made by others and ask questions to deepen understanding

✓ analyze similarities and differences in the interpretations of group members

✓ identify further research to deepen an investigation of the themes

✓ synthesize and evaluate conclusions reached by group members

Rubric for Self-Assessment

Criteria for Discussion	not very					very
To what extent did you come to the discussion prepared to discuss the themes of the literary work?	1	2	3	4	5	6
How effectively and clearly did you present your ideas?	1	2	3	4	5	6
To what extent did you listen attentively and ask probing questions that deepened understanding?	1	2	3	4	5	6
How thoroughly did you explore the similarities and differences in the interpretations of themes?	1	2	3	4	5	6
To what extent did the group identify issues that could be clarified by further research?	1	2	3	4	5	6
How well did you and others synthesize comments, claims, and evidence presented by the group?	1	2	3	4	5	6

For use with Literature 2

Name _____ Date _____ Assignment _____

Performance Task 3A

> **Literature 3   Analyze the impact of the author's choices regarding how to develop and relate elements of a story or drama (e.g., where a story is set, how the action is ordered, how the characters are introduced and developed.)**

Task: Analyze an Author's Choices

Write an analysis of a literary text in which you focus on the author's choices regarding how to develop and relate elements of a story or drama, such as setting, sequence of action, and characterization.

Tips for Success

Produce an analysis in which you focus on an author's choices regarding how to develop and relate elements of a story or drama. In your analysis, include these items:

✓ a brief, objective summary of the work

✓ an analysis of setting and how that setting influences the work

✓ an analysis of ways in which the author introduces and develops characters

✓ an analysis of how the sequence of action creates suspense or surprise

✓ an analysis of any other important influences, such as organization, voice, or literary devices

✓ a formal style and objective tone appropriate for your audience and the genre

Rubric for Self-Assessment

Criteria for Success	not very					very
How effectively have you summarized the work?	1	2	3	4	5	6
To what extent have you explained how the setting influences other elements of the work, such as the action and characters?	1	2	3	4	5	6
How effectively have you analyzed the author's choices regarding character development?	1	2	3	4	5	6
How well have you explained the overall effect of the sequence of action?	1	2	3	4	5	6
How well have you supported your analysis with strong evidence from the text?	1	2	3	4	5	6
To what extent have you used a formal style and appropriate tone for your audience?	1	2	3	4	5	6

* Other standards covered include Writing 1, 1a, 1b, 1d, 1e, 2, 2b, 2e, 4, 9; Speaking 1a, 1b, 1d, 3, 4, 6

For use with Speaking and Listening 1c

Name _____ Date _____ Assignment _____

Performance Task 3B

Speaking and Listening 1c Propel conversations by posing and responding to questions that probe reasoning and evidence; ensure a hearing for a full range of positions on a topic or issue; clarify, verify, or challenge ideas and conclusions; and promote divergent and creative perspectives.

Task: Discuss the Analysis of Author's Choices

As part of a group discussion, explain your analysis of a literary text and use probing questions to clarify, verify, or challenge the ideas and conclusions of others.

Tips for Success

Participate in a discussion focusing on an analysis of an author's choices in a literary text. As part of your participation in the discussion, include these elements:

✓ preparation by having read and analyzed the literary text

✓ guidelines that ensure a hearing for a full range of analyses by all participants in the group

✓ participation by everyone to clarify, illustrate, or expand on a response when asked to do so

✓ questions that probe reasoning and respectfully challenge the speaker to clarify, verify, or defend conclusions

✓ thoughtful consideration of divergent and creative perspectives

Rubric for Self-Assessment

Criteria for Discussion	Assignment Rubric					
To what extent did you come to the discussion prepared to discuss and make a thoughtful analysis of the literary work?	1	2	3	4	5	6
How effective were the groups' guidelines in insuring that everyone had an opportunity to explain their ideas and respond to questions?	1	2	3	4	5	6
How effectively did you answer questions and provide textual examples to support your ideas?	1	2	3	4	5	6
To what extent did you respectfully challenge other speakers to clarify, verify, or defend conclusions?	1	2	3	4	5	6
To what extent were you open to consideration of divergent and creative perspectives?	1	2	3	4	5	6
To what extent were you polite and respectful of other points of view?	1	2	3	4	5	6

Name _____ Date _____ Assignment _____

Performance Task 4A

> **Literature 4** Determine the meaning of words and phrases as they are used in the text, including figurative and connotative meanings; analyze the impact of specific word choices on meaning and tone, including words with multiple meanings or language that is particularly fresh, engaging, or beautiful.

Task: Analyze Word Choice

Write an essay in which you examine the author's choice of connotative, denotative, and figurative language, especially in terms of how they influence the meaning and tone of the work.

Tips for Success

Produce an essay about a literary selection you have read. In your essay, include these elements:

- ✓ a brief, objective summary of the work

- ✓ an explanation of how the author uses denotations, connotations, and figurative language

- ✓ identification of specific words, phrases, or language that you found fresh, engaging, or beautiful

- ✓ examples of how figurative language and literary devices contribute to the meaning and tone of the work

- ✓ a formal style and objective tone appropriate for your audience and the genre

Rubric for Self-Assessment

Criteria for Success	not very					very
To what extent does your summary provide the reader with the information needed to understand your essay?	1	2	3	4	5	6
To what extent have you focused on the author's choices of particular words and phrases?	1	2	3	4	5	6
How effectively have you analyzed the influence of specific word choices on the meaning and tone of the work?	1	2	3	4	5	6
How extensively have you identified specific words, phrases, or language that you found particularly fresh, engaging, or beautiful?	1	2	3	4	5	6
How well have you supported your analysis with evidence from the text, as well as your own reasoning, word choice, and tone?	1	2	3	4	5	6
To what extent have you used a formal style and appropriate tone?	1	2	3	4	5	6

* Additional standards covered include Writing 1, 1c, 1d, 2, 2b, 2c, 2d, 4, 5, 9; Speaking 1d, 4, 6

For use with Speaking and Listening 3

Name _____ Date _____ Assignment _____

Performance Task 4B

> **Speaking and Listening 3** Evaluate a speaker's point of view, reasoning, and use of evidence and rhetoric, assessing the stance, premises, links among ideas, word choice, points of emphasis, and tone used.

Task: Evaluate a Speaker's Presentation

In small groups, take turns sharing your reflections on the word choices made by the author in a literary work. Focus on your own use of reasoning, evidence, word choice and tone as you present your reflection. When listening to others present, evaluate the speaker's point of view, reasoning, and use of evidence and rhetoric.

Tips for Success

Participate in a discussion about an author's word choices in a literary text. As part of your participation, follow these tips for success:

✓ prepare by reading and taking notes on the literary text that will be discussed

✓ identify the point of view and major premises put forth by the speaker

✓ evaluate the extent to which the speaker supported ideas through reasoning and evidence

✓ evaluate the extent to which the speaker's word choice, organization, emphasis, and tone supported his or her ideas

Rubric for Self-Assessment

Criteria for Discussion	not very					very
To what extent were you prepared to discuss the literary work and the word choices in it?	1	2	3	4	5	6
How effectively did you identify each speaker's point of view?	1	2	3	4	5	6
How well did you follow each speaker's reasoning and evidence?	1	2	3	4	5	6
To what extent did you notice any bias, ambiguity, stereotypes, or cultural assumptions in each speaker's presentation?	1	2	3	4	5	6
To what extent did you consider the effect of word choice, emphasis, and tone as you evaluated each presentation?	1	2	3	4	5	6
To what extent did you offer respectful, constructive criticism to the speakers?	1	2	3	4	5	6

Name _____ Date _____ Assignment _____

Performance Task 5A

> **Literature 5** **Analyze how an author's choices concerning how to structure specific parts of a text (e.g., the choice of where to begin or end a story, the choice to provide a comedic or tragic resolution) contribute to its overall structure and meaning as well as its aesthetic impact.**

Task: Analyze Structure

Write an analysis of a literary text in which you examine the author's choices concerning how to structure and organize the work. Explain how these choices contribute to the overall meaning and aesthetic impact of the work.

Tips for Success

Produce a literary analysis of a short story you have read. In your essay, include these elements:

✓ a brief, objective summary of the work

✓ a clear thesis statement that sums up your conclusions

✓ a discussion of the work's structure or pattern of organization

✓ an analysis of ways in which the author creates mood and tone

✓ a reflection on how the author's choices influence the overall meaning of the work, as well as its aesthetic impact

✓ a formal style and objective tone appropriate for your audience and the genre

Rubric for Self-Assessment

Criteria for Success	not very				very	
To what extent does your summary provide readers with a basis for understanding your thesis and conclusions?	1	2	3	4	5	6
How detailed is your analysis of the work's structure or pattern of organization?	1	2	3	4	5	6
How thoroughly have you supported your analysis of structure with textual examples?	1	2	3	4	5	6
How effectively have you analyzed the relationship between the structure and the mood and tone?	1	2	3	4	5	6
How effectively have you reflected on the meaning and aesthetic impact of the work?	1	2	3	4	5	6
To what extent have you used a formal style and appropriate tone for your audience?	1	2	3	4	5	6

* Additional standards covered include Writing 1, 1a, 1b, 1c, 1d, 2, 2b, 2c, 2d, 9; Speaking 1d, 6

Name _____ Date _____ Assignment _____

Performance Task 5B

> **Speaking and Listening 4** Present information, findings, and supporting evidence, conveying a clear and distinct perspective, such that listeners can follow the line of reasoning, alternative or opposing perspectives are addressed, and the organization, development, substance, and style are appropriate to purpose, audience, and a range of formal and informal tasks.

Task: Discuss Author's Choice of Structure

Present your analysis on the author's choice of structure in a manner that clearly conveys and supports your perspectives, including a comparison and defense of your ideas against opposing or alternative perspectives.

Tips for Success

Present your reflection about an author's choice of structure in a literary text. As part of your presentation, follow these tips for success:

✓ prepare by reading and reflecting on the literary text

✓ present your reflection in a clear and organized manner to engage your audience and allow them to follow your reasoning

✓ make effective use of reasoning, evidence, word choice, and tone

✓ explain alternative or opposing perspectives objectively, while arguing for your own interpretation

✓ make use of a tone and language appropriate to your purpose and audience

Rubric for Self-Assessment

Criteria for Discussion	not very					very
How well prepared were you for your presentation?	1	2	3	4	5	6
How clear and organized was your presentation?	1	2	3	4	5	6
How effectively did you engage your audience?	1	2	3	4	5	6
To what extent did you use reasoning, evidence, and effective word choice and tone to persuade your audience?	1	2	3	4	5	6
How successfully did you explain alternative or opposing perspectives and counter them with evidence supporting your own conclusions?	1	2	3	4	5	6
How effectively did you vary the tone and pacing of your presentation?	1	2	3	4	5	6
How successfully did you use a tone and language appropriate to your purpose and audience?	1	2	3	4	5	6

For use with Literature 5

Name _____ Date _____ Selection _____

Performance Task 6A

Literature 6 Analyze a case in which grasping point of view requires distinguishing what is directly stated in a text from what is really meant (e.g., satire, sarcasm, irony, or understatement).*

Task: Analyze a Text and Its Point of View

Write an analysis of a literary text in which you identify and discuss the author's use of literal and figurative meaning, and other literary devices, such as satire, sarcasm, and irony. Use your analysis to develop a thesis about the work's point of view. Provide textual evidence to support any conclusions you draw.

Tips for Success

Produce an analysis of a literary selection you have read. In your analysis, include these elements:

- ✓ a brief, objective summary of the work

- ✓ a thesis statement that describes the author's point of view

- ✓ evidence from the text that supports your thesis and any inferences you make

- ✓ evidence from the text that supports your conclusions about how the author's use of literary devices reveals point of view

- ✓ a clear and coherent analysis that leads to a strong and compelling conclusion

- ✓ a formal style and objective tone appropriate for your audience and the genre

Rubric for Self-Assessment

Criteria for Success	not very					very
How effective is your summary of the work?	1	2	3	4	5	6
How well does your thesis statement describe the author's point of view?	1	2	3	4	5	6
To what extent have you provided textual evidence to support your thesis and inferences?	1	2	3	4	5	6
To what extent have you described the relationship between the author's use of literary devices and the author's point of view?	1	2	3	4	5	6
How successfully have you concluded your analysis?	1	2	3	4	5	6
To what extent have you used a formal style and appropriate tone for your audience?	1	2	3	4	5	6

* Other standards covered include: Writing 1c, Writing 1d, Writing 1e, Writing 2b, Writing 2c, Writing 2f, Writing 4, Writing 9, Speaking 2, Speaking 4, Language 3, Language 4, Language 5

Name _____ Date _____ Selection _____

Performance Task 6B

> **Speaking and Listening 6** Adapt speech to a variety of contexts and tasks,
> demonstrating a command of formal English when indicated or appropriate.

Task: Present an Analysis

Present to the class your analysis of the devices used in a literary text. Incorporate into your presentation readings of sections of the text that support your interpretation and conclusions. Invite questions and comments at the end of your presentation.

Tips for Success

Present your analysis of a literary text. Follow these tips for success:

✓ prepare by revising your written analysis, adapting it for an oral presentation while maintaining a formal tone

✓ incorporate dramatic readings of supporting sections of text at appropriate points in your analysis

✓ assemble the analysis and readings into a coherent presentation

✓ rehearse your presentation, adapting your tone to suit your tasks

✓ demonstrate a command of English usage by avoiding incorrect tenses, and temporizing slang such as *you know* and *I mean*.

Rubric for Self-Assessment

Criteria for Discussion	not very					very
How clearly organized and professional was your presentation?	1	2	3	4	5	6
How effectively did you integrate your analysis of the text with dramatic readings from the text?	1	2	3	4	5	6
How coherent was your presentation?	1	2	3	4	5	6
To what extent did you demonstrate a command of formal English?	1	2	3	4	5	6
To what extent did you avoid slang and words and phrases such as *like* and *you know*?	1	2	3	4	5	6
How effectively did you adapt your presentation to your audience?	1	2	3	4	5	6

Name _____ Date _____ Assignment _____

Performance Task 7A

Literature 7 Analyze multiple interpretations of a story, drama, or poem (e.g., recorded or live production of a play or recorded novel or poetry), evaluating how each version interprets the source text. (Include at least one play by Shakespeare and one play by an American dramatist.).*

Task: Analyze Multiple Interpretations of a Literary Work

Write an evaluative analysis of two or more interpretations of a literary work, such as Shakespeare's play *The Tragedy of Macbeth*. In your essay, tell how each version interprets the original work.

Tips for Success

Read the original text and then compare and contrast the different versions in a written, critical response. In your analysis, include the following:

✓ a synopsis of the work

✓ a summary of analyses from scholars about the underlying meaning of the work

✓ a description of each of the versions you watched or listened to

✓ an evaluation of how closely each version adhered to the original

✓ an analysis of the strengths and weaknesses of each version

✓ a formal style and objective tone appropriate for your audience and the genre

Rubric for Self-Assessment

Criteria for Success	not very					very
How well does your synopsis summarize the work?	1	2	3	4	5	6
To what extent have you researched analyses of the work by scholars?	1	2	3	4	5	6
How concisely have you described each of the versions you watched or listened to?	1	2	3	4	5	6
How effectively have you compared and evaluated each version with respect to the original?	1	2	3	4	5	6
How thoroughly have you analyzed the strengths and weaknesses of each version?	1	2	3	4	5	6
To what extent have you used a formal style and appropriate tone?	1	2	3	4	5	6

* Other standards covered include: Writing 1a, Writing 1b, Writing 1d, Writing 1e, Writing 2b, Writing 2c, Writing 2d, Writing 2f, Writing 4, Writing 8, Writing 9, Speaking 4, Speaking 5, Speaking 6, Language 3, Language 4, Language 5

Name _____ Date _____ Assignment _____

Performance Task 7B

> **Speaking and Listening 2** Integrate multiple sources of information presented in diverse formats and media (e.g., visually, quantitatively, orally) in order to make informed decisions and solve problems, evaluating the credibility and accuracy of each source and noting any discrepancies among the data.

Task: Present an Analysis Using Multiple Media

Present your analysis of how various versions of a literary work adhere to the original version. During your presentation, include video and audio clips from the versions, as well as dramatic reading of the original work to support your evaluation.

Tips for Success

Prepare a multimedia presentation of your analysis of several versions of a literary text. Follow these tips for success:

✓ familiarize yourself with the original work as well as with the selected versions

✓ identify sections of the works and its versions that demonstrate their similarities and differences

✓ combine audio and video clips into a multimedia program that supports your evaluation

✓ practice your presentation so that it flows smoothly and effectively

✓ invite your audience to participate in a question and answer discussion

Rubric for Self-Assessment

Criteria for Discussion	not very					very
How well did you study the literary work and the chosen versions?	1	2	3	4	5	6
How successfully did you choose sections of the play and other versions to demonstrate their similarities and differences?	1	2	3	4	5	6
How effectively did you combine audio and video clips and incorporate them into your evaluation?	1	2	3	4	5	6
How smooth, seamless, and effective was your presentation?	1	2	3	4	5	6
To what extent did you invite your audience to participate in a question and answer discussion?	1	2	3	4	5	6

For use with Literature 7

Name _____ Date _____ Assignment _____

Performance Task 8

Literature 9 Demonstrate knowledge of eighteenth-, nineteenth- and early
twentieth-century foundational works of American literature, including how two
or more texts from the same period treat similar themes or topics.*

Task: Write a Comparative Essay

Write an essay that compares and contrasts how the writings of Ralph Waldo Emerson, Emily
Dickinson, and Henry David Thoreau embody the ideas of Transcendentalism.

Tips for Success

Read works expressing Transcendentalist ideas by all three authors and then write a comparative
essay on the similarities and differences in their points of view and include:

✓ a thesis statement about the common point of view of the three authors

✓ an analysis of the similarities between the works related to this common
   point of view

✓ an analysis of the differences between the works related to this common
   point of view

✓ an evaluation of how well the authors expressed the ideas of
   Transcendentalism

✓ an effective organizational pattern

✓ a formal style and objective tone appropriate for your audience and the genre

Rubric for Self-Assessmentt

Criteria for Success	not very					very
How clearly have you identified the common philosophical point of view in the works of these authors?	1	2	3	4	5	6
How effective is your analysis of similarities and differences in the works?	1	2	3	4	5	6
To what extent have you analyzed the ideas of Transcendentalism found in the works of these authors?	1	2	3	4	5	6
To what extent is your essay logically and effectively organized?	1	2	3	4	5	6
To what extent have you used a formal style and appropriate tone for your audience?	1	2	3	4	5	6

* Other standards covered include: Writing 1a, Writing 1c, Writing 1d, Writing 1e, Writing 2b, Writing 2c, Writing 2d, Writing 2f,
Writing 4, Writing 9, Speaking 2, Speaking 4, Speaking 6, Language 2, Language 3, Language 4, Language 5, Language 6

For use with Speaking and Listening 5

Name _____ Date _____ Assignment _____

Performance Task 8B

> **Speaking and Listening 5** Make strategic use of digital media (e.g., textual, graphical, audio, visual, and interactive elements) in presentations to enhance understanding of findings, reasoning, and evidence and to add interest.

Task: Present an Oral Report Using Digital Media

Transform your comparative essay into an oral report that integrates digital media, such as a computer slideshow or Powerpoint. Use the digital components to enhance your analysis of the authors' ideas about Transcendentalism.

Tips for Success

Prepare a visual presentation of your analysis of the work of several authors. Follow these tips for success:

✓ select the most relevant and important points in your analysis

✓ prepare a slide on each key point, while summarizing the content

✓ vary the look of your slides, including video, audio, and other effects, where appropriate

✓ assemble your slides into a coherent, logical presentation

✓ rehearse your presentation, seamlessly integrating commentary with the slides

Rubric for Self-Assessment

Criteria for Discussion	not very				very	
How effectively did you integrate digital components throughout your oral report?	1	2	3	4	5	6
How well do your slide illustrate your major points?	1	2	3	4	5	6
To what extent did you make your slideshow appealing by varying the look of the slides?	1	2	3	4	5	6
To what extent were your slides well organized and easy to follow?	1	2	3	4	5	6
How interesting and effectively organized was your presentation?	1	2	3	4	5	6

Name _____ Date _____ Assignment _____

Performance Task 9A

> **Literature 10** By the end of grade 12, read and comprehend literature, including stories, dramas, and poems, at the high end of the grades 11–CCR text complexity band independently and proficiently.

Task: Write in the Style of an Author

Select a favorite author of stories, novels, or drama. Demonstrate your comprehension of the author's unique style and use of literary devices by writing in the style of the author, but on a different theme. Publish your writing and share with the class.

Tips for Success

Write in the style of one of your favorite authors. Follow these tips for success:

✓ read several works by your chosen author and take notes on his or her style and the themes he or she explores

✓ in your writing, explore themes like those explored by the author

✓ in your writing, create a mood and tone similar to those in works by the author

✓ in your writing use structures and syntax that reflect your author's style

✓ revise your work to strengthen its impact

Rubric for Self-Assessment

Criteria for Success	not very					very
How closely did analyze the works of your chosen author?	1	2	3	4	5	6
How effectively have you explored themes like those explored by the author?	1	2	3	4	5	6
How well have you emulated the author's style?	1	2	3	4	5	6
How closely have you followed the author's use of sentence structure and patterns of organization?	1	2	3	4	5	6
To what extent have you strengthened your writing by editing?	1	2	3	4	5	6

* Other standards covered include: Writing 3a, Writing 3b, Writing 3c, Writing 3d, Writing 3e, Writing 5, Writing 6, Speaking 1b, Speaking 1c, Speaking 1d, Speaking 3, Speaking 6, Language 1, Language 2, Language 3, Language 5

For use with Speaking and Listening 1a

Name _____ Date _____ Assignment _____

Performance Task 9B

> **Speaking and Listening 1a** Come to discussions prepared, having read and researched material under study; explicitly draw on that preparation by referring to evidence from texts and other research on the topic or issue to stimulate a thoughtful, well-reasoned exchange of ideas.

Task: Engage in a Discussion of an Author

Form a group with other students who have written in the style of a particular author. Prepare for a discussion of each student's writing by reading a variety of selections from the author, making note of particularly characteristic use of literary devices and other features of style. After each student's presentation, contribute to a thoughtful, well-reasoned exchange of ideas.

Tips for Success

Prepare for a discussion of the style and point of view of a particular author. Follow these tips for success:

- ✓ read selections by the author that clearly convey the author's unique style
- ✓ make note of word usage and literary devices that exemplify the author
- ✓ summarize the elements that make the author unique and memorable
- ✓ listen attentively to the passages, scenes, or poems written by others in the group
- ✓ analyze the extent to which each piece of writing has successfully imitated the author
- ✓ contribute to a thoughtful and courteous exchange of ideas

Rubric for Self-Assessment

Criteria for Discussion	not very					very
How thoroughly did you familiarize yourself with the author's style?	1	2	3	4	5	6
How well did you make note of examples of the author's style?	1	2	3	4	5	6
How well did you summarize the elements that make the author unique?	1	2	3	4	5	6
How attentively did you listen to the speaker?	1	2	3	4	5	6
How well did you evaluate the extent to which the speaker imitated the author?	1	2	3	4	5	6
How effectively did you contribute to a thoughtful and courteous exchange of ideas?	1	2	3	4	5	6

Name _____ Date _____ Assignment _____

Performance Task 10A

> **Informational Text 1** Cite strong and thorough textual evidence to support analysis of what the text says explicitly as well as inferences drawn from the text, including determining where the text leaves matters uncertain.*

Task: Support Inferences and Conclusions

Write an analysis of a work of informational nonfiction in which you present a thesis and cite textual evidence to support your analysis of the text. In addition to including literal interpretation, provide strong and thorough textual support for any inferences you make. Identify instances of the author's use of literary devices to advance his or her thesis, supporting your conclusions with textual evidence.

Tips for Success

Produce a response to an informational text. In your response, include these elements:

✓ a brief, objective summary of the text

✓ a thesis statement that clearly and concisely describes your conclusions

✓ evidence from the text that identifies both explicit details and ambiguities

✓ inferences and conclusions about the work

✓ evidence from the text that supports your conclusions, interpretation, and any inferences you make

✓ a formal style and objective tone appropriate for your audience and the genre

Rubric for Self-Assessment

Criteria for Success	not very					very
How clearly and objectively have you summarized the text?	1	2	3	4	5	6
How clearly does your thesis reveal your conclusions?	1	2	3	4	5	6
To what extent have you provided evidence from the text that identifies explicit details and ambiguities?	1	2	3	4	5	6
To what extent have you made inferences and drawn conclusions about the text?	1	2	3	4	5	6
To what extent have you provided textual evidence that supports your conclusions, interpretation, and inferences?	1	2	3	4	5	6
To what extent did you use a formal style and appropriate tone for your audience?	1	2	3	4	5	6

* Other standards covered include: Writing 1c, Writing 1d, Writing 1e, Writing 2b, Writing 2c, Writing 2d, Writing 2e, Writing 4, Writing 9, Speaking 4, Speaking 6, Language 3, Language 6

For use with Speaking and Listening 1

Name _____ Date _____ Assignment _____

Performance Task 10B

Speaking and Listening 1 Initiate and participate effectively in a range of
    collaborative discussions (one-on-one, in groups, and teacher-led) with diverse
    partners on grade 11–12 topics, texts, and issues, building on others' ideas and
    expressing their own clearly and persuasively.

Task: Discuss the Responses to a Text

Participate in a group discussion in which you explain your analysis of an informational text and
respond thoughtfully to the points of view of others.

Tips for Success

Participate in a discussion in which you analyze a work of informational text. Follow these tips for
success:

✓ prepare by reading the work and identifying explicit details and ambiguities

✓ with group members, develop discussion guidelines that ensure equal and
   full participation for each person

✓ prepare questions that will evoke further discussion from participants and
   propel the discussion forward

✓ craft complete and concise responses to questions asked by others in the group

✓ summarize different points of view presented in the responses

Rubric for Self-Assessment

Criteria for Discussion	not very					very
To what extent did you prepare for the discussion of the work?	1	2	3	4	5	6
How effectively did the guidelines established by the group ensure full and fair inclusion of ideas from all members?	1	2	3	4	5	6
To what extent did you provide complete, concise, and convincing responses to questions?	1	2	3	4	5	6
To what extent did you ask thoughtful questions that helped explore the points of view presented?	1	2	3	4	5	6
How effectively did you and other group members build on one another's ideas?	1	2	3	4	5	6
How well did the discussion summarize the main perspectives of participants?	1	2	3	4	5	6
To what extent were you polite and respectful of other points of view?	1	2	3	4	5	6

For use with Informational Text 1

Name _____ Date _____ Assignment _____

Performance Task 11A

Informational Text 2 Determine two or more central ideas of a text and analyze their development over the course of the text, including how they interact and build on one another to provide a complex analysis; provide an objective summary of the text.*

Task: Analyze Details That Contribute to Central Ideas

Write a complex analysis of an informational text in which you examine how central ideas are conveyed through key details, and how those ideas interact and build on another in the course of the text. Be sure to support your ideas with textual evidence.

Tips for Success

Produce an analysis of an informational work of nonfiction. In your analysis, include these elements:

✓ an objective summary of the work

✓ identification of two or more central ideas in the text

✓ identification of particular details relevant to two or more central ideas

✓ an analysis, supported by textual evidence, of how the details are developed to express central ideas

✓ analysis of how the central ideas work together to convey the overall message of the work

✓ revision and editing to produce a well-organized, coherent analysis

✓ language that is formal, precise, and follows the rules of standard English

Rubric for Self-Assessment

Criteria for Success	not very					very
How objectively have you summarized the work?	1	2	3	4	5	6
How effectively have you identified key details relevant to the central ideas?	1	2	3	4	5	6
To what extent have you described how the central ideas are developed?	1	2	3	4	5	6
How effectively have you analyzed how the central ideas work together to convey the author's point of view?	1	2	3	4	5	6
To what extent did revise and edit your writing to produce a stronger analysis?	1	2	3	4	5	6

For use with Speaking and Listening 1c

Name _____ Date _____ Assignment _____

Performance Task 11B

> **Speaking and Listening 1c** Propel conversations by posing and responding to questions that probe reasoning and evidence; ensure a hearing for a full range of positions on a topic or issue; clarify, verify, or challenge ideas and conclusions; and promote divergent and creative perspectives.

Task: Discuss Multiple Perspectives

Participate in a group discussion with other students who have analyzed the central ideas of the same informational text. After each student identifies central ideas and how they are developed in the text, discuss any differences among the group's ideas ideas and creative perspectives by posing and responding to questions that probe reasoning and evidence.

Tips for Success

Participate in a discussion about an analysis of an informational text. Follow these tips for success:

✓ prepare by anticipating questions about your analysis

✓ with group members, develop discussion guidelines that ensure equal and full participation for each person

✓ develop questions that require group members to clarify, verify, or challenge ideas and conclusions

✓ formulate clear and convincing responses to other students' questions about your conclusions

✓ use non-verbal cues that convey your attention to the speaker

Rubric for Self-Assessment

Criteria for Discussion	not very					very
How thoroughly did you prepare to defend your ideas?	1	2	3	4	5	6
How effectively did the group establish guidelines for the discussion?	1	2	3	4	5	6
To what extent did you ask thoughtful questions that required others to clarify and verify their ideas and conclusions?	1	2	3	4	5	6
How effectively and convincingly did you respond to questions asked by others?	1	2	3	4	5	6
To what extent did you use non-verbal cues to convey your attention to the speaker?	1	2	3	4	5	6

Performance Task 12A

> **Informational Text 3** Analyze a complex set of ideas or sequence of events and explain how specific individuals, ideas, or events interact and develop over the course of the text.*

Task: Explain the Ideas in a Work of Nonfiction

Write an essay in which you analyze the ideas developed in a work of nonfiction that you have read. In the essay, show how the author's ideas develop and evolve over the course of the work and identify the strategies the author employs to development those ideas.

Tips for Success

Provide an analysis of an informational text. In your analysis, include these elements:

✓ a clear explanation of the events and ideas in the text and the relationships among them

✓ an explanation of the development of the ideas and events over the course of the work

✓ a description of how the ideas, events, and individuals interact

✓ sufficient information and details to support your explanation

✓ an appropriate tone and formal style that uses standard English

Rubric for Self-Assessment

Criteria for Success	not very					very
How clear and thorough is your description of the ideas in the work?	1	2	3	4	5	6
How effectively have you described the ideas and their development over the course of the work?	1	2	3	4	5	6
How effectively have you explained the interaction between the ideas, events, and individuals over the course of the work?	1	2	3	4	5	6
How well have you described the strategies the author used to organize and develop the ideas?	1	2	3	4	5	6
How well have you supported your ideas with sufficient textual details?	1	2	3	4	5	6
To what extent have you maintained an appropriate tone and a formal style?	1	2	3	4	5	6

* Other standards covered include: Writing 2a, Writing 4, Writing 5, Writing 9b, Speaking 4, Speaking 6, Language 1, Language 2, Language 3, Language 6

Name _____ Date _____ Assignment _____

Performance Task 12B

Speaking and Listening 5 Make strategic use of digital media (e.g. textual, graphical, audio, visual, and interactive elements) in presentations to enhance understanding of findings, reasoning, and evidence and to add interest.

Task: Develop a Media Presentation

Create a media presentation in which you show the development and interaction of ideas, events, and individuals in a work on nonfiction. Utilize various and strategic visual, audio, and interactive elements to enhance your audience's understanding of the work, your reasoning, and the evidence that supports your reasoning.

Tips for Success

Create a presentation in which you explain the development of ideas, events, and individuals in a work of nonfiction. In your presentation, include these elements:

- ✓ a description of the strategy used by the author to develop the ideas in the work

- ✓ visual, audio, and interactive elements that enhance the audience's understanding of the work, your reasoning, and the details that support your reasoning

- ✓ the use of gestures, eye contact, and varied tone and volume to maintain audience interest

- ✓ an appropriate tone and formal style

Rubric for Self-Assessment

Criteria for Discussion	not very				very	
How effective was your presentation in explaining the development of the events, ideas, and individuals over the course of the work?	1	2	3	4	5	6
How well did you explain the author's strategy for presenting his or her ideas?	1	2	3	4	5	6
To what extent did you add text, graphics, audio, and multimedia to enhance the audience's understanding?	1	2	3	4	5	6
To what extent were you able to enhance your presentation with text, visuals, audio, or even interactive digital elements?	1	2	3	4	5	6
How effective were your use of eye contact, gestures, and varied tone and volume in maintaining audience interest?	1	2	3	4	5	6
To what extent did you maintain an appropriate tone and formal style in your presentation?	1	2	3	4	5	6

For use with Informational Text 3

Name _____ Date _____ Assignment _____

Performance Task 13A

> **Informational Text 4** Determine the meaning of words and phrases as they are used in a text, including figurative, connotative, and technical meanings; analyze how an author uses and refines the meaning of a key term or terms over the course of a text (e.g., how Madison defines *faction* in Federalist No. 10).*

Task: Analyze the Literal and Figurative Language in a Personal Essay

Write an analysis of a personal essay in which you identify and determine how words and phrases are used in a denotative, connotative, figurative, and/or technical way. In addition, analyze how the author uses and refines the meaning of key terms over the course of the essay.

Tips for Success

Produce a written analysis of a personal essay. In your analysis, include these elements:

- ✓ an analysis of key words or terms in each paragraph
- ✓ an analysis of the effect of figurative language in advancing the author's purpose
- ✓ an analysis of the author's word choices in producing a compelling message
- ✓ description of the author's word choices and insights
- ✓ strong textual evidence to support your inferences and conclusions
- ✓ an appropriate tone and formal style that uses standard English

Rubric for Self-Assessment

Criteria for Success	not very					very
How well have you identified the key words or terms that reflect the author's beliefs?	1	2	3	4	5	6
How effectively have you analyzed the effect of figurative language in describing his or her beliefs?	1	2	3	4	5	6
To what extent have you analyzed the effectiveness of the author's word choices in producing a compelling message?	1	2	3	4	5	6
How effectively have you commented on the extent to which the author focuses on and/or returns to key ideas?	1	2	3	4	5	6
To what extent have you cited strong textual evidence to support your inferences and conclusions?	1	2	3	4	5	6
How well have you maintained an appropriate tone and a formal style?	1	2	3	4	5	6

*Other standards covered include: Writing 1b , Writing 1c , Writing 1d, Writing 1e, Writing 2b, Writing 2c, Writing 2d, Writing 2f, Writing 4, Writing 9b, Speaking 1a, Language 3, Language 4, Language 5, Language 6

For use with Speaking and Listening 3

Name _____ Date _____ Assignment _____

Performance Task 13B

> **Speaking and Listening 3** Evaluate a speaker's point of view, reasoning, and use of evidence and rhetoric, assessing the stance, premises, links among ideas, word choice, points of emphasis, and tone used.

Task: Engage in a Discussion

Participate in a discussion in which you evaluate a speaker's point of view, reasoning, and use of evidence and rhetoric in a speech, and then compare evaluations with other group members.

Tips for Success

Prepare an evaluation form and use it as you watch a speech. Follow these tips for success:

✓ with the group, agree on a videotaped speech to view and analyze

✓ list and evaluate the speaker's underlying assumptions and logic of those assumptions

✓ list and evaluate the speaker's word choice, particularly emotionally-charged words and their effect

✓ list and evaluate the speaker's use of evidence and rhetoric in explaining key points

✓ list and evaluate the speaker's use or avoidance of ambiguities, bias, stereotypes, cultural assumptions, and propaganda

✓ list and evaluate the speaker's ability to smoothly link his or her ideas

✓ compare your evaluations with those of other group members

Rubric for Self-Assessment

Criteria for Discussion	not very					very
How well did you evaluate the logic of the speaker's assumptions?	1	2	3	4	5	6
How well did you list and evaluate word choice, particularly emotionally-charged words and their effect?	1	2	3	4	5	6
To what extent did you evaluate the speaker's use of evidence and rhetoric in explaining key points?	1	2	3	4	5	6
To what extent did you identify ambiguities, bias, stereotypes, cultural assumptions, or propaganda in the presentation?	1	2	3	4	5	6
How well did you evaluate the speaker's use of smooth transitions to link ideas and conclusions?	1	2	3	4	5	6
How thoughtfully did you compare your evaluation of the speaker's overall effectiveness with other listeners?	1	2	3	4	5	6

For use with Informational Text 4

Name _____ Date _____ Assignment _____

Performance Task 14A

Informational Text 5 Analyze and evaluate the effectiveness of the structure an author uses in his or her exposition or argument, including whether the structure makes points clear, convincing, and engaging.*

Task: Compare the Effectiveness of Organizational Structure

Write an analysis in which you compare and contrast the effectiveness of the organizational structure of two informational texts. Include texts with two or more of the following methods of organization: chronological or sequential, cause-and-effect; compare and contrast; and order of importance. Note whether the organization has produced an engaging text.

Tips for Success

Produce a written comparison of the effectiveness of the organizational structure of two informational texts. In your comparison, include these elements:

- ✓ a discussion of the organizational structure of each work
- ✓ evidence to support your identification of the organization in each work
- ✓ an analysis of the strengths and weaknesses of each organizational structure
- ✓ an analysis of the effectiveness of each text's organizational structure
- ✓ a strong closing statement summarizing your conclusions
- ✓ an appropriate tone and formal style that uses standard English

Rubric for Self-Assessment

Criteria for Success	not very					very
How effectively have you identified the organizational structure of each work?	1	2	3	4	5	6
To what extent have you provided textual evidence to support your identification of organizational structure?	1	2	3	4	5	6
How effectively have you analyzed the strengths and weakness of each text's organizational structure?	1	2	3	4	5	6
How thoroughly have you analyzed the effectiveness of each text's organizational structure?	1	2	3	4	5	6
How effectively does your closing summarize your conclusions?	1	2	3	4	5	6
How well did you maintain an appropriate tone and a formal style?	1	2	3	4	5	6

*Other standards covered include: Writing 1b , Writing 1d , Writing 1e, Writing 2b, Writing 2c, Writing 2d, Writing 2e, Writing 2f, Writing 4, Speaking 2, Speaking 4, Language 1, Language 3, Language 4a, Language 6

Name _____ Date _____ Assignment _____

Performance Task 14B

> **Speaking and Listening 6** Adapt speech to a variety of contexts and tasks, demonstrating a command of formal English when indicated or appropriate.

Task: Present a Formal Oral Analysis

Give a formal oral presentation of your comparison of the effectiveness of organizational structure in two informational texts. Incorporate readings from the texts as part of your presentation. Invite questions from the audience at the conclusion of your presentation.

Tips for Success

Present a formal oral presentation of your comparison of organizational structure. Follow these tips for success:

✓ prepare by practicing your presentation until it is polished

✓ develop an organization that is interesting, appealing, and thought-provoking for your audience

✓ incorporate relevant excerpts from the works

✓ vary your tone, volume, and pacing to add interest to your presentation

✓ use formal English for your presentation; switch to a less formal tone when responding to questions

Rubric for Self-Assessment

Criteria for Discussion	not very				very	
How thoroughly did you prepare for your presentation?	1	2	3	4	5	6
How effectively did you organize your presentation to make it interesting, appealing, and thought-provoking for your audience?	1	2	3	4	5	6
How effectively did you integrate relevant excerpts from the speeches you are comparing?	1	2	3	4	5	6
To what extent did you vary your voice qualities, pacing, and tone to engage your audience?	1	2	3	4	5	6
To what extent did you adapt your presentation to suit the needs of your audience?	1	2	3	4	5	6

For use with Informational Text 5

Name _____ Date _____ Assignment _____

Performance Task 15A

Informational Text 6   Determine an author's point of view or purpose in a text in which the rhetoric is particularly effective, analyzing how style and content contribute to the power, persuasiveness, or beauty of the text.*

Task: Identify and Analyze Author's Purpose or Point of View

Write an analysis of a speech or persuasive essay in which you identify how the author's style and choice of content contribute to the power and persuasiveness of the text in advancing a particular purpose or point of view.

Tips for Success

Write an analysis of the author's point of view and purpose in a speech or persuasive essay. In your analysis, include these elements:

✓ a strong opening, clear thesis, and a strong conclusion

✓ identification of the speaker's purpose or point of view

✓ analysis of how the speaker uses literary elements to advance a particular purpose or point of view

✓ examples of how the speaker expresses point of view through word choice and/or figurative language

✓ examples and analysis of the way in which the speaker's style and content contribute to the power, beauty, and persuasiveness of the speech

Rubric for Self-Assessment

Criteria for Success	not very					very
How effective were your opening, thesis, and conclusion?	1	2	3	4	5	6
How well did you identify the speaker's purpose and point of view?	1	2	3	4	5	6
To what extent did you analyze the author's purpose and the speaker's use of literary elements?	1	2	3	4	5	6
To what extent did you provide examples of the author's use of word choice and figurative language to express a point of view?	1	2	3	4	5	6
How effectively did you analyze the way in which the author's style and content contribute to the power, beauty, and persuasiveness of the speech?	1	2	3	4	5	6

*Other standards covered include: Writing 1, Writing 1c, Writing 1d, Writing 1e, Writing 2, Writing 2c, Writing 2d, Writing 2e, Writing 2f, Writing 4, Speaking 1a, Speaking 1d, Speaking 3, Speaking 6, Language 1, Language 2, Language 3, Language 6

For use with Speaking and Listening 4

Name _____ Date _____ Assignment _____

Performance Task 15B

> **Speaking and Listening 4** Present information, findings, and supporting evidence, conveying a clear and distinct perspective, such that listeners can follow the line of reasoning, alternative or opposing perspectives are addressed, and the organization, development, substance, and style are appropriate to purpose, audience, and a range of formal and informal tasks.

Task: Present a Clear and Distinct Perspective

Present your analysis of a speaker's point of view or purpose in a speech, editorial, or persuasive essay. Your presentation should include your own line of reasoning as well as addressing alternative or opposing perspectives.

Tips for Success

In groups of four or five, each student should give an oral presentation about his or her analysis of an informational text, followed by a discussion and questions from other group members. As your part of the discussion, include these elements:

✓ passages from the speech integrated into your presentation

✓ evidence from the text to support your line of reasoning

✓ discussion of alternative or opposing perspectives about the purpose and point of view

✓ questions that probe the reasoning of other group members

✓ effective responses to the questions from others in the group about your conclusions

Rubric for Self-Assessment

Criteria for Discussion	not very					very
How well did you integrate passages from the text into your presentation?	1	2	3	4	5	6
How effectively did you include evidence from the text to support your line of reasoning?	1	2	3	4	5	6
To what extent did you include alternative or opposing perspectives about the purpose or point of view?	1	2	3	4	5	6
To what extent did you ask thoughtful questions about the ideas of other group members?	1	2	3	4	5	6
How effectively and convincingly did you respond to questions asked by other members in the group?	1	2	3	4	5	6

For use with Informational Text 6

Name _____ Date _____ Assignment _____

Performance Task 16A

> **Informational Text 7** Integrate and evaluate multiple sources of information presented in different media or formats (e.g., visually, quantitatively) as well as in words in order to address a question or solve a problem.*

Task: Use Multiple Sources of Information

Integrate a variety of informational sources and formats to describe a historical issue or event, such as the role of Theodore Roosevelt in America's entry into and participation in the Spanish-American War. Evaluate information from biographical, autobiographical, and historical sources, as well as information in a variety of formats, in your summary.

Tips for Success

Write a summary describing a historical issue or event. As you do, synthesize various types of informational texts and sources and include these elements:

✓ multiple sources of information in various formats

✓ comparison and analysis of the information each source provides

✓ evaluation of the reliability of the information from each source

✓ integration of information into a chronological organization

✓ supporting textual evidence from each source

✓ conclusion that sums up your perspective on the event

Rubric for Self-Assessment

Criteria for Success	not very					very
How effectively did you incorporate multiple sources of information in various formats?	1	2	3	4	5	6
How well did you compare and analyze the types of information provided by each source?	1	2	3	4	5	6
To what extent did you analyze the reliability of the information from each source?	1	2	3	4	5	6
How effectively did you integrate the information into a chronological organization?	1	2	3	4	5	6
To what extent did you include textual evidence from each source?	1	2	3	4	5	6
How effective was your conclusion?	1	2	3	4	5	6

*Other standards covered include: Writing 1a, Writing 1b, Writing 1d, Writing 1e, Writing 2b, Writing 2c, Writing 2e, Writing 2f, Writing 4, Writing 6, Writing 7, Writing 8, Writing 9, Speaking 1d, Speaking 2, Speaking 4, Speaking 6, Language 1, Language 2, Language 3, Language 6

For use with Speaking and Listening 5

Name _____ Date _____ Assignment _____

Performance Task 16B

> **Speaking and Listening 5** Make strategic use of digital media (e.g., textual, graphical, audio, visual, and interactive elements) in presentations to enhance understanding of findings, reasoning, and evidence and to add interest.

Task: Produce a Digital Multimedia Presentation

Present a summary of a historical issue or event, such as the role of Theodore Roosevelt in America's entry and participation in the Spanish-American War. Research the issue from a variety of sources and integrate it into a well-organized, informative, and interesting presentation.

Tips for Success

Prepare and present a summary on a historical issue or event. Include some kind of digital media in the presentation, as well as these elements:

✓ opening that introduces the event in an appealing way

✓ research from a variety of different sources and types of sources

✓ integration of digital elements, such as graphics, sound, animations, and text

✓ chronological organization that is easy to follow

✓ include visual or auditory support from the sources to enhance understanding

✓ question and answer session after the presentation with other members of your group

Rubric for Self-Assessment

Criteria for Discussion	not very				very	
How effective was your opening in introducing the event in an interesting, appealing manner?	1	2	3	4	5	6
How well were you able to integrate research from a variety of different sources into your presentation?	1	2	3	4	5	6
How effectively were you able to integrate digital elements?	1	2	3	4	5	6
How well were you able to produce an easy-to-follow sequential organization?	1	2	3	4	5	6
To what extent did you include visual or auditory support from the sources to enhance understanding?	1	2	3	4	5	6
How useful was the question and answer session afterwards?	1	2	3	4	5	6

Name _____ Date _____ Assignment _____

Performance Task 17A

Informational Text 8 Delineate and evaluate the reasoning in seminal U.S. texts, including the application of constitutional principles and use of legal reasoning (e.g., in U.S. Supreme Court majority opinions and dissents) and the premises, purposes, and arguments in works of public advocacy (e.g., *The Federalist*, presidential addresses).*

Task: Analyze and Evaluate the Reasoning in a Supreme Court Ruling

Write an analysis of a seminal Supreme Court ruling. In your analysis, identify, analyze, and evaluate the effectiveness of legal reasoning and constitutional principles.

Tips for Success

Write an analysis of a written opinion in a seminal Supreme Court ruling in which you identify, analyze, and evaluate the judge's legal reasoning. In your analysis, include these elements:

- ✓ identification of the judge's legal point of view

- ✓ analysis and evaluation of appeals to reason, emotion, ethics, or authority

- ✓ identification, analysis, and evaluation of the judge's use of rhetorical devices, such as parallelism, rhetorical questions, and anecdotes

- ✓ evaluation of the constitutional evidence used to support the judge's premises, purposes, arguments, and legal reasoning

- ✓ analysis that includes the most significant and relevant facts and quotations

Rubric for Self-Assessment

Criteria for Success	not very					very
How clearly did you identify the judge's legal point of view?	1	2	3	4	5	6
How effectively did you analyze and evaluate appeals to reason, emotion, ethics, and authority?	1	2	3	4	5	6
How well did you analyze the speaker's use of rhetorical devices?	1	2	3	4	5	6
How effectively did you evaluate the Constitutional evidence used to support the speaker's premises, arguments, and legal reasoning?	1	2	3	4	5	6
How thoroughly did you develop the topic by supporting it with relevant facts, quotes, and examples?	1	2	3	4	5	6

*Other standards covered include: Writing 1, Writing 2b, Writing 2c, Writing 2e, Writing 2f, Writing 4, Writing 5, Writing 7, Writing 8, Writing 9, Speaking 1b, Speaking 1c, Speaking 1d, Speaking 3, Speaking 4, Language 1, Language 2, Language 5

Name _____ Date _____ Assignment _____

Performance Task 17B

Speaking and Listening 6 Adapt speech to a variety of contexts and tasks, demonstrating a command of formal English when indicated or appropriate.

Task: Take Part in a Panel Discussion

Hold a conversation with a partner and take part in a group discussion in which you analyze the legal reasoning and constitutional principles in a Supreme Court ruling. Each member of the group should focus a different aspect of the ruling, such as persuasive appeals; word choice, connotation, and emotion; and constitutional reasoning and precedent.

Tips for Success

Prepare for the group discussion by holding a conversation with a partner about the requirements of this assignment and your role in it. As you converse, decide which topic each of you will present. Then, as a part of your participation in the group discussion, include these elements:

✓ description of how the ruling illustrates your assigned topic

✓ examples from the ruling to illustrate the points you make

✓ evaluation of the effectiveness of rhetorical elements in the ruling on its persuasive power

✓ analysis of how effectively elements were used to support legal reasoning

✓ discussion among group members regarding their agreement with the Court's position

Rubric for Self-Assessment

Criteria for Discussion	not very				very	
How well did you describe your assigned element in your introduction?	1	2	3	4	5	6
How effectively did you integrate examples of your assigned element?	1	2	3	4	5	6
How well did you analyze the effectiveness of your element relative to the persuasive power of the ruling?	1	2	3	4	5	6
To what extent did you analyze the effectiveness of rhetorical elements in supporting legal reasoning?	1	2	3	4	5	6
To what extent did you discuss as a group your agreement with the Court's position?	1	2	3	4	5	6

Name _____ Date _____ Assignment _____

Performance Task 18A

Informational Text 9   Analyze seventeenth-, eighteenth-, and nineteenth-century foundational U.S. documents of historical and literary significance (including The Declaration of Independence, the Preamble to the Constitution, the Bill of Rights, and Lincoln's Second Inaugural Address) for their themes, purposes, and rhetorical features.*

Task: Analyze a Foundational U.S. Document

Write an analysis of a foundational U.S. document, such as the 1841 argument of John Quincy Adams before the Supreme Court regarding the capture of the schooner *Amistad*. Identify and analyze Adam's thesis, purpose, and the rhetorical devices used to persuade the Court.

Tips for Success

Write a brief analysis of the document you chose, identifying and analyzing its theme, purpose, and use of rhetorical features. In your analysis, include these elements:

✓ description of the theme, purpose, and background of the document

✓ analysis of appeals to reason, emotion, ethics, or authority used in the document

✓ identification, analysis, and evaluation of rhetorical devices used, such as parallelism, rhetorical questions, and anecdotes

✓ textual examples to support your analysis of rhetorical devices

✓ conclusions about the effectiveness of the document

Rubric for Self-Assessment

Criteria for Success	not very				very	
How clearly did you describe the thesis, purpose, and background of the document you chose?	1	2	3	4	5	6
How thoroughly did you analyze its appeals to reason, emotion, ethics, and authority?	1	2	3	4	5	6
To what extent did you identify, analyze, and evaluate the use of rhetorical devices?	1	2	3	4	5	6
To what extent did you provide examples to support your analysis?	1	2	3	4	5	6
How effectively were you able to draw conclusions about what makes the document of lasting historical significance?	1	2	3	4	5	6

*Other standards covered include: Writing 1, Writing 2b, Writing 2c, Writing 2e, Writing 2f, Writing 4, Writing 9, Speaking 1a, Speaking 1b, Speaking 1c, Speaking 3, Speaking 4, Language 1, Language 2, Language 3, Language 5

Common Core
Companion
Workbook

A Student Workbook for Mastering the Common Core State Standards

- Instruction and Practice for every Common Core State Standard
- Writing Workshops
- Listening and Speaking Workshops
- Support for Research and Technology
- Performance Tasks

PEARSON

COMMON CORE Literature

Name _____ Date _____ Assignment _____

Performance Task 18B

> **Speaking and Listening 1d.** Respond thoughtfully to diverse perspectives; synthesize comments, claims, and evidence made on all sides of an issue; resolve contradictions when possible; and determine what additional information or research is required to deepen the investigation or complete the task.

Task: Compare and Contrast Perspectives

Participate in a group discussion in order to compare and contrast each group member's analyses of a foundational U.S. document. Discuss each of the diverse perspectives among the analyses, ask probing questions to elicit deeper thinking. At the end of the discussion, determine what other information may be needed to expand the discussion and resolve contradictions.

Tips for Success

Participate in a group discussion on an analysis of a major U.S. document, such as John Quincey Adam's argument before the Supreme Court regarding the capture of the schooner *Amistad*. As a part of your participation in the discussion, include these elements:

✓ present your own position on the document and its significance

✓ listen attentively to the analyses of others and compare them to your own

✓ identify diverse perspectives among the group participants

✓ probe and clarify differences through thoughtful questions

✓ resolve contradictions through discussion and identify opportunities for additional research

Rubric for Self-Assessment

Criteria for Discussion	not very					very
How well did you present and describe your own position on the significance of the document?	1	2	3	4	5	6
How attentively did you listen to the analyses of other group members and compare them to your own?	1	2	3	4	5	6
How well were you able to identify differences in perspectives of other group members?	1	2	3	4	5	6
To what extent did you ask thoughtful questions designed to probe and clarify differences?	1	2	3	4	5	6
How effectively were you able to resolve contradictions through discussion or identify opportunities for additional research?	1	2	3	4	5	6

For use with Informational Text 9

Name _____ Date _____ Assignment _____

Performance Task 19A

Informational Text 10 By the end of grade 12, read and comprehend literary nonfiction at the high end of the grades 11–CCR text complexity band independently and proficiently.*

Task: Write a Critical Response to a Work

Write a critical response to a work of literary nonfiction in which you demonstrate your comprehension by discussing the elements of writing, such as the quality of content, clarity of the thesis, organization, themes, sentence variety, word choice, and the use of rhetorical devices.

Tips for Success

Write a critical response to a work of literary nonfiction and include these elements:

✓ summary of the work including description of the thesis and themes

✓ evaluation of the quality and clarity of content with supporting examples

✓ analysis of the author's use of word choice, sentence variety, and style to advance the themes

✓ analysis of the author's use of rhetorical and literary devices, such as metaphor, repetition, and appeals to emotion or reason

✓ thoughtful comparison of your own personal response to literary criticism of the work

Rubric for Self-Assessment

Criteria for Success	not very					very
How clearly did you summarize the work and identify the thesis and themes?	1	2	3	4	5	6
How effectively did you evaluate the quality and clarity of the work?	1	2	3	4	5	6
To what extent did you support your evaluation with textual examples?	1	2	3	4	5	6
To what extent did you analyze the effect of the author's sentence structure, word choice, and style to advance the themes of the work?	1	2	3	4	5	6
How well did you analyze the author's use of rhetorical and literary devices?	1	2	3	4	5	6
How effectively did you compare your own personal response to literary criticism of the work?	1	2	3	4	5	6

*Other standards covered include: Writing 1, Writing 2b, Writing 2c, Writing 2e, Writing 2f, Writing 4, Writing 7, Writing 9, Speaking 1a, Speaking 1b, Speaking 1c, Speaking 3, Speaking 4, Language 1, Language 2, Language 3, Language 5

For use with Speaking and Listening 6

Name _____ Date _____ Assignment _____

Performance Task 19B

> **Speaking and Listening 6.** Adapt speech to a variety of contexts and tasks, demonstrating a command of formal English when indicated or appropriate.

Task: Participate in a Literature Circle

Participate in a literature circle in which you discuss a work of literary nonfiction with others who have read the same work. Before beginning, work with peers to promote civil democratic discussions, set clear goals, and insure equal participation by all group members.

Tips for Success

Participate in a literature circle with others who have read and formed a critical response to the same work of literary nonfiction. As a part of your participation, include these elements:

✓ present your own thoughts on the work clearly and concisely

✓ compare and contrast your responses with the responses of others

✓ listen attentively to the comments and responses of other group members

✓ ask thoughtful questions to clarify and expand upon the ideas of others

✓ convincingly answer questions about your own responses and conclusions

✓ summarize the responses of all group members regarding the work

Rubric for Self-Assessment

Criteria for Discussion	not very					very
How clearly and concisely did you present your own comments on the work?	1	2	3	4	5	6
To what extent did you compare and contrast your responses with the responses of others?	1	2	3	4	5	6
How attentively did you listen to the comments and responses of other group members?	1	2	3	4	5	6
To what extent did you ask thoughtful questions designed to clarify the ideas of others?	1	2	3	4	5	6
How convincingly did you answer questions about your own responses and conclusions?	1	2	3	4	5	6
To what extent did your group summarize responses?	1	2	3	4	5	6